20th-Century United States History

HARPERCOLLINS COLLEGE OUTLINE

20th-Century
United States History

Daniel Preston

HarperPerennial
A Division of HarperCollins*Publishers*

This book is dedicated to the memory of Richard Farrell.

All maps are reprinted from Gary B. Nash, Julie Roy Jeffrey, John R. Howe, Peter J. Frederick, Allen F. Davis, and Allan M. Winkler, *The American People: Creating a Nation and a Society*, 2nd ed., (New York: HarperCollins Publishers, Inc., 1990). Reprinted with permission.

An American BookWorks Corporation Production
Project Manager: Jonathon E. Brodman
Editor: Robert A. Weinstein

Library of Congress Catalog Card Number: 91-55400
ISBN: 0-06-467132-1

92 93 94 95 96 ABW/RRD 10 9 8 7 6 5 4 3 2 1

Contents

Preface vii

1 The Industrial Age: 1880–1910 1

2 A World Power: 1890–1908 19

3 The Progressive Era: 1901–1917 35

4 World War I: 1914–1920 54

5 Postwar Conservatism: 1919–1929 71

6 The Great Depression and the New Deal: 1929–1939 88

7 World War II: 1939–1945 108

8 The Postwar Era: 1945–1960 125

9 The Civil Rights Movement: 1954–1972 147

10 War and Protest: 1961–1975 161

11 The Shift to Conservatism: 1976–1988 192

Epilogue 215

Appendix A: Presidential Profiles: 1901–1991 217

Appendix B: Presidential Elections: 1900–1988 224

Appendix C: Presidential Cabinets: 1901–1991 234

Index 247

Preface

THE CHALLENGE OF
THE TWENTIETH CENTURY

At the beginning of the twentieth century the United States began to reap the profits of the rapid economic and physical expansion of the late nineteenth century. The great industrial expansion, which began in the midnineteenth century and continued until the 1950s, was at the root of this change. Increased national wealth, combined with an expanding labor force, new and better markets both at home and abroad, and great advancements in technology, propelled the United States into the front rank of nations. The acquisition of overseas territory during the 1890s was just one manifestation of this expansion which gave the United States new and greater influence in global affairs. The American people approached this new role cautiously at first, but the country's decisive participation in World War I confirmed the country's place as a world leader. America's victory in World War II and the great economic boom that followed the war justified the claim that the United States was the world's strongest nation.

And yet, all was not smooth sailing. Even as the country grew and prospered, a large number of people were denied a share of economic prosperity and political liberty. Suppression of political dissent was not unusual, grim poverty beset many of the nation's citizens, labor unrest accompanied industrial expansion, and racism and discrimination against minority groups was an everyday fact of life. Even prosperity did not seem guaranteed, for in the 1930s the national economy sank into a depression so severe that only the massive mobilization for World War II could revive it.

In the postwar era, the United States found that its wealth and power brought a whole new series of challenges. The Soviet Union also emerged from World War II as one of the world's great powers. The spread of communism through Europe, Asia, and the Third World presented an economic, political, and ideological challenge to the United States and its Western European allies. For many Americans the defeat of communism was the country's primary task. At the same time, European empires crumbled, and their former colonies struggled to overcome the limitations of imperialism and form themselves into healthy independent nations. This presented the United States with a twofold problem: how to assist these fledgling nations to become free and wealthy democracies while maintaining the economic advantages gained from these weaker states. The problem was particularly tough because many people in the Third World considered the United States, the leader of the Western nations, to be symbolic of imperialism.

An equally serious challenge presented itself on the domestic front. Since the founding of the nation, America's large and expanding middle class had enjoyed unequaled freedom and prosperity, a freedom and prosperity denied to blacks, immigrants, and the poor. In the 1950s a vast social movement began that demanded social justice for all Americans. The movement began as a campaign to guarantee civil rights to blacks and quickly expanded to include women, other minority groups, and people suffering from economic and social disadvantages. The movement also demanded that the United States apply the same principles of justice in its dealings with foreign nations. Thus the country faced the challenge of not only improving its high standard of living but also of extending it to all citizens.

Daniel Preston

1

The Industrial Age: 1880–1910

1881 Electric dynamo invented

Municipal electric power plant constructed in New York

1882 First hydroelectric power plant built

Standard Oil Trust organized

1883 United States begins construction of steel warships

1884 Steel framing first used in building construction

1886 Electrolytic process for extracting aluminum developed

American Federation of Labor organized

Labor unrest highlighted by railroad strikes and Haymarket Riot in Chicago

1887 Trusts organized in sugar, whiskey, lead, and other industries

First successful electric trolley system introduced

1888 Electric motor invented

First electric-powered automobile in the U.S.

1889 Electric sewing machine introduced

Holding companies first organized

1890 United Mine Workers organized

American Tobacco Company organized

1892 Labor unrest highlighted by nationwide coal strike, silver mine strike in Idaho, and the Homestead Steel Company strike in Pennsylvania

General Electric Company organized

First gas-driven automobile in U.S.

Financier Jay Gould dies, leaving an estate worth $72 million

1894 Labor unrest includes Pullman strike in Chicago, coal strike in Ohio, garment workers' strike in New York City, and nationwide railroad strike

1896 Henry Ford builds his first automobile

1897 Coal strikes

1901 United States Steel Company organized

First oil wells in Texas

1902 International Harvester Company organized; controls manufacture of 85 percent of farm machinery in U.S.

Nationwide coal strike

1903 Ford Motor Company organized

Wright brothers build first airplane

1904 Diesel engine introduced in U.S.

1905 Population of some portions of New York's slums reaches 1,000 people per acre

Industrial Workers of the World organized

1907 Coal mine explosions in December kill over 700 people; between 1905 and 1909 over 2,500 miners die in accidents

1908 Model-T Ford introduced; 19,000 manufactured in 1909

The emergence of the United States as a major industrial nation in the late nineteenth century was an essential factor in the continuing prosperity of the nation and in the rise of the United States as a world power in the twentieth century. The availability of new machines, new sources of capital, new modes of industrial power, and new methods of business organization contributed to the rise of industrialism. This new economic order brought many benefits to the country, but it also introduced a number of problems that continued to plague the nation throughout the following century.

THE EMERGENCE OF INDUSTRIALISM

Elements of Growth

Industrialization began in the United States in the early nineteenth century, but it was not until the decade of the 1880s that manufacturing became the dominant sector of the American economy. Manufacturing had always been a component of the American economy; it was during the 1880s, however, that a number of factors combined to establish the industrial age. First among these was the proliferation of machinery—not just in the factory, but also on the farm, in offices and stores, in transportation, and in the home. Another factor was the increased availability of raw materials. The rich North American continent yielded a great variety of agricultural products, timber, minerals, and ores needed by manufacturers. The development of machine technology eased the production and extraction of these materials, thereby increasing their availability and reducing their cost. Materials not found at home were imported from abroad.

Manufacturing was an expensive undertaking, and a third element in its emergence was the availability of the huge amounts of money needed to finance it on a massive nationwide scale. By the 1880s the United States was prosperous enough to spawn investors willing to underwrite these projects. Financing also came from wealthy investors in Europe. A fourth stimulus to growth—and another source of money—was the expansion of the market for American manufactured products. The population of the United States continued to grow at a high rate, producing an ever-increasing number of consumers. Prosperity was widespread, so many of these consumers had money to spend on manufactured goods. At the same time, American producers were successful at finding new markets for their goods in foreign countries and at increasing their share of existing overseas markets. A final asset for the emergence of industrialization was the availability of a large labor force. The end of the nineteenth century and the beginning of the twentieth was a period of heavy immigration. The arrival of thousands of workers during these years provided an immense source of cheap labor for the nation's factories.

4   20th-Century United States History

Table 1.1 Population of the United States, 1860–1980	
1860	31,443,000
1870	39,818,000
1880	50,155,000
1890	62,947,000
1900	75,994,000
1910	91,972,000
1920	105,710,000
1930	122,775,000
1940	131,669,000
1950	150,697,000
1960	179,323,000
1970	203,235,000
1980	226,545,000

Table 1.2 Value of products manufactured in the United States, 1880–1910	
1880	$3,748,000,000
1890	5,406,200,000
1900	7,925,800,000
1910	13,685,200,000

The Shift from Agriculture

From colonial times through the end of the nineteenth century, agriculture dominated the American economy. At the turn of the century this began to change. As manufacturing increased, it gradually replaced agriculture as the most important sector of the nation's economy. In 1890 the value of manufactured products exceeded the value of farm products for the first time. In 1920 the number of Americans living in urban areas surpassed the number living in the countryside. Also in 1920, the farm population decreased for the first time. The rising ascendancy of manufacturing did not mean that agriculture was on the decline. On the contrary, both farm production and agricultural exports continued to increase as more land came under cultivation and improved farming methods produced record harvests.

Table 1.3 Urban and rural population of the United States, 1880–1920		
	rural	urban
1880	36,970,881	13,184,902
1890	40,388,347	22,559,367
1900	45,411,164	30,583,411
1910	49,348,883	42,623,383
1920	51,406,017	54,304,603

Table 1.4 Farm population, 1880–1920	
1880	21,973,000
1890	24,771,000
1900	29,875,000
1910	32,077,000
1920	31,974,000

Table 1.5 Value of farm products, 1880–1900	
1880	$4,129,000,000
1890	4,990,000,000
1900	6,409,000,000

The Proliferation of Machinery

One of the hallmarks of industrialization was the mechanization of manufacturing. During the early and mid-1800s certain types of manufacturing, particularly textile production, began to mechanize. By the end of the century practically all factories used power-driven machinery. Mechanization spread through other sectors of the economy as well. Agriculture proved to be a particularly fertile field for the use of machine technology. Horse-drawn and horse-powered implements predominated, but steam-driven machines, particularly tractors and threshers, were common. After the turn of the century the internal combustion engine began to completely revolutionize farming. In railroading, technological developments such as air brakes, refrigerator cars, and improved engines were important innovations.

STEAM TECHNOLOGY

A number of mechanical innovations resulted from improvements in power sources. Prior to 1870 most machinery was water-driven. Water power was cheap and efficient, but it had its drawbacks, the primary one being that the machines had to be located near a source of moving water. Steam technology, which improved constantly during the nineteenth century, offered a number of advantages over water power. First, steam engines could be constructed anywhere, thus allowing factories to be built in areas without access to running water. Furthermore, improved steam engines produced more power and allowed better regulation of the power that was generated. By the end of the century, steam power propelled 80 percent of the factories in the country.

Another advantage to the steam engine was that it was portable. The most important application of portable engines was on the railroad, but once mechanics and engineers had learned to build sturdy enough engines, they could be used for other applications as well. Steam engines could be hauled into the forest to power sawmills and into fields to power threshers. They were also used as motive power in tractors, automobiles, and heavy construction equipment.

ELECTRICITY

An even greater innovation was the harnessing of electricity. Thomas Edison's many inventions paved the way for the application of electricity to a great many uses. Electric generators provided an incomparable amount of power, and electric motors provided an even, steady stream of power to machinery. A strong, efficient electric motor was invented in 1888. This device was adapted to all sorts of machinery, and after the turn of the century electric power became increasingly important in manufacturing. Because generators could be centrally located and the power transmitted through wires, electrical power became available to practically any location, including individual households. The widespread availability of electricity stimulated manufacturing by creating markets for such innovations as electric streetcars, electric public lighting, and electric household appliances.

INTERNAL COMBUSTION ENGINE

A final source of motive power developed during this period, the internal combustion engine, was admirably suited for use in transportation. These engines, though comparatively small and light-weight, were capable of generating a large amount of power. The fuel supply—gasoline and diesel oil—was also lightweight and compact. The great application of the internal combustion engine was in the automobile. These small gas-driven engines made the automobile practical and affordable. The availability of these engines was also a key factor in the invention of the airplane. Another important use of the internal combustion engine was on the railroad, where diesel engines eventually replaced the steam engine.

IMPACT ON INDUSTRIALIZATION

The spread of machinery contributed to the rise of industrialization in several ways. First, improved power sources and the increased manufacturing capacity of machines made large-scale production economical and feasible. Second, mechanized transportation made it possible to ship large inventories of heavy manufactured goods. Third, the manufacture of machinery became an industry in itself. The widespread demand for heavy industrial machinery created thousands of jobs and fueled the demand for steel and other materials used in their production. And finally, because of the proliferation of machinery, particularly household appliances, machines became, literally, household items. This familiarity with machinery, combined with admiration for speed and efficiency and a desire for manufactured goods, made large-scale manufacturing acceptable to the general public.

Investment and Financing

FINANCIAL INSTITUTIONS

Throughout the nineteenth century the United States depended heavily on foreign investment, particularly from England. But as the country grew and prospered, more and more of the financing for industrial activity came from American investors. By the 1880s institutions such as banks and insurance companies as well as private individuals had amassed considerable capital. These financial institutions applied their vast resources to manufacturing in two ways: They made loans, and they invested directly in the burgeoning corporations. The primary means of investing was the purchase of stock in the many new industrial corporations. Joint-stock companies were nothing new, but as factories grew in size, stock investment reached new proportions.

FINANCIERS

Also new to the scene was a class of extremely wealthy and extremely powerful financiers who commanded millions of investment dollars. The prince of these money brokers was New York banker John Pierpont Morgan. Like most brokers, Morgan rose to power through his investments in railroading and later turned his attention to manufacturing. Many manufacturers courted these financiers, but some industrialists—most notably Andrew Carnegie and John D. Rockefeller—distrusted them and strove to keep their companies out of the control of bankers. They did this by setting aside a considerable portion of their profits for reinvestment. This approach worked for men like Carnegie who commanded huge resources, but most businessmen relied heavily on investors and lending institutions.

Expanding Markets

DOMESTIC MARKETS

An essential part of the expansion of manufacturing was a demand for manufactured goods. There had always been a healthy market for consumer goods in the United States, but prior to the 1880s a large portion of these products were imported, particularly from England. As the country prospered, the demand for factory-made products increased. This development, aided by a series of protective tariffs designed to raise the price of imports, encouraged American manufacturers to increase their output, and domestic goods began to replace imports. As the country grew there were more people with more money to spend. An increasingly prosperous middle class, supplemented by an expanding upper class, created a huge demand for household and personal goods. The trend toward mass production drove down the cost of manufactured goods, thereby stimulating the market even more. The continued demand for consumer goods was a major factor in the demand for producer goods (heavy industrial items such as machinery and railroad equipment).

FOREIGN MARKETS

American manufacturers also found an outlet in foreign markets. The United States had always had a strong export trade in agricultural products. As manufacturing increased, finished goods began to find their way into these same markets, particularly in Latin America. At the same time, producers began to seek additional markets—in the European colonies of Africa and Asia and in Europe itself. Europe was heavily industrialized, but by 1900 the manufacturing capacity of the United States had surpassed that of England and Germany combined. This great productive capability, combined with aggressive marketing tactics, enabled American manufacturers to expand their overseas markets, penetrating even into the heartland of European industrialism.

Immigration

LABOR FOR MANUFACTURING

The United States is a nation of immigrants, and during the nineteenth century a substantial portion of the population was foreign-born. Each year hundreds of thousands of immigrants arrived in the country. Many headed for the newly opened farming regions of the west, but the majority settled in cities, where the prospects for employment were better. This influx was a great boon for manufacturers. Machine operation required very little training, and the flood of immigration provided a great pool of labor to fill these jobs. And it was cheap labor. Most immigrants came from countries with standards of living considerably lower than that of the United States. Desperate for jobs and with low expectations, they were willing to work for low wages.

NATIONS OF ORIGIN

The wave of immigration that hit the United States at the turn of the century was different than that of previous years. Most of the earlier immigrants came from northern European countries: Great Britain, Ireland, Germany, and Scandinavia. After 1880 immigration from these countries declined. In their place came an even larger number of people from eastern and southern Europe. Between 1901 and 1920 over 3 million immigrants arrived from Italy, 2.5 million from Russia, and almost 4 million from other eastern and southern European countries. Immigration reached its peak between 1903 and 1914, when almost 12 million people entered the country.

Table 1.6 Immigration into the United States, 1881–1920	
1881–1890	5,245,000
1891–1900	3,689,000
1901–1910	8,796,000
1911–1920	5,736,000

Urban Growth   INFLUENCE OF MANUFACTURING

Manufacturing required the support of many people working outside the factory and had, therefore, always been an important incentive to urban growth. Something as simple as a flour mill, for example, required the support of coopers to make barrels; teamsters to transport wheat and flour to and from the mill; wagon and harness makers to build and maintain wagons and equipment; blacksmiths to manufacture and repair metal parts; carpenters for woodworking; merchants to market the flour; railroad workers, river boatmen, and mariners to transport it long distances; a host of craftsmen to maintain the transportation system; and merchants, artisans, and professionals to provide goods and services to all these people. Convenience and efficiency dictated that these various activities cluster together in an urban setting. The more industries concentrated in one place, the larger the town or city.

Technological innovations of the late nineteenth century intensified this pattern of urban concentration. The increased use of steam engines (and later electricity) freed manufacturers from their dependence on water power and allowed them to choose locations with prime access to markets, raw materials, shipping facilities, and labor supplies. This freedom from water power meant that manufacturers could build larger factories and that a great number of factories could locate in one place. The railroad, by freeing manufacturers from their dependence on water transportation, did the same.

Great industrial centers such as New York, Chicago, Philadelphia, and Pittsburgh emerged and experienced tremendous growth rates.

TRANSPORTATION IMPROVEMENTS

Improvements in urban transportation also contributed to an increase in the size of cities. Before the invention of the street railroad in the late 1860s, people walked to work. City size was, therefore, limited. With the introduction of the horse-drawn, and later the electric, streetcar (or in New York and Boston, the subway), people could live farther away from their places of employment and from shopping districts and still have access to them.

Table 1.7 Growth of selected U. S. cities, 1880–1910				
	1880	1890	1900	1910
New York	1,911,678	2,507,414	3,437,202	4,766,883
Chicago	503,185	1,099,850	1,698,575	2,185,283
Philadelphia	847,170	1,046,946	1,293,697	1,549,008
Boston	362,839	448,477	560,892	670,585
St. Louis	350,518	451,770	575,238	687,029
Baltimore	332,313	434,439	508,957	558,485
Pittsburgh	156,389	238,617	321,616	533,905
Los Angeles	11,183	50,395	102,479	319,198
Seattle	3,533	42,837	80,671	237,194
Atlanta	37,409	65,533	89,872	154,839
Dallas	10,358	38,067	42,638	92,104
Oklahoma City	—	4,151	10,037	64,205

FOUR IMPORTANT INDUSTRIES

Steel

A key element in the development of American industry was the breakthrough in the manufacture of steel. In the early nineteenth century steel-making was a slow, expensive process, and most metal products were made of iron, which was easier to produce but less durable. The invention of the Bessemer converter and the development of the open-hearth process in the late 1860s greatly simplified steel-making and drastically lowered its cost. The discovery of vast iron ore deposits in Minnesota, Michigan, and Alabama and the widespread availability of coal throughout the Appalachians provided the raw materials needed in the steel industry. The effect of these developments was immediate. In 1867 the United States produced just over 1.5 million tons of steel. In 1900 production exceeded 10 million tons, and by 1910 it had jumped to 24 million tons. The manufacture of tools, hardware, machinery, and, later, automobiles, and the con-struction of railroads, ships, bridges, and buildings created an unending demand for steel. For most of the twentieth century steel was the predominant material used in manufacturing.

ANDREW CARNEGIE

The growth of the steel industry brought changes in industrial manage-ment as well as in production. The chief innovator was Andrew Carnegie, who began to manufacture steel in Pittsburgh in 1873. Carnegie's operations were too large to be managed by one or two men, so he established a hierarchy in which managers supervised different aspects of production and lower-level managers reported to their superiors through a chain of com-mand. This management system and the immense size of Carnegie's opera-tions required hundreds of office workers. Their ability to handle such a large volume of business depended upon the use of newly developed business machines such as typewriters and the telephone, which provided easy communication for the widespread managerial network.

Another Carnegie innovation is known as vertical integration. Carnegie figured it would be cheaper for him to own all aspects of steel production than it would be to contract with others to provide raw materials and transportation. He therefore began to buy iron and coal mines, rail lines, and steamships, thus bringing all operations from the digging of the ore to the selling of the raw steel under his control. He also began to buy out his competitors, thereby eliminating competition and gaining almost total con-trol of the steel market in the United States. By 1900 Carnegie had assembled a vast industrial empire.

U.S. STEEL

Carnegie Steel, while the largest, was only one of the large steel companies in the country. In the late 1890s several manufacturers, backed by New York financier John Pierpont Morgan, launched a drive to con-solidate the steel industry. A trend toward amalgamation was already well underway. In 1880 there were over a thousand companies producing steel; by 1900 this number had dropped to seventy. Any large merger within the steel industry obviously needed Andrew Carnegie's cooperation. But Car-negie, who lacked the resources to bring the industry entirely under his own control, opposed any plan that required him to surrender his empire. He eventually acquiesced and agreed to sell his company for half a billion dollars. The result was the organization of the United States Steel Corporation in 1901, a company that controlled three-fifths of the steel business in the country. If nothing else, the creation of U.S. Steel confirmed that great fortunes could be made in manufacturing. Carnegie, who retired from business after the sale with a fortune worth $400 million, made a profit of $250 million on the deal. Morgan, for his part in the sale, earned $62 million.

Railroads

INFLUENCE ON MANUFACTURING

The railroad was not an industry in the same sense that the steel industry was; that is, it did not manufacture anything. The railroad did, however, play an integral part in the expansion of American manufacturing. It did this in three ways. First, the railroad provided fast, efficient transportation for bulky raw materials such as coal and for heavy manufactured goods. Second, it stimulated manufacturing by its need for manufactured goods: steel rails, engines, cars, and a wide variety of machines and other equipment needed in the management and operation of the lines. And third, like the steel industry, the railroads were innovators in large-scale management.

EXPANSION AND CONSOLIDATION

The second half of the nineteenth century was a period of great expansion and improvement for the railroads. In 1860 there were 31,000 miles of railroads, a figure that grew to 200,000 by the end of the century. The first transcontinental line linked the Mississippi Valley with the Pacific in 1867; by the end of the century there were five transcontinental railways. Innovations such as sleeping and dining cars, stronger engines, refrigerator cars, better constructed beds, steel rails, and a uniform gauge for tracks improved service for both passengers and freight.

As the railroad mania spread, businessmen across the country organized companies and built railroads. Hundreds of companies operated railroads that ran only forty or fifty miles. The creation of so many companies led to a duplication of service and resulted in intense and often cutthroat competition. Railroaders used this competition to force other companies out of business. But this competition scared many railroad owners, who feared that it might lead to a collapse of the whole rail system. These executives turned toward consolidation as a way of ending this competition and providing more efficient service. Companies began to merge, and the large railroads bought the smaller lines.

By 1900 the nation's railroads were controlled by a handful of large rail corporations such as the New York Central, the Pennsylvania, the Baltimore and Ohio, and the Northern Pacific. Like the steel companies, the railroad companies applied new management techniques and employed professional managers to oversee their various operations. Other industries, beset by many of the same problems as the railroads, watched these developments carefully. This pattern of nationwide consolidation and professional management served as a model for other businesses.

Oil

A third large industry that emerged and consolidated during this period was the oil business. Oil was used in factories to keep machinery lubricated. It was also used, in the form of kerosene, for lighting streets, factories, and homes. By the end of century a vast new market had opened for gasoline. The central figure in the oil industry was John D. Rockefeller, owner of the Standard Oil Company. During the 1870s Rockefeller formed a cartel of oil refiners that controlled 90 percent of the oil refining in the country. Rockefeller's control of these various businesses ran afoul of several state antimonopoly laws. In 1882 he organized a new company, the Standard Oil Trust, that resolved the legal conflict. The new arrangement also increased his control of the oil industry. Like Carnegie, Rockefeller established a vertical integration of the business by building pipelines and buying oil fields. He also employed modern management techniques, including the creation of a system of sales districts across the country under the direction of managers responsible for sales in each area. And also like Carnegie, Rockefeller became extremely wealthy. When he retired in 1911 his fortune exceeded $530 million.

Automobile

EARLY DEVELOPMENT

The introduction of the automobile came late in the nineteenth century. There was some experimentation with steam-driven automobiles, but the gasoline-driven internal combustion engine, which was developed in Europe in the 1870s, proved to be much more practical. In the 1890s Charles and Frank Duryea, Henry Ford, and a number of other American inventors built gas-driven automobiles. The automobile was one of the most popular inventions of all time—Americans fell in love with it immediately. In 1900 automakers produced more than 4,000 cars, a figure that jumped to 187,000 in 1910. By 1917 over 5 million cars were on the road. Like the railroad, the automobile stimulated other industries. Construction of cars added to the demand for steel, oil, and other products. Furthermore, it spawned another major economic undertaking—road building. At the beginning of the twentieth century the roads in America were dirt. The automobile led to the paving of old roads and the construction of new ones. Soon the construction of highways and their continual maintenance became an industry in itself.

CONSOLIDATION

Automobile manufacturers, like other industries, followed the trend of consolidation and mass production. At first, automobiles were built by small companies all across the country. Competition and consolidation gradually put an end to the small companies and led to the formation of several large car-building companies. Like other industries, automakers employed new management and production methods to increase their efficiency. Henry Ford introduced a moving assembly line that allowed his company to reduce the amount of time needed to manufacture a car. This innovation allowed Ford to reduce the price of his cars, a move that greatly increased sales.

PROBLEMS RESULTING FROM INDUSTRIALIZATION

Industrialization brought prosperity, wealth, and other great benefits to the United States. These advances came at a price, however, for industrialization also created many problems for the country.

Labor Problems

Industrialization brought great wealth to a small group of Americans and prosperity to the growing middle class, but for many others it brought a mere subsistence or poverty.

WORKING CONDITIONS

Many manufacturers looked upon labor as a commodity—something to be purchased at the cheapest price. The flood of immigrants from abroad and the migration of people from the countryside to the city supplied employers with a vast pool of laborers willing to work for low wages. And because labor was a commodity, its price was flexible. If business improved, workers could be paid more. But if it declined, wages, which were barely adequate to support a family, could be cut. For many Americans, particularly immigrants who were happy to find jobs so quickly after their arrival, factory work looked good. In many cases, however, they had little choice, for the only jobs available were in the factories. Workers soon found themselves trapped in jobs they did not like and taking home too little pay. They also found themselves working in conditions that were abysmal. Factory workers put in a seventy-two-hour week in shops that were dark, hot, dirty, crowded, noisy, and dangerous. Some tried to improve their lots by changing jobs, but one factory was pretty much like another. Others tried to supplement their family incomes by sending their wives and children to work under equally intolerable conditions.

UNIONS

Faced with these conditions, factory workers began to unionize. Traditionally, unions were organized by trades. Carpenters, blacksmiths, coopers, and other craftsmen banded together with others of their trade to set wages and prices for their wares. As industrialization progressed, workers began to form unions to represent all the workers in a factory. Some labor leaders, such as Eugene Debs, argued that workers could have more power if all the employees of a particular industry—such as the railroad—combined into one large union.

Unions had a very hard time during the late nineteenth and early twentieth centuries. Owners argued that, as proprietors, they would make management decisions; no one, particularly employees, had the right to tell owners what to do with their businesses. Politicians and many members of the general public looked upon unions and the tactics they used as a threat to public safety and a disruption of order. Another problem was that the workers themselves were divided and without any agreed-upon goals. Skilled craftsmen refused to unite with unskilled laborers. Socialists claimed that labor problems were endemic to capitalism and called for a complete economic reorganization of the country. Other unionists accepted the capitalist system and merely called upon owners to increase wages and improve working conditions.

UNION LEADERSHIP

Samuel Gompers and Eugene Debs—the two most important labor leaders of the era—represented the two different approaches to union organization and agitation. Gompers, as head of the American Federation of Labor, represented primarily skilled workers. Gompers believed that labor problems were economic in nature, rather than political, and urged the unions in the AFL to restrict their goals to higher wages, shorter work days, and better working conditions. Debs, on the other hand, was a confirmed socialist who believed that political change was necessary to insure economic justice. The Socialist party was the political wing of the socialist labor organization, and Debs ran for president four times. Gompers and Debs also differed on their approach to organization. The AFL was a federation of skilled crafts unions, and Gompers supported their efforts to maintain their independence. Debs was more radical in his belief that all workers—from the lowliest unskilled laborer on up—should belong to a single industry-wide union. He encountered strong resistance from the crafts unions, but in 1894 Debs won a major victory when his American Railway Union staged a nationwide strike.

LABOR UNREST

Workers quickly became dissatisfied with their low pay and poor working conditions, and strikes occurred frequently. The great number of strikes—between 1881 and 1905 there were over 36,000 strikes in the United States—indicated the widespread dissatisfaction of workers. The failure of many of these strikes reflected the continued strength of the owners. Feelings ran high among strikers and owners alike, and it was not unusual for a labor dispute to turn into a violent confrontation. The most notorious labor violence of the decade occurred at Andrew Carnegie's Homestead Steel Mill in Pennsylvania in 1892 and at the Pullman Company in Chicago in 1894. Owners of both companies used private guards, police, and state militia to suppress the strikes. Most of the workers who participated in the labor movement were not interested in overthrowing capitalism or destroying their employers; they simply wanted more pay and better working conditions. Socialism remained an influential part of the labor movement, and Debs continued to be an important labor leader. But after 1900 Gompers and the AFL were in the ascendancy, and most union activity focused on attaining improvements and not on changing the system.

Monopoly

As industrialization expanded across the country, owners sought to increase production and efficiency and to increase their power and wealth. Many manufacturers saw consolidation—the elimination of competition and the amalgamation of different companies that produced the same product—as the best means of accomplishing these goals. Industrialists argued that consolidation increased efficiency and was good for the national economy. It also made them lots of money.

Industrialists used several methods in their quest for consolidation. The simplest was to form a monopoly. One business would, by a variety of tactics, either buy out its competitors or force them out of business, thereby becoming the sole manufacturer of a certain commodity or the sole supplier of a certain service. Monopolies, with their ability to set prices and control the availability of goods and services, frequently provoked hostile reactions from the public and local governments. When this happened the owners tried a more subtle approach. One method was for manufacturers of a certain commodity to form a pool, an arrangement under which they agreed to set prices and limit competition. Another was the holding company. Holding companies were businesses that owned other businesses. Individual companies within an industry would retain their own names and managers, but they would all be controlled by one central group. Holding companies frequently diversified and owned businesses in a variety of industries. A final form of consolidation was the trust. The trust was a rather vague sort of arrangement in which a parent company directly owned all the operations under it. It was half way between a monopoly and a holding company. The trust was a legal nicety that allowed companies to avoid state antimonopoly laws. The public was not fooled, however, and by 1900 *trust* became another name for *monopoly*.

An even more subtle form of consolidation occurred in the boardrooms of the large corporations. Industrialization produced a small class of extremely wealthy individuals who invested in a variety of industries. Their large investments enabled them to become members of the directorates of these companies. It was not unusual for a wealthy manufacturer or financier to be on the boards of two dozen or more different corporations. This development placed a great amount of power in the hands of a small group of men and gave them great influence in economic and political affairs.

Urban Problems

The urban growth that accompanied industrialization spawned a number of problems. Rapid population growth taxed the resources of the cities; services and infrastructures proved inadequate as thousands of people poured into the cities. Some cities turned to urban planning in an attempt to regulate growth, but in most cases expansion was uncontrolled. An inadequate supply of low-cost housing was one of the most pressing problems. Overcrowding became widespread as thousands of newcomers sought inexpensive shelter. It was not unusual for ten or twelve people to occupy a space designed for four, in buildings that lacked proper ventilation, heat, and plumbing. Immigrants and blacks in particular suffered because of inadequate housing, and ethnic slums became a regular feature of the urban landscape.

Poverty

Increased poverty also accompanied industrialization. Many of the people flocking to the cities seeking jobs were unskilled farm laborers. Most were able to find work, though frequently for very low pay. The result was a large class of working poor who lived at or just below the poverty level. When business slowed, these workers suffered a pay cut or, even worse, were laid off. Also in this lower class were those people who worked only sporadically and those who were unable to find work.

Environmental Problems

In the 1880s the United States occupied a vast expanse of land rich in resources. The idea that these resources could be exhausted or that air and water could be damaged was unthinkable. It is not surprising, therefore, that Americans paid little or no attention to environmental concerns. Factories belched smoke into the air and dumped their wastes into rivers, miners dug as fast as they could, logging companies started at one end of a forest and cut their way through to the other. On the Great Plains hunters slaughtered millions of buffalo so that their hides could be made into the belts used to drive machinery.

When manufacturing moved to the forefront of the American economy in the late nineteenth century it began to exert a tremendous influence on American society. A majority of Americans either worked in the manufacturing sector or else depended upon it in some way for their livelihood. It became so important to the national economy that the protection and expansion of markets for American-made goods became a central concern of American foreign policy. Manufacturing produced untold wealth and prosperity for the United States and was a central element in the rising power of the nation. But it also created a host of problems that confronted government officials throughout the country. In short, manufacturing became one of the most important factors in defining the United States in the twentieth century.

Selected Readings

Chandler, Alfred. *The Visible Hand: The Managerial Revolution in American Business* (1977)

Daniels, Roger. *Coming to America: A History of Immigration and Ethnicity in American Life* (1990)

George, Peter. *The Emergence of Industrial America: Strategic Factors in American Economic Growth Since 1870* (1982)

Gutman, Herbert. *Work, Culture, and Society in Industrializing America: Essays in Working-Class and Social History* (1976)

Hogan, William. *Economic History of the Iron and Steel Industry in the United States* (1971)

Hollingsworth, John. *The History of American Railroads* (1983)

Hughes, Thomas. *American Genesis: A Century of Invention and Technological Enthusiasm, 1870–1970* (1989)

Jackson, Stanley. *J. P. Morgan: A Biography* (1983)

Jardim, Anne. *The First Henry Ford: A Study in Personality and Business Leadership* (1970)

Kaufman, Stuart. *Samuel Gompers and the Origins of the American Federation of Labor, 1848–1896* (1973)

McKelvey, Blake. *The Urbanization of America, 1860–1915* (1963)

Nevins, Allan. *Study in Power: John D. Rockefeller, Industrialist and Philanthropist*, 2 vols. (1953)

Porter, Glenn. *The Rise of Big Business, 1860–1910* (1973)

Salvatore, Nick. *Eugene V. Debs: Citizen and Socialist* (1982)

Wall, Joseph. *Andrew Carnegie* (1970)

2

A World Power: 1890–1908

1867 U.S. acquires Alaska

1870 Attempt to annex Santo Domingo fails

1882 Commercial treaty with Korea

1883 U.S. begins construction of steel warships

1893 Americans in Hawaii stage successful revolution; U.S. refuses to annex islands

1894 Republic of Hawaii established

1895 Revolution begins in Cuba

1896 U.S. commission established to arbitrate boundary dispute between Venezuela and British Guiana

1897 William McKinley begins first term as president

1898 DeLome letter criticizing McKinley published

USS *Maine* sinks in Havana harbor

Congress authorizes president to use force in Cuba

Spain declares war on U.S.

U.S. wins battle of Manila Bay

U.S. troops occupy Guam

U.S. wins battle of Santiago, Cuba

U.S. troops occupy Puerto Rico

Spain asks for peace negotiations

U.S. captures Philippine Islands

Peace treaty signed

Cuba granted independence

U.S. acquires Hawaii, Philippines, Puerto Rico, Guam, Midway, Wake Island

1899 U.S. acquires portion of Samoa

Revolt begins in the Philippines

1900 Boxer Rebellion in China

1901 McKinley begins second term as president

McKinley assassinated; Theodore Roosevelt becomes president

Cuba becomes a protectorate of the U.S.

1902 Denmark rejects U.S. offer to purchase Virgin Islands

1903 Colombia rejects U.S. treaty on Panama Canal

Panama revolts against Colombia

U.S. recognizes independence of Panama

U.S. and Panama sign canal treaty; canal zone placed under U.S. jurisdiction

1904 Roosevelt Corollary to the Monroe Doctrine stating the right of the U.S. to intervene in Latin American affairs announced

1905 Roosevelt begins second term as president

President Roosevelt mediates an end to the Russo-Japanese War

1906 U.S. troops sent to Cuba to quell revolt

Philippine revolution suppressed

U.S. mediates dispute between France and Germany over African territory

1907 Work begins on the Panama Canal

Dominican Republic becomes a protectorate of the U.S.

U.S. troops sent to Central America

U.S. sponsors peace conference in Washington to end fighting in Central America

1909 U.S. troops sent to Nicaragua

1914 Panama Canal opens

*A*t the beginning of the twentieth century the United States emerged as one of the most powerful nations on earth. This new-found status was exemplified by worldwide economic and territorial expansion. Several factors influenced this expansion. One was a desire to secure overseas markets for the country's industrial and agricultural products. Another was manifest destiny—the belief that the United States was God's chosen country and, as such, destined to dominate world affairs. The third factor was a reform impulse. Americans had always been great believers in improving society. They looked upon reform as a duty that applied to the improvement of foreign people as well as of those at home. A final influence on expansion was domestic politics. Americans found their new status as a world power to be a source of national pride. As a result, national leaders received widespread support for an aggressive foreign policy.

BACKGROUND TO EXPANSION

Basic Tenets of American Foreign Policy

FREE TRADE

Since the beginning of the nation in 1789 two rules guided American foreign policy. The first was a strong support for the principle of free trade. During its early years as a nation the United States had a very large merchant fleet that thrived on international trade. Naturally, the government took a position in support of this trade. The United States maintained that ports should be open to ships of all nations and that merchants, manufacturers, and shippers should have access to worldwide markets. As the nation's economy grew and as American manufacturing increased, the government had even more reason to support this policy.

This position was not absolute, however. On the one hand, the government claimed that exporters and shippers from all nations had the right to compete equally in world markets. At the same time, it also believed that a country had the right to enact tariffs that would give domestic manufacturers and businessmen an advantage over foreign competition. Trade regulations should not, however, grant concessions to or place restrictions upon particular nations. A tariff on wheat, for example, should apply equally to imports from all nations. The result of these beliefs was a policy of modified free trade based upon two premises: one, that a nation had the right to enact reasonable and non-discriminatory (that is, not favoring any particular nation) protective tariffs; and two, that all nations have the right to compete equally for foreign trade.

ISOLATION

The second principle of American foreign policy was that the United States should not form any alliances with foreign nations. For years, Americans watched the European nations get pulled into wars because of military alliances. The United States took advantage of its geographic isolation from other nations to pursue a policy of isolationism. The United States became increasingly active in world affairs in the late nineteenth and early twentieth century, but national leaders were careful to avoid any commitments that could pledge the country to military action.

Early Overseas Interests

TERRITORIAL INTERESTS

During the nineteenth century United States overseas activity was primarily economic in nature. The country did give some support to the independence movements in South America and Greece early in the century, but to a very limited extent only. There was also a limited territorial interest in the Caribbean and Central America. At different times, the United States considered acquiring Cuba, Mexico, and Santo Domingo, but nothing came of these plans. Efforts to gain control of territory for an inter-ocean canal across the Central American isthmus also failed to bear fruit.

EUROPE AND LATIN AMERICA

As the United States grew and prospered, certain regions of the globe became increasingly important for foreign trade. Europe was, of course, attractive as a trading area, but the advanced state of the continent's economy severely restricted American activity in this market. More accessible was Central and South America and the Caribbean. The United States had a long history of trade with this region, dating back to the colonial period. During the late nineteenth century Latin America was an important source of raw materials and one of the main markets for American exports.

ASIA

Trade with Asia grew steadily as the nineteenth century progressed. New England merchants had begun trading with China and India early in the century, and in 1854 the United States became the first Western nation to trade with Japan. The Pacific islands likewise proved to be attractive sources of trade. American merchants and planters found their way to Hawaii in the 1850s. When steamships began to replace sailing vessels, the Pacific islands became important as coaling stations.

OPPOSITION TO EXPANSION

Throughout the nineteenth century Americans satisfied their territorial ambitions by occupying the continental United States. But even as this settlement progressed some Americans dreamed of an extended overseas empire in Central America, the Caribbean, and the Pacific. Others, however, opposed this scheme. The main objection was that the United States possessed a vast expanse of productive territory at home and had no need for overseas possessions. Another objection was the expense of an overseas empire, especially the maintenance of a large navy and the staffing of colonial governments. In fact, some critics raised the same objection to extended foreign trade. The country would, they claimed, need a large navy to protect shipping and a large diplomatic corps to maintain relations with foreign nations.

Racism was also an issue. The United States had a policy of incorporating all its territory into the nation as states and—with the big exception of Indians—granting citizenship to all inhabitants. Critics of expansion objected to the notion of acquiring foreign territory occupied by non-white people and granting them equal status as citizens. Critics also opposed the conquest of foreign lands. Traditionally the United States had acquired foreign territory by purchase or by annexation treaties. It would be a violation of American ideals, critics argued, to conquer foreign lands and force the inhabitants to accept American rule. (A glaring contradiction to this argument was, of course, the acquisition of Indian land. American Indian policy was always ambivalent, and the government justified its acquisitions by arranging treaties which forced the natives to sell their land to the United States.)

Overseas Expansion at the Turn of the Century

By the 1890s the idea of an American overseas empire was a notion that had gained widespread acceptance. There was still a powerful element that opposed foreign expansion, but the anti-imperialists (as the opposition as called) were unable to stop the expansionists. A number of developments in the United States greatly promoted overseas expansion.

COMMERCIAL EXPANSION

The United States had always been a major exporter of agricultural produce. As the nation expanded, farmers brought more land under cultivation and adopted improved farming methods that allowed them to produce far beyond the needs of the continually growing domestic market. Late in the century America's vast manufacturing capacity far exceeded domestic demand, and manufactured goods joined agricultural products in the export market. As a result, the United States found itself in competition with the industrial nations of Europe for a share of the world market. It also found itself competing with these nations for raw materials. The diversified nature of American manufacturing created a demand for ores, timber products, and agricultural goods from Africa, Asia, South America, the Caribbean, and the Pacific islands. The immense production capacity of American manufacturers and farmers, the demand for raw materials, and the competition from other nations for markets and resources placed tremendous pressure on the government to open new avenues of trade.

The European nations had been confronted with many of these commercial problems as early as the fifteenth century. They had resorted to colonization as a means of securing foreign markets and resources. By the 1890s the United States realized that it too needed to strengthen its position in world markets and seriously began to consider the viability of an overseas empire. The possession of foreign territory (or at least the possession of exclusive trading concessions) would guarantee the flow of needed raw materials as well as markets for the country's exports. These colonies would also provide friendly ports for the country's wide-ranging merchant fleet and for the navy needed to protect overseas commerce.

NATIONAL PRIDE

In 1845 a New York newspaper writer coined the term "manifest destiny." Although the phrase was new, the concept was not. From the earliest days of colonial settlement, Americans believed that they were a special people and their land a special place. They believed that divine providence had intended from the time of creation for European settlers to come to North America and establish a nation destined to be the greatest on earth. Throughout the nineteenth century they believed that they had a divine mandate to conquer and occupy North America. By 1890, when the continental United States was completely settled, Americans began to extend this vision abroad. If the United States was destined to be the greatest nation and the American people the greatest people, then, they reasoned, it was only natural for Americans to dominate lesser peoples. This sense of national superiority received a boost late in the century with the evolution of social darwinism. This theory, which applied Charles Darwin's theories on natural selection to international politics, argued that people of northern European descent (particularly those of English origin) were genetically superior to other races. Like manifest destiny, social darwinism provided a rationale for American domination of other parts of the globe.

Closely allied with this sense of greatness was a concern about the status of the United States in the world community. All the great European nations had overseas empires. If the United States was to take its proper place among the great nations, then it must match or surpass those nations in power and prestige. If the other great nations had empires, then, argued the expansionists, the United States should have one as well.

IDEALISM

The concept of manifest destiny included another important aspect in addition to the territorial imperative. If the United States, as God's chosen country, was the best nation on earth—or in the terms of social darwinism, the most genetically advanced—then it necessarily followed that American institutions such as republican government, individual liberty, protestantism, and capitalism were also superior. But being the best not only presented benefits; it also created responsibilities. According to the theory of manifest destiny, it was the responsibility of the United States to be an example to the rest of the world, to show other nations how a country should be organized and governed. In the 1880s and 1890s the expansionists put forth a new interpretation, in which they argued that it was the duty of the United States to move beyond being just an example. The United States should, they claimed, take an active role in spreading those institutions around the globe. Blessed with the benefits of a superior civilization, Americans had a moral responsibility to offer guidance and improvement to those less fortunate. American expansion was not just a campaign for power and economic expansion. It was a moral crusade to remodel the world in the image of the United States. It was a campaign waged not just by diplomats, merchants, industrialists, and the military, but by religious and cultural missionaries as well.

THE SPANISH-AMERICAN WAR

Background to War

SPAIN'S DWINDLING EMPIRE

By 1890 the islands of Cuba and Puerto Rico were all that remained of Spain's once far-flung American empire. When the wars of independence swept through Latin America in the early nineteenth century, Spain was careful to maintain these two islands, her most valuable possessions in the western hemisphere. A revolution wracked Cuba in the late 1860s and early 1870s, but it proved to be unsuccessful.

AMERICAN INTEREST IN CUBA

The United States had always taken a strong interest in these two nearby islands. Southerners, in particular, were attracted by Cuba's great wealth and its system of slave-worked agriculture. Indeed, in the 1850s southern nationalists envisioned the island as part of a great southern slave empire. After the Civil War American businessmen invested heavily in the island's great sugar plantations.

REVOLUTION IN CUBA

In 1895 revolution broke out in Cuba once again. Ironically, the United States was partially responsible for the miserable conditions that sparked the revolt. In 1892 the United States enacted a new tariff that placed a high

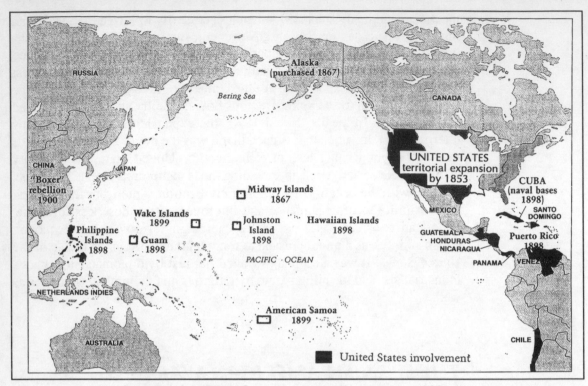

RUSSIA

Alaska
(purchased 1867)

Bering Sea

CANADA

CHINA

JAPAN

UNITED STATES
territorial expansion
by 1853

CUBA
(naval bases
1898)

"Boxer"
rebellion
1900

Midway Islands
1867

MEXICO

SANTO
DOMINGO

Wake Islands
1899

Johnston
Island
1898

Hawaiian Islands
1898

GUATEMALA
HONDURAS
NICARAGUA

Puerto Rico
1898

Philippine
Islands
1898

Guam
1898

PACIFIC OCEAN

PANAMA

VENEZ

NETHERLANDS INDIES

American Samoa
1899

AUSTRALIA

CHILE

■ United States involvement

Fig. 2.1 United States Territorial Expansion to 1900

duty on foreign sugar. This tariff put an end to Cuban exports to the United States and devastated the island's economy. This calamity, combined with Spain's repressive colonial government, set off the uprising. The war quickly degenerated into a series of atrocities committed by both sides. The rebels, unable to defeat the Spanish militarily, hoped to force their withdrawal by destroying Cuba's sugar plantations and ruining the island's economy. The government used equally harsh methods to suppress the rebellion.

NEWSPAPER COVERAGE

The Cuban revolution became a great popular issue in the United States. The American people were, for the most part, sympathetic to the revolutionaries. The government, however, under the leadership of President Grover Cleveland, remained aloof from the struggle and maintained the country's traditional policy of neutrality in the colonial affairs of other nations. But as the war dragged on, pressure on the government to intervene increased.

A major factor in the growing war fever in the United States was the great competition among American newspapers. Editors across the country discovered that they could sell newspapers by providing sensational coverage of the revolution. William Randolph Hearst and Joseph Pulitzer, the two leading publishers in the country, were particularly adept at exploiting the Cuban situation. The newspapers reported in lurid detail the atrocities committed by the Spanish, thus inflaming the sympathy that already existed for the Cubans. The growing popular support for intervention added great weight to the arguments of the expansionists, who wanted to increase American influence in the Caribbean.

War with Spain

THE DELOME LETTER

William McKinley succeeded Cleveland as president in 1897. McKinley took a stronger stance toward Spain than his predecessor had, but he continued to resist the demands for war. In early 1898, however, several events forced the president's hand. In February the Spanish ambassador to the United States, Dupuy deLome, wrote a private letter containing remarks highly critical of McKinley. This letter fell into the hands of a Cuban agent, who gave it to the American newspapers. The publication of the letter, which characterized McKinley as a weak-willed opportunist, greatly incensed the American public.

SINKING OF THE *MAINE*

This report was immediately followed by even more alarming news: On February 15 the American battleship *Maine* blew up in Havana harbor. An investigating committee concluded that the ship had been destroyed by an underwater mine; whether this had been the work of the Spanish or the Cubans could not be determined. Who the culprit actually was did not matter to the American public. In their minds the Spanish were responsible.

DECLARATION OF WAR

The public outcry for war was great, but still McKinley resisted. In one last attempt to avoid war, the administration demanded that Spain declare an armistice to end the fighting in Cuba. Popular pressure became too great, however, and before Spain could comply, McKinley asked Congress for authority to send troops to Cuba. Congress granted the authority on April 11. This measure was followed on April 20 by a series of resolutions that not only empowered the president to use military force but also declared Cuba to be an independent nation and denied any territorial ambitions in Cuba. Spain, which had belatedly agreed to the armistice, declared war on the United States on April 24. For the first time in over fifty years the United States found itself at war with a foreign nation.

THE PHILIPPINES

The war itself was almost an anticlimax. Spain, a declining power with an outdated navy, proved to be no match for America's burgeoning strength and its modern navy. Undersecretary of the Navy Theodore Roosevelt, an ardent expansionist, kept the navy on alert and as soon as war was declared sent the Pacific fleet to attack the Spanish-controlled Philippine Islands. Commodore George Dewey sailed into Manila Bay on May 1 and demolished the Spanish fleet anchored there. With this stroke a war supposedly for the liberation of Cuba became a war of territorial conquest. American troops arrived shortly thereafter, and in August the Spanish governor of the Philippines surrendered. American forces en route to the Philippines captured the island of Guam without a struggle; the Spanish garrison did not even know there was a war.

CUBA

The conquest of Cuba also proceeded quickly. American troops landed in Cuba in mid-June and on July 1 captured the outposts of the fortified city of Santiago. The Spanish forces in Cuba greatly outnumbered the Americans, but the Spanish officers, demoralized by Spain's deteriorating fortunes, failed to press their advantage. On July 3 the American navy destroyed the Spanish fleet at Santiago and forced the surrender of the city, a victory that effectively ended Spanish control of Cuba. Later in July American troops occupied the nearby island of Puerto Rico.

THE PEACE TREATY

The destruction of the fleets at Manila and Santiago proved disastrous to the Spanish war effort. On July 26, only ten weeks after the fighting had started, the Spanish government sued for peace. Commissioners met in Paris and negotiated a treaty, which they signed on December 10, 1898. Spain granted independence to Cuba and "sold" the Philippines to the United States for $20 million. It ceded Puerto Rico and Guam to the United States as indemnity for the war.

AFTERMATH

Americans, for the most part, rejoiced in the victory. Dewey's whirlwind victory at Manila Bay and the highly publicized charge of the Rough Riders—a regiment led by former undersecretary of the navy and now Colonel Theodore Roosevelt—at San Juan Hill in Cuba created new national heroes and glamorized the exploits of the military. The light casualties suffered by the American troops in their rapid conquest of the Spanish islands—379 killed, 1,600 wounded, and 5,000 dead from disease—added to the sense of glory. In the short space of a year, the United States had proved itself to be a major military power and had acquired an overseas empire.

Not all Americans were pleased with this adventure, however. Critics claimed that the war had been fought without provocation and for the benefit of large business interests. They also argued against the acquisition of far-away territory, particularly the Philippines. Expansionists responded that the war had been fought for good cause and that expansion would benefit all Americans and the residents of the new territories as well. They proudly pointed out that the United States had guaranteed the independence of Cuba and that it would grant independence to the Philippines as soon as it was feasible.

THE AMERICAN EMPIRE

Expansion into the Pacific

The increasing importance of Asian trade and the Spanish-American War convinced American officials of the necessity of controlling strategic islands in the Pacific Ocean. In the late 1890s, the United States took possession of Guam, Samoa, Midway, and Wake Island. More important, however, were the large island chains of Hawaii and the Philippines.

HAWAII

United States interests in Hawaii were represented by a large group of American sugar planters who, by 1890, dominated the islands' economy. In 1893 the planters, aided by the American ambassador and a contingent of Marines, seized control of the government and applied to the United States for annexation. President Cleveland condemned the action of the ambassador and refused to take possession of the islands. Defeated in their bid for annexation, the revolutionaries established the Republic of Hawaii and bided their time. Cleveland's successor, William McKinley, advocated annexation but was unable to persuade Congress to take action. When the war with Spain started, the strategic importance of Hawaii became obvious. The United States annexed the islands on July 7, 1898.

THE PHILIPPINES

The acquisition of the Philippines created a special problem for the United States. Many people questioned the wisdom of annexing a distant territory occupied by a foreign, non-white population. At first President McKinley hesitated to acquire the islands, but their strategic and commercial value convinced him to push for annexation. In explaining his decision, McKinley argued that he had little choice. Indeed, he claimed, he had only three options: surrender the islands to a foreign nation, grant the Filipinos a premature independence, or annexation. This last option, the president said, was the only humane and Christian action to take.

Part of the debate over annexation focused on the questions of how the Philippines would be governed and what rights the inhabitants would have. In the past it had been assumed that territories occupied by the United States would eventually be incorporated into the union as states. Inhabitants of the territories possessed full rights as citizens of the United States. But those territories had been in North America and the inhabitants were, for the most part, white American settlers. What arrangement, critics asked, was the government going to make for an Asiatic people occupying a land so distant from the United States?

The colonial government created for the Philippines (and used in Puerto Rico as well) resembled the traditional form of territorial government used in the past. At its head was a governor appointed by the president. The governor exercised broad administrative and legislative powers and was assisted by a board of commissioners (comprised of both American and Filipino members), which was also appointed by the president. The governor shared legislative power with a popularly elected assembly. The inhabitants of the islands were granted many of the rights and privileges of residents of the United States, but they were not awarded citizenship. This arrangement, although far short of autonomy, did provide the Filipinos with a degree of self-government. The colonial government, in an effort to establish a benign administration, launched a program of building schools, roads, and other civic improvements designed to Americanize the islands.

This arrangement proved unsatisfactory to the Filipinos. When the war broke out in 1898 the islanders organized an army and a provisional government and declared their independence from Spain. When American troops arrived, the Filipino army fought alongside them against the Spanish. The Filipinos, who expected the United States to recognize their independence, were shocked at annexation. They refused to accept this new colonial status, and the insurrection against Spain became an insurrection against the United States. Both sides fought a ruthless guerrilla war, and casualties ran high—American losses exceeded 7,000 (out of 70,000 men sent to suppress the rebellion), and the Filipinos suffered even more. Although the American army was successful in quelling the rebellion, the harsh tactics employed to defeat the rebels alienated many islanders. The war ended in 1902, but anti-colonial sentiment remained rampant; in 1908 the pro-independence party won a majority of the seats in the first election for the new national assembly.

Expansion into the Caribbean and Central America

THE ROOSEVELT COROLLARY

Following its victory in the Spanish-American War, the United States looked upon the Caribbean and Central America as its special province. Even more than Hawaii or the Philippines, the Caribbean basin was of great economic and strategic value to the United States. Other nations maintained colonies and exercised influence in the area, but their power was eclipsed by the rising might and international activism of the United States. In 1904 President Theodore Roosevelt announced his intention to broaden the diplomatic and military role of the United States in the western hemisphere. The new policy, known as the Roosevelt Corollary to the Monroe Doctrine, stated that the United States reserved the right to intervene in the internal affairs of the Central American and Caribbean nations in order to insure the peace and stability of the region.

INTERVENTION

Intervention took several forms. The most common means of intervention was the use of military force to suppress rebellion or to maintain order. But there were other ways as well. When war broke out in Central America in 1908 President Roosevelt sent troops to protect American interests. But he also persuaded representatives of the Central American nations to meet in Washington, where, under the guidance of the United States, they negotiated a peace treaty. A third method of intervention was the protectorate, an arrangement in which a large power assumed administrative duties in a small nation when local officials were unable to maintain order to the satisfaction of the more powerful country.

CUBA

The first American protectorate was established in Cuba in 1903. Although the United States guaranteed Cuban independence, American government officials questioned the political stability of the island and feared that it might fall under the power of another nation. The United States sought to forestall such an event by drafting a series of provisions designed to maintain stability and having the Cubans insert them in their constitution. Among these provisions was the right of the United States to intervene in Cuban affairs to maintain order. The United States tried to persuade other Latin American nations to accept similar provisions but was unsuccessful.

THE PANAMA CANAL

The United States had a strong interest in the entire region, but Panama proved to be of particular importance. The United States and the western European nations had long favored the construction of a canal connecting the Atlantic and the Pacific. All that had been accomplished, however, was an American-operated steamboat-railway line across Nicaragua. A French company attempted to dig a canal across the isthmus in Panama, but it went bankrupt in 1888. When the expansion of the American empire in the Pacific made a canal across Central America a necessity, a commission appointed by President Roosevelt recommended that the canal be built at the same location as the abandoned French project. At the time, Panama was a province of Colombia. The United States attempted to negotiate a treaty for canal rights with Colombia, but the South American nation rejected the proposal. Roosevelt contemplated seizing Panama by force, but this proved unnecessary, for in November 1903 the Panamanians, with support from the United States, launched a successful revolt against Colombia. The United States recognized the independence of the Republic of Panama on November 13, 1903; on November 18 the two countries signed a treaty granting the United States the right to build and operate a canal. Major construction began in 1905, and on August 15, 1914, the Panama Canal was opened to traffic.

INTERNATIONAL RELATIONS

Asia

CHINA

Throughout the nineteenth century China had been a major center of Asian trade. The vast Chinese feudal system greatly weakened the nation, and by the end of the century the Europeans were able to force the Chinese to grant liberal trading concessions. Indeed, foreign influence had advanced to the point where China had been divided into spheres of influence, with each foreign nation exercising exclusive control of the trade (including tariff rates, ports, and railroads) within its sphere. The United States, afraid that it would be denied access to trade, decided to oppose this arrangement. In 1899 Secretary of State John Hay initiated his Open Door Policy. This plan, adopted from an earlier British proposal, called upon nations trading in China to guarantee all nations access to China's ports, to grant citizens of all nations equal trading rights within the various spheres of influence, and to allow the Chinese government to set tariff rates. The ultimate goal of Hay's policy was the gradual reduction of foreign control in China and the emergence of an independent nation committed to free trade. Such a policy would have benefited the United States, but it would have been of little use to the nations that already enjoyed trading concessions. These nations rejected this proposal at first, but increasing anti-foreign agitation in China forced them into a degree of compliance.

If the United States was alarmed by this commercial division of China, the Chinese were outraged. Antiforeign nationalists organized the secret Society of Fists (or "Boxers," as they were commonly known) and began to attack foreigners. In 1900 the Boxers gained control of Peking and laid siege to the foreign legations there. A multinational military force, which included Americans, landed in China and drove the Boxers out of Peking. For the third time in the space of three years American troops found themselves in combat in Asia.

JAPAN

American economic interests in Asia mandated a foreign policy designed to promote the unity and independence of China. Those same interests dictated an entirely different policy for Japan. Japan was an emerging imperial power with strong territorial ambitions in mainland Asia. The United States looked favorably upon Japan's increasing power, for a strong Japan would be in a position to limit the commercial advances of the European nations. It would also serve as a check against Russia, the other empire with territorial interests in mainland Asia. This was a difficult policy to pursue, however. The United States wanted Japan to be strong enough to block the ambitions of other nations in China, but not so strong that it could dominate the mainland itself. The United States received an opportunity to shape the balance of power in eastern Asia when Japan and Russia went to war in 1904. The United States took an active diplomatic role in the conflict by advising the warring nations to respect the territorial sovereignty of China. This role increased in 1905 when the Japanese government asked President Roosevelt to mediate a settlement between the two nations. Roosevelt accepted the task and served as arbitrator in the peace negotiations, an action that earned him the Nobel Peace Prize in 1906.

Europe

While the United States broadened its involvement in affairs around the globe, it was careful to maintain its traditional policy of neutrality in European affairs. But even while maintaining this policy of neutrality, the country took a greater interest in Europe. President Roosevelt repeatedly reminded the nation that a new world order had emerged. Improvements in transportation and communications and the rapid expansion of colonial empires brought the nations of the world closer together. The United States should maintain its neutrality, Roosevelt argued, but as American markets and influence expanded, it became increasingly important for the United States to take a more active role in world affairs, even in Europe. American leaders believed that peace and order were conducive to commerce and prosperity; a war in Europe or a colonial war involving European nations would be a threat to American economic well-being. These concerns, coupled with a need to win respect as a world leader from the Europeans, persuaded Roosevelt and other like-minded men that the United States could no longer afford to remain aloof from European affairs. This led to a new foreign policy for Europe that focused on encouraging a balance of power and the arbitration of international disputes. This new position drew a fine line for American diplomats to walk, for most Americans agreed that if the country embarked on this course, it should be careful to adhere to its traditional policy of neutrality and nonalignment.

An opportunity for the United States to take an active part in European affairs came in 1906. In an attempt to expand its territorial holdings in Africa, France sought to bring the country of Morocco under its control. Great Britain, Italy, and Spain gave approval to the French initiative, but Germany opposed it. When it looked like war might erupt, President Roosevelt persuaded French and British officials to meet with American diplomats at Algeciras, Spain, and draft a proposal to resolve the crisis. Roosevelt then persuaded Germany to accept the terms of the proposal. As in Asia, Roosevelt had used arbitration to maintain a balance of power and avert war.

In the years between 1890 and 1910 expanding American economic and diplomatic interests projected the United States into a leading role in the international arena. Many Americans questioned the wisdom of this new role, but the expansion of American interests undermined these objections. The new-found might of the United States, triggered by an era of vigorous economic growth and piloted by the aggressive leadership of men such as Theodore Roosevelt, placed the nation at the forefront of world affairs. The United States still held to its traditional policy of neutrality in European affairs, but America's new role as a world leader placed this policy in jeopardy. How long, critics wondered, could the United States pursue its goal of trying to maintain international order and stability before it was drawn into a major international war?

Selected Readings

Beale, Howard. *Theodore Roosevelt and the Rise of America to World Power* (1956)

Beisner, Robert. *Twelve Against Empire: The Anti-Imperialists, 1898–1900* (1968)

Campbell, Charles. *The Transformation of American Foreign Policy, 1865–1900* (1976)

Clemens, Samuel (Mark Twain). *The War Prayer* (1968)

Gould, Lewis. *The Presidency of William McKinley* (1980)

McCullough, David. *The Path Between the Seas: The Creation of the Panama Canal, 1870–1914 (1977)*

Porter, William S. (O. Henry). *The Complete Works of O. Henry* (1926)

Morgan, H. Wayne. *America's Road to Empire: The War with Spain and Overseas Expansion* (1965)

Trask, David. *The War with Spain in 1898* (1981)

Welch, Richard. *Response to Imperialism: The United States and the Philippine-American War, 1899–1902* (1979)

Young, Marilyn. *Rhetoric of Empire: American China Policy, 1895–1901* (1968)

3

The Progressive Era: 1901–1917

1880 Salvation Army begins operations in the United States

1886 First settlement house in the U.S. opens in New York

1887 Interstate Commerce Commission established

1889 Hull House established in Chicago

1890 Sherman Antitrust Act

1901 President William McKinley assassinated; Theodore Roosevelt becomes president

1902 "Wisconsin Idea"—series of political reforms introduced in Wisconsin

1905 Roosevelt begins second term as president

1906 Upton Sinclair's *The Jungle* published

William Howard Taft becomes president

1909 NAACP organized

1913 Woodrow Wilson becomes president

1916 New York Birth Control League (predecessor of Planned Parenthood) founded

1917 Wilson begins second term as president

Americans have always had a strong reform impulse. From the Pilgrims who landed at Plymouth in 1620 to the patriots of the revolutionary generation to the reform movements of the 1830s and 1840s to the abolitionists of the Civil War era, numerous Americans have turned to social activism in order to correct iniquities and improve the condition of life. The progressive reform movement of the early 1900s was a continuation of this same spirit and concern.

PROGRESSIVISM

Middle-Class Reform

DIVERSITY OF MOVEMENT

Like the earlier reform efforts, progressivism was not a unified movement. As Americans entered the twentieth century they found themselves facing a number of problems resulting from the rapid industrialization and urbanization of the previous twenty years. Some people, especially socialists, believed that these problems were caused by capitalism and argued for a new economic and political system. Most reformers, however, accepted capitalism and believed that the best remedy for the nation's ills was to apply specific reforms to specific problems. At the same time, reform-minded citizens agreed that these problems were widespread and serious enough to endanger the nation's well-being.

MIDDLE-CLASS SUPPORT

The progressive reform movement drew much of its support from middle-class Americans who were afraid that their position in American society was vulnerable to the changes engendered by industrialization. The rise of the fantastically wealthy and powerful industrialists and the corresponding growth of a poor, frustrated, and frequently violent lower class threatened the order and stability craved by those in the middle. This polarization frightened many people who believed that if reform did not occur the country would be ripped by disorder, revolution, and civil war. The only hope for continued peace and prosperity was to bridle the power of the great corporations and alleviate the suffering of the poor. The progressive reform movement was not, therefore, just an effort to correct a variety of social problems; it was a multifaceted effort by the middle class to save itself by combating the threat posed by these problems.

TYPES OF REFORM

In general, progressive reform can be divided into three large categories. One was the social justice movement. Industrialization brought great wealth to the United States, but it also brought poverty, inequality, and injustice. Reformers, driven by a sincere wish to improve the lot of the poor and by a fear of the social chaos that would result if they did not, launched attacks on a multitude of social evils. The second was a program of government reform. As concerns about corruption in city and state government increased, progressives initiated a number of measures to improve bureaucratic efficiency and increase the power of the electorate. The third part of the movement, embodied in a series of antitrust suits and legislation designed to protect workers and consumers, was an effort to force large corporations to conduct their affairs in a more socially responsible manner. The campaign to win these reforms was fought by private individuals and organizations as well as by city, state, and federal governments.

Influences on the Reform Movement

SPIRIT OF REFORM

The spirit that drove progressive reform was similar to the spirit that fostered expansionism. Americans felt that the wealth, power, and prestige that would enable them to solve problems abroad could also be brought to bear on problems at home. Middle-class reformers sought to create the same order and stability at home that the expansionists hoped to bring to the rest of the world. Reformers worked to instill the same American values in the hearts of immigrants and the poor that expansionists sought to implant in the nation's new colonies. In short, just as the expansionists claimed that they could bring peace and stability to the chaotic and diverse international arena, so the reformers believed that they could maintain order and efficiency in modern society.

SOCIAL THEORY

In addition to the feeling that Americans, with their great wealth, energy, and divinely mandated destiny, could accomplish anything, several sociological theories led the reformers to believe that they could overcome the problems confronting the country. One was the belief that environment shaped personality. Philosophers and theologians have long debated the nature of man: Are human beings innately good, bad, or neutral? Reformers of the nineteenth and early twentieth centuries considered this question unimportant. They believed that it was not the state of a person's soul at birth that defined character and behavior but the conditions in which that person lived. For them it was poverty, injustice, and improper family life that caused problems—conditions that could be changed with positive results.

GOVERNMENT RESPONSIBILITY

Equally important to the reform movement was an increasing belief that government had a responsibility to protect public welfare. The basic goal of American political philosophy has been to balance the rights of the individual with the welfare of society as a whole. For many years the rights of the individual had been paramount. But in the early twentieth century the tremendous physical and economic growth of the country, combined with the trend toward bigness and consolidation, convinced many people that events had moved beyond the control of the individual. A single individual did not seem to count for much in such a large nation. Faced with what they perceived to be a decline in status within the body politic, people turned to government to represent their interests and protect them from the large and powerful forces of modern society. Individuals and private organizations played an important role in progressive reform, but it was government action that scored the really big victories for the movement.

PUBLICITY CAMPAIGN

The reformers maintained a great trust in the American sense of justice. They believed that if the people and their government became aware of the many problems confronting the country they would take action to alleviate them. To achieve this end the reformers engaged in a thorough documentation of the social, political, and economic ills of the United States. Photographers such as Jacob Riis took their cameras into the slums and realistically illustrated the horrible living conditions there. Other reformers compiled table upon table of statistics relating to poverty, crime, and unemployment. Magazines and newspapers regularly carried articles exposing corruption and social problems and reported on the efforts to end them. Books such as *Poverty* by Robert Hunter; *The Treason of the Senate* by David Phillips; *The Octopus* by Frank Norris; and *Maggie, A Girl of the Streets* by Stephen Crane were of great importance in bringing problems to light and stimulating reforms to solve them.

PRIVATE EFFORTS AT REFORM

Government action was essential to the success of many of the reforms proposed by the progressives, but the campaign for reform was not undertaken by the government alone. Individual citizens, either acting alone or as members of civic and professional organizations, lent great support to the reform movement. This civic activism aided the movement in several ways. The most obvious, of course, were their direct efforts on behalf of reform.

But beyond this, the many middle-class Americans who worked for reform became familiar with the problems confronting the country and eventually recognized that private efforts alone could not bring about the necessary changes. This realization made them supportive of government action. Conversely, as interest in and support for reform grew, politicians, aware that they could not afford to ignore the concerns of their constituents, became more and more committed to reform legislation.

Civic Organizations

The primary vehicle for private reform efforts was the civic organization. The problems confronting Americans ranged from issues of national importance to matters of local interest, from the age-old problem of poverty to a newly awakened concern for personal health. In some cases, reformers mobilized already existing associations such as fraternal or professional organizations; in others they formed new organizations charged with the duty of combating a single evil.

PROHIBITION

A particular concern of these civic organizations was the physical and moral well-being of the American people. Reformers worked for better health care and improved sanitation, supported physical-fitness programs, and encouraged their fellow citizens to practice better physical hygiene. They also launched attacks on what they considered the greatest source of moral decay—the consumption of alcoholic beverages. Temperance advocates had been fairly successful during the first half of the nineteenth century in their efforts to reduce the amount of alcohol consumed in the United States. Late in the century, however, consumption once again began to rise. A particular target of prohibition forces was the saloon. These neighborhood taverns became symbols of public drunkenness, wholesale vice, and moral degeneracy. Middle-class reformers were likewise disdainful of the lower-class immigrants who frequented the saloons. The Women's Christian Temperance Union (WCTU) and the Anti-Saloon League led an assault on the sale and consumption of liquor. Their tactics included public demonstrations, attacks on saloons—Carrie Nation, a Kansas prohibitionist, became famous for her axe-wielding raids on saloons—and political organization. The Prohibition party represented the goals of the temperance movement and ran candidates for office from president on down (see Appendix B). The prohibitionists, who campaigned at the local, state, and federal level for restrictions on alcoholic consumption, won the ultimate victory in 1919 when the eighteenth amendment to the Constitution outlawed the manufacture and sale of alcoholic beverages in the United States.

SUFFRAGE AND BIRTH CONTROL

At the beginning of the twentieth century middle-class American women were, for the most part, better educated and more economically secure than their mothers or grandmothers and possessed more leisure time than women of previous generations. Endowed with time, energy, and a desire to be of service to society, these women eagerly embraced the reform movement, serving not only as foot soldiers but as leaders. Women's organizations—local clubs, church groups, and national associations such as the WCTU—exercised tremendous influence.

Given this involvement, it is not surprising that issues of special interest to women received attention. Women's suffrage, like prohibition, had been a subject of public debate for almost a century. The campaign by women to win the right to vote gained strength in the late nineteenth century when a number of states granted women the franchise. Victory at the state level frustrated women as much as it pleased them. Wyoming granted women the complete right to vote in 1869, but by 1900 only three other states had followed suit. The movement picked up momentum in the early 1900s, and efforts to rally support began to bear fruit. By 1919 women could vote in twenty-nine states. In 1920 the states ratified the nineteenth amendment to the Constitution, guaranteeing the right of women to vote.

Another issue important to women—birth control—proved to be not so popular. Margaret Sanger, the founder of the New York Birth Control League (the predecessor of Planned Parenthood), led the campaign for birth control, arguing that it was a public health measure. For most Americans, birth control or even a public discussion of reproduction were forbidden subjects. Indeed, federal law prohibited the advocacy of contraceptives. When Sanger opened a birth-control clinic in New York City in 1916 she was arrested for creating a public nuisance. On another occasion she had to leave the country to avoid prosecution for her writings.

CIVIL RIGHTS

Civil rights was also an unpopular subject. Most progressive reforms were designed to benefit or protect the white middle class. The large black population of the South could certainly pose a threat if it were ever mobilized and united, but there was not much chance of this happening in the early twentieth century. The middle-class urban whites who comprised the core of the reform movement considered blacks to be an inferior rural underclass and were content to leave them so. Black leaders, however, shared the same reform impulses as whites. Booker T. Washington, W. E. B. Dubois, and other black reformers led the fight for social and economic improvements for blacks. With the support of a few liberal whites, black reformers organized the National Association for the Advancement of Colored People in 1909 and the National Urban League in 1911.

Reform Movements from England

SETTLEMENT HOUSES

Two other popular reform measures were imported from England. The first, the settlement house movement, was created to provide a moral living environment for young women who moved to the cities seeking employment. These houses, which started as residences, evolved into social and educational centers that offered a wide range of programs and activities to both men and women. Settlement houses proliferated in many American cities, with Hull House in Chicago being the most famous.

RESCUE MISSIONS

The other English import was the rescue mission. Unlike settlement houses, which were intended for the benefit of lower-middle-class working women and men, rescue missions were religious organizations created to win converts among the poor and to provide emergency food, shelter, and clothing for the destitute. Some of the rescue missions were sponsored by large organizations such as the Salvation Army; most, however, were operated by local clergy and church groups intent on bringing relief to the impoverished in their own communities. Although rescue missions and settlement houses began operating in the United States in the 1880s—long before the beginning of the progressive movement—both gained great popularity in the early twentieth century and became bastions of progressive reform.

Philanthropy

An important source of funding for these private reform efforts was philanthropy. Philanthropy had always existed in the United States, but the great wealth created by industrialization enabled philanthropists to support charities and civic improvement projects at a level that had not been dreamed of before. There were several reasons for this increase in public benefaction. Many wealthy men and women possessed a sense of *noblesse oblige* and considered it their duty to support public institutions and charities. Men such as Andrew Carnegie who had amassed huge fortunes felt obliged to return part of it to the country that had allowed them to become so wealthy. Carnegie, who retired from business in 1901, gave away $350 million before he died in 1919. There were also less charitable reasons for giving. Many unscrupulous businessmen who found themselves under indictment for illegal activities felt they could improve their chances in court by becoming public benefactors. Less cynical were those donors who sought to use their wealth as a means of social control. Many progressives argued that reform was the only alternative to revolution. Wealthy individuals who shared this view donated readily in an effort to protect their social and economic standing. These donations also enabled them to control the direction of reform, molding it to fit their needs and desires. They could also use reform organizations to instill their religious and moral values on the working poor in an effort to make them better and more obedient employees.

Public Art
One goal of the progressive movement was to preserve moral values in the seemingly chaotic and immoral world of the city. Reformers used several methods to do this. One was public art. The new-found wealth of the late nineteenth century financed a flowering of the arts in the United States. Artists and patrons alike believed that art was a strong moral force and that it should be put on public display. Museums proliferated, murals and paintings decorated public buildings, and public monuments became common features of cities and towns. Public sculpture, in particular, played an important part in this movement. Private organizations across the country commissioned statues and monuments to celebrate the great achievements of the past. Monuments such as Augustus St. Gaudens's *Sherman Memorial* in New York and the statue of Abraham Lincoln by Daniel Chester French in the Lincoln Memorial in Washington were designed to offer inspiration to the nation's citizens and to instill immigrants with the virtues of their new home.

URBAN REFORM

Ideological Bias
Throughout the nineteenth century and into the twentieth, Americans maintained a bias against big cities. Most Americans lived on farms and in small towns and believed cities to be centers of corruption, crime, poverty, and moral degradation. Their distrust of the city was caused, in part, by a national ideology that proclaimed farming the greatest occupation and rural living superior to urban living. This attitude remained central to American thinking even as the number of urban dwellers increased and cities became an essential feature of the national landscape. Gradually, economic reality overcame ideology. Thousands of Americans abandoned the precarious life on the farm for more secure and better paying jobs in the city. But when these people migrated from the countryside to the city they carried their fears and suspicions with them. These new urbanites, already convinced that cities were overwhelmed with great problems, eagerly embraced the progressive reforms that promised to bring order out of the chaos of the city. Businessmen and professionals, convinced that urban reform was the key to economic growth, led the movement to make cities more attractive places in which to live and work.

Reform Measures
CITY GOVERNMENT
One of the great scandals of turn-of-the-century urban life was corruption in city government. Big-city bosses sold offices and contracts for public services; received payments from operators of illegal businesses such as

brothels and gambling houses; took kickbacks from city employees; and used intimidation, election fraud, and bribery to maintain their power. It was not unusual for employees at all levels of government to demand bribes or payments in exchange for service. The progressives rebelled not only against the corruption of this system but its inefficiency as well. Urban dwellers across the nation rallied behind reform candidates for mayor, city council, judgeships, and prosecuting attorney in an effort to drive corrupt officials from office. Although not entirely successful in defeating the bosses, reformers made significant improvements in city government and services. The most important innovation was the city manager. These professional managers—in some cases individuals and in others members of a board of commissioners—were hired to supervise the daily administration of city business. Assisted by other professionals who worked as department heads, city managers provided new efficiency and improved the quality of services delivered by city government.

PUBLIC UTILITIES

Another important reform came in the area of public utilities. As cities grew, general access to a reliable source of electricity, gas, water, and sewerage facilities became essential. Water and sewerage systems were usually operated by municipal governments, but the gas and electric networks were privately owned. Reformers feared that the privately owned utility companies would charge exorbitant rates for these essential services and deliver them only to people who could afford them. Some city and state governments responded by regulating the utility companies, but a number of cities began to supply these services themselves. Proponents of these reforms argued that public ownership and regulation would insure widespread access to these utilities and guarantee a fair price.

PUBLIC VICE

A special target for middle-class urban reformers was public vice. Private organizations such as the WCTU waged war against public drunkenness, but some activities, particularly gambling and prostitution, were too entrenched to be threatened by private action. In many cases, they were protected by their ties to the city bosses. As part of the drive for urban reform, the progressives pressured city police forces to take action against these "immoral" crimes. The police, under the direction of reform mayors and prosecuting attorneys, responded by organizing vice squads charged with putting an end to gambling, prostitution, and other kinds of public vice. There was an adverse side to this campaign, however, for some anti-vice crusaders saw immorality and pornography everywhere and attacked the theater, literature, movies, and other forms of legitimate recreation.

CITY PLANNING

While some reformers focused on government and public behavior, others looked at the cities as a whole. Civic leaders, convinced that physical environment influenced human behavior, argued that cities should develop master plans to guide their future growth and development. City planning was nothing new, but the rapid industrialization and urban growth of the late nineteenth century took place without any consideration for order. Urban renewal in the early twentieth century followed several courses. Some cities, such as Washington, Chicago, and Cleveland, introduced plans to completely rebuild the city core. Most other cities contented themselves with plans for regulating future growth. The most common practice was to establish zones for different types of buildings and activities. Under this arrangement certain parts of town were restricted to residential use, while others were set aside for industrial or commercial development. City planners also placed a strong emphasis on the development of parks and playgrounds. These recreational areas served several functions: They maintained a vestige of the rural countryside within the city, and they provided space where urban dwellers could relax and exercise, thereby improving both their mental and physical health.

HOUSING

Housing also received attention. The thousands of people moving into the cities discovered that these urban areas lacked sufficient housing. Many, particularly immigrants, were forced to lived in overcrowded, substandard housing in rapidly spreading slum areas. A major goal of the progressives was to eliminate slums and to provide decent housing for all—a goal that continues to elude urban reformers.

STATE REFORM

Economic Reform

BUSINESS REGULATION

State governments played a central role in the implementation of progressive reform. States traditionally had the responsibility to protect the rights and welfare of their citizens. They were active particularly in the area of business regulation. The states had the authority to regulate businesses operating within their borders, and it was not unusual for states to pass laws designed to protect their citizens from unfavorable business practices. In the late nineteenth century, state governments took the lead in fighting the railroads by passing legislation to regulate the rates charged by the rail companies.

LABOR LAWS

These actions encouraged citizens' groups to lobby the state governments for other business-related reforms. The National Child Labor Committee, for example, launched a campaign that persuaded most of the states to pass some sort of child-labor legislation. Other state laws designed to protect workers included the six-day work week, the eight-hour day, worker's compensation for on-the-job injuries, a minimum wage, old-age pensions, and the protection of women workers. Like most progressive reform legislation, the states enacted these laws in a piecemeal fashion. There was no comprehensive plan of labor legislation, and there was no provision for large-scale projects such as unemployment insurance, pension plans, or universal health care. Even so, the battles for the reforms that did pass were long and hard, and the courts struck down much of the reform legislation.

STATE LEADERSHIP

Even with these defeats, state governments gained the reputation of being bastions against corporate abuse, and a number of governors—most notably Robert LaFollette of Wisconsin, Woodrow Wilson of New Jersey, and Hiram Johnson of California—rose to national prominence on the strength of their reform campaigns. Furthermore, the states served as laboratories for progressive reform measures. Reformers across the country looked to states such as Wisconsin and Oregon for models of reform. All state governments were not advocates of reform, however. Indeed, some state legislatures were notoriously hostile to any restrictions on business. But overall, the states compiled an impressive record of reform.

Political Reform

The states were also pioneers in political reform. They introduced tax reform, established regulatory commissions, and instituted new election practices. Changes in the method of conducting primary elections gave voters the power to select candidates. The introduction of recall gave the electorate greater control over their representatives. In 1904 Oregon gave voters the right to initiate legislation; it also passed a referendum law that allowed the electorate to vote upon laws passed by the legislature. The states also took the lead in granting women suffrage: Sixteen states gave women full voting rights and another thirteen granted a partial franchise before the passage of the nineteenth amendment.

Educational Reform

Theoretically, universal education was a mainstay of the American republic, but public schools were under the control of local school districts, and the quality and amount of education that students received varied greatly. Under the leadership of the progressives, state governments became more active in education and worked to improve schools. State legislatures passed compulsory education laws, and reformers introduced changes in curriculum and teaching methods that led to greater uniformity in the nation's school systems.

FEDERAL REFORM

State and local government and private organizations were successful in bringing reform to many areas, but it was clear to all that some problems—particularly those relating to corporations—required action by the federal government. Some conservatives argued that the federal government lacked the authority to interfere in private matters, but the reformers countered that regulation of the corporations had become a matter of public welfare. In fact, the progressives claimed, the emergence of giant corporations that operated on a national scale required an extension of federal power.

Business Regulation

THEODORE ROOSEVELT

The role of the federal government in the regulation of business increased when Theodore Roosevelt became president in 1901. Roosevelt realized that the great corporations played an essential role in America's rise to international prominence. But he also believed that they were out of control and needed to be tamed. He did not wish to destroy the corporations; he simply wanted them to be more responsive to the public welfare. Roosevelt believed that the protection of public welfare was one of his prime duties as president and set out to establish the federal government as a regulator of the business community. In his battle to protect the public against the power of the large corporations, Roosevelt used the same aggressive tactics that he used in dealing with foreign nations. He also set the tone for progressive reform at the federal level. William Howard Taft and Woodrow Wilson, the two presidents who followed him, continued the program of reform and adhered to Roosevelt's philosophy of protecting the public welfare.

REGULATORY COMMISSIONS

A central element in the government's plan to regulate business was the establishment of commissions to study the problems associated with big business, recommend a course of action, and administer the regulatory laws. Some of these were special presidential commissions appointed to report on a specific issue; others were permanent bodies. The most important regulatory agency of the progressive period was the Interstate Commerce Commission (ICC), which had been in existence since 1887. When Roosevelt assumed office in 1901 the ICC had very little power; over the next ten years, however, Congress passed several laws that increased the power of the commission and widened its jurisdiction. Regulatory commissions established during this period include the Industrial Relations Commission in 1912 and the Federal Trade Commission in 1914. Congress also established the Department of Commerce and Labor in 1903 (divided into the Department of Commerce and the Department of Labor in 1913).

ANTITRUST SUITS

In 1903 Congress passed the Elkins Act, a law that defined a number of interstate trade violations and granted the courts authority to issue injunctions against these practices. Once this legislation was in place, the Justice Department launched an aggressive campaign of lawsuits against corporations operating in violation of interstate trade laws. The first victory came in 1904 when the Supreme Court ruled against the Northern Securities Company and ordered the breakup of this holding company. Other suits led to the dissolution of trusts in the meat, oil, and tobacco industries. In all, Roosevelt initiated forty-four anti-trust suits and Taft ninety. The major outcome of the antitrust suits was not the breakup of the large corporations but rather a realization on the part of business that the government was serious about antitrust legislation. The corporations also realized that federal antitrust regulations were not that restrictive. The result was a modification of corporate operations that brought interstate trade practices into compliance with federal law.

PROTECTIVE LEGISLATION

In addition to its campaign to break up the trusts, the federal government took action to provide more direct protection to the public. In 1906 Upton Sinclair published *The Jungle*, a novel about a poor immigrant working in the Chicago stockyards. Sinclair's graphic description of the unsanitary facilities maintained by the meat-packing industry aroused public disgust and anger. This book came hard on the heels of a progressive campaign against medicines that contained large quantities of alcohol and addictive drugs but little curative power. Public indignation was so great that Congress passed a pure food and drug law and a meat inspection law. Heartened by these victories, reformers pushed for other protective legislation. In 1916 and again in 1919 Congress passed child labor laws, but these were struck down when the Supreme Court ruled that regulation of labor contracts was a prerogative of state, not federal, government.

Conservation

President Roosevelt was an avid hunter and outdoorsman who took a special interest in the protection of the country's great natural beauty and the conservation of its natural resources. Roosevelt believed that federal control of natural resources would slow the rate of depletion and help conserve them for the future. He also valued the land for its natural beauty and as a place of recreation. During his presidency, Roosevelt added some 125 million acres to the national forest reserves, oversaw the creation of several national parks (most notably Yosemite), and placed restrictions on coal lands, phosphate beds, and water-power sites. He was also instrumental in the passage of the Newlands Reclamation Act of 1902, which provided federal funding for massive irrigation projects in the West. In 1908 Roosevelt sponsored a national conservation conference at the White House, and one of his last acts as president was the establishment of the National Commission for the Conservation of Natural Resources.

Constitutional Amendments

The great influence of the progressive reformers and the diversity of their interests is exemplified by the ratification of four constitutional amendments during this period. The sixteenth amendment, ratified in 1913, gave the federal government the authority to collect an income tax. Prior to this, the national government had depended on the sale of land and import tariffs as sources of revenue. Tariffs, which amounted to a form of sales tax, had always been unpopular; by 1913 land sales had, for the most part, ended. The progressive income tax, which laid a heavy burden on the rich and exempted poorer citizens, was considered a major reform.

The seventeenth amendment, also ratified in 1913, provided for the direct election of U.S. senators. This amendment was as much a state reform as it was a federal one. The Constitution originally allowed the state legislatures to elect senators. The seventeenth amendment deprived powerful state legislatures of this privilege and transferred it to the electorate. The ratification of this amendment is another example of the election reforms approved by the states during the progressive era.

The states ratified the eighteenth amendment, which prohibited the manufacture and sale of alcoholic beverages, in 1919. Prohibitionists had been successful in persuading many state and local governments to ban alcohol. But, they argued, prohibition could not be enforced properly until it was enacted nationwide. The Volstead Act, passed in 1919 over President Wilson's veto, gave the federal government the authority to enforce prohibition.

The nineteenth amendment, passed the following year, guaranteed the right of women to vote. Many states had granted some degree of suffrage to women, but others completely denied the right. By 1918 popular support for a constitutional amendment had become so great that opponents were forced to give up. Congress passed the amendment in January 1919; by the end of the summer of 1920 it had been ratified by the states.

Table 3.1 Progressive Reforms Enacted by the Federal Government, 1901–1920	
1903	Department of Commerce and Labor established
	Elkins Act: strengthened Interstate Commerce Commission
1904	*Northern Securities Co.* v. *U.S.*: successful prosecution of railroad holding company
1905	*Swift and Co.* v. *U.S.*: successful prosecution of the beef trust
1906	Hepburn Act: strengthened Interstate Commerce Commission
	Pure Food and Drug Act
	Meat Inspection Act
1908	Aldrich-Vreeland Act: banking regulation
	White House Conservation Conference; National Commission for the Conservation of Natural Resources appointed by President Roosevelt
1910	Mann-Elkins Act: placed interstate communications system under the jurisdiction of the Interstate Commerce Commission
	Mann Act: prohibited interstate prostitution
1911	*Standard Oil of New Jersey* v. *U.S.*: successful prosecution of the oil trust
	U.S. v. *American Tobacco Co.*: court-ordered reorganization of tobacco trust
1913	Department of Commerce and Labor divided into two departments
	Sixteenth amendment to the Constitution ratified: enacted federal income tax
	Seventeenth amendment to the Constitution ratified: provided for direct election of U. S. senators
	Federal Reserve System established
1914	Federal Trade Commission established
	Clayton Antitrust Act
1916	Child Labor Act (struck down by Supreme Court in 1918)
1919	Child Labor Act (struck down by Supreme Court in 1922)
	Eighteenth amendment to the Constitution ratified: prohibition of the manufacture and sale of alcoholic beverages
1920	Nineteenth amendment to the Constitution ratified: guaranteed women's suffrage

THE ELECTION OF 1912

Theodore Roosevelt

THE ELECTION OF 1904

Theodore Roosevelt became president in 1901 when recently reelected President William McKinley was killed by an assassin in Buffalo, New York. Roosevelt, an aggressive and ambitious man, quickly assumed control of both the government and the Republican party. Many conservative Republicans opposed Roosevelt's policies, particularly his use of the federal government to implement economic reform. The president was an astute politician, however, and was able to win conservative support for his renomination in 1904. His commitment to reform assured his popularity with the voters. It also deprived the Democrats—the nominal party of reform—of an issue. The Democratic nominee, Judge Alton Parker of New York, ran a lackluster campaign and never posed a serious threat to Roosevelt, who won easily (see Appendix B).

AN ACTIVIST PRESIDENT

Roosevelt believed that the president was the "steward of the public welfare" and, as such, should take an active role in the formulation and implementation of both foreign and domestic policy. Committed to the principle of federal regulation of business and to the expansion of American power and influence overseas, Roosevelt used his office to promote his goals. A skilled politician and a popular figure with the electorate, he was the central figure of his era. When Roosevelt won the election in 1904 he announced that he would not run in 1908. Despite pressure to run again in an election he was sure to win, Roosevelt held to his promise.

William Howard Taft

1908 ELECTION

Roosevelt's hand-picked successor was William Howard Taft, an able administrator who had risen to prominence as governor of the Philippines and Roosevelt's secretary of war. The 1908 election pitted Taft against William Jennings Bryan, who had been the unsuccessful Democratic candidate in 1896 and 1900. Bryan was a brilliant speaker and a noted reformer, but the popularity of the Roosevelt administration assured Taft's victory (see Appendix B).

THE TAFT ADMINISTRATION

Taft was a well-known advocate of reform, and his administration compiled an impressive record, both in legislation and in the courts. At the same time, Taft supported a number of measures—particularly a new tariff—that were favorable to big business. This position hurt Taft, but his greatest problem was that he was not Theodore Roosevelt. Taft was more conservative than Roosevelt, and he did not share his predecessor's belief that the president should be an aggressive advocate of the public welfare. According to Taft, reform was the responsibility of Congress, the states, and the courts, not the president. This attitude, along with Taft's lack of political skill, alienated many progressives who saw the president's stance as a retreat from the strong commitment of previous years. More important, it alienated Roosevelt, who was growing bored with life as a private citizen. The final split between the two former friends came in 1910 over a dispute concerning the Department of the Interior. When Gifford Pinchot, the director of the U.S. Forest Service and a political ally of Roosevelt, accused Secretary of the Interior Richard Ballinger of misconduct in office, Taft dismissed Pinchot. This move cost Taft whatever support he had left among the progressives.

The Candidates

Roosevelt, outraged at Taft's performance in office, announced that he would seek the Republican nomination for the presidency in the election of 1912. When the convention renominated Taft, Roosevelt and his supporters left the Republican party and joined up with the newly formed Progressive party. This party, comprised mainly of disaffected Republicans, named Roosevelt as their presidential candidate. The Democrats nominated Woodrow Wilson, the reform governor of New Jersey, as their candidate.

THE SOCIALIST PARTY

Also in the running was Eugene Debs, the candidate of the Socialist party. Debs, who had been imprisoned for his activities as leader of the American Railway Union, was making his fourth bid for the presidency. Socialism never attracted many adherents in the United States, but it was an influential movement nevertheless. Many reformers and intellectuals, disheartened by the halfway measures of the progressives, turned to socialism. Some workers also joined the socialist ranks, and they occasionally succeeded in electing one of their leaders to political office. The progressives, for their part, greatly feared socialism. Indeed, a great incentive to reform was the fear that if measures were not taken to alleviate social and labor problems, a socialist revolution would result and the middle class would lose its preeminent place in American society.

The Election

The campaign, which centered largely on the best methods for implementing reform, quickly boiled down to a race between Roosevelt and Wilson. Roosevelt easily commanded the support of reformers within the Republican party but was unable to take any Democratic votes away from Wilson. The division in the Republican ranks between supporters of Taft and Roosevelt assured a Democratic victory. Wilson easily beat Roosevelt, with Taft coming in a poor third. Debs, who advocated the most radical plan of reform, polled almost a million votes and placed fourth (see Appendix B).

Woodrow Wilson

Wilson was not as reform-minded as Roosevelt, but he was more progressive in his outlook than Taft. Among the notable achievements of his administration was a new tariff with lower rates; the creation of the Federal Reserve System—the nation's first major banking reform since the Civil War; the Clayton Antitrust Act, which outlawed a number of abusive corporate practices; and the establishment of the Federal Trade Commission, which greatly increased the federal government's ability to combat unfair practices in interstate commerce. Most important, however, was Wilson's attitude toward the presidency. Like Roosevelt, he believed that the president should exercise an active role in national leadership. He used the prestige of his office to promote reform and exercised his influence to assure the passage of legislation in Congress. Even so, federal reform efforts declined during his presidency. As war clouds gathered in Europe, Wilson became increasingly preoccupied with foreign affairs and paid less attention to the reform movement. The progressives continued to work for reform, but when war broke out in 1914 the public's support for the movement waned. From 1917 through 1920 the United States directed its energy toward fighting a war and settling the terms of the peace. Congress and the state assemblies continued to pass progressive reform measures up through 1920, but America's entry into World War I marked the end of the progressive period.

The progressive movement produced many notable reforms, but it was not an unqualified success. The movement comprised many different elements wanting many different things, and it was impossible for all the proposed changes to be implemented. Even so, many of the reforms, such as women's suffrage and election reform, were significant gains. Also of great importance was the emergence of the federal government as an economic regulator. Like other reform efforts, federal regulation of business was at best a moderate success. But the public's acceptance of this new regulatory role paved the way for the more extensive economic and social legislation that came in later years. This era also saw the president assume a more active role in legislative and political affairs. Roosevelt and Wilson were the strongest and most aggressive presidents since Lincoln. They redefined the duties of the president and established a pattern of strong executive leadership that was, for the most part, followed through the rest of century.

Selected Readings

Addams, Jane. *Forty Years at Hull House, with Autobiographical Notes* (1938)

Blum, John M. *The Republican Roosevelt* (1954)

Bogart, Michele. *Public Sculpture and the Civic Ideal in New York City, 1890–1930* (1989)

Coletta, Paolo. *The Presidency of William Howard Taft* (1973)

Dreiser, Theodore. *Sister Carrie* (1900)

Gould, Lewis. *The Presidency of Theodore Roosevelt* (1991)

Hays, Samuel. *Conservation and the Gospel of Efficiency: The Progressive Conservation Movement, 1890–1920* (1969)

_____. *The Response to Industrialism, 1885–1914* (1957)

Hofstadter, Richard. *The Age of Reform: From Bryan to FDR* (1955)

Kolko, Gabriel. *The Triumph of Conservatism: A Re-Interpretation of American History, 1900–1916* (1963)

Kraditor, Aileen. *The Ideas of the Women's Suffrage Movement, 1890–1920* (1965)

Link, Arthur. *Woodrow Wilson and the Progressive Era, 1910–1917* (1954)

McCullough, David. *Mornings on Horseback* (1981)

O'Neill, William. *The Progressive Years: America Comes of Age* (1975)

Patterson, James T. *America's Struggle Against Poverty, 1900–1980* (1981)

Porter, William S. (O. Henry). *The Complete Stories of O. Henry* (1926)

Riis, Jacob. *How the Other Half Lives: Studies Among the Tenements of New York* (1890)

Sinclair, Upton. *The Jungle* (1906)

Thelen, David. *Robert LaFollette and the Insurgent Spirit* (1976)

Wiebe, Robert. *The Search for Order, 1877–1920* (1967)

4

World War I: 1914–1920

1913 Revolution begins in Mexico

1914 U.S. troops occupy Vera Cruz, Mexico

World War I begins

U.S. declares neutrality in European war

President Wilson makes unsuccessful attempt to initiate peace talks in Europe

1915 British ship *Lusitania* sank by German U-boat; 128 Americans killed

Haiti becomes U.S. protectorate

U.S. recognizes new government in Mexico

1916 President Wilson makes second attempt to initiate peace talks in Europe

U.S. troops sent to Mexico

U.S. troops sent to Dominican Republic

President Wilson makes third effort to initiate peace talks in Europe

1917 U.S. troops withdrawn from Mexico

U.S. severs diplomatic relations with Germany

Zimmermann letter made public

Wilson begins second term as president

U.S. acquires Virgin Islands from Denmark

U.S. declares war on Germany

Selective Service Act passed

U.S. troops arrive in France

Bolsheviks gain control of Russian government; Russia withdraws from the war

U.S. declares war on Austria-Hungary

1918 Wilson announces his "Fourteen Points" peace plan

U.S. troops help repulse German offensive

U.S. troops participate in Allied offensive

German government asks Wilson for an armistice

Austria-Hungary surrenders

Kaiser Wilhelm II abdicates

Armistice declared

1919 Wilson attends peace conference in France

Treaty of Versailles signed; includes provisions for League of Nations

Wilson suffers a stroke

1920 Senate rejects the Treaty of Versailles

Wilson wins Nobel Peace Prize for efforts on behalf of the League of Nations

1921 Warren Harding becomes president

Congress passes joint resolution ending war

Senate ratifies treaties of peace with Germany, Austria, and Hungary

*W*hen war erupted in Europe in August 1914 most Americans, although alarmed at the international scope of the conflict, felt safe from it. Once again the Atlantic barrier between Europe and North America and the traditional commitment of the United States to neutrality in European affairs saved the country from involvement. Americans took a lively interest in the war, and most sided with the British and the French rather than the Germans. Overall, however, they were happy to be out of it. It was, after all, just another European war.

This isolation was not destined to last, however. As the war progressed, American sympathy for the Allies increased, as did antagonism toward Germany. Tension with Germany continued to build, and in 1917 the United States entered the war. The American people were reluctant to go to war. But when they did, they approached it with the same zeal that they exhibited in their campaign for reform and their drive for overseas expansion. Indeed, the three were very similar, for the Americans (and particularly President Wilson) saw the war and the *subsequent peace settlement as a chance to reform Europe and promote the spread of American ideals.*

The war in Europe became the focus of American foreign policy during this period, but the country never lost sight of its other interests, particularly in the Caribbean and Central America. The United States kept a firm grip on its control of this area, dispatched troops to several countries, and came close to war with Mexico.

THE BEGINNING OF THE GREAT WAR

During the first decade of the twentieth century the European nations were engaged in an intense struggle for power, both on the continent of Europe and abroad. Two central features of this contest were a massive arms buildup and an intricate web of military alliances and mutual defense pacts. These measures were designed to help maintain a balance of power, but when war broke out they had they opposite effect and quickly drew all the great powers into the conflict.

The Opening of Hostilities

The war started when Archduke Ferdinand, the nephew and heir of the emperor of Austria-Hungary, was assassinated in June 1914. At the time, Austria was embroiled in a dispute with Serbia (a small Balkan nation) over the independence of parts of the Austrian empire. A Serb shot Ferdinand, and Austria, with the support of its ally Germany, retaliated by invading Serbia in August. Russia went to the assistance of Serbia, and France, allied with Russia, was pulled into the conflict. Great Britain, allied with both Russia and France, was reluctant to join the fight and did not do so until Germany invaded Belgium. Turkey and Bulgaria entered the war on the side of Germany. Italy, Greece, Romania, and Japan eventually joined the Allies. The nations of the British Commonwealth participated in the war, and the Arabs in the Middle East revolted against their Turkish rulers. Germany, stronger and more aggressive than Austria, became the primary enemy of the British, French, and Russians.

American Neutrality

This chain of events vindicated the traditional American policy of neutrality in European affairs. As the country increased its overseas empire it took a greater interest in European affairs. Even so, the government was careful to avoid any treaty agreements and was not, therefore, drawn into the conflict. On August 4, 1914, President Wilson reinforced this position by issuing a proclamation of neutrality, which forbade Americans from giving military aid to the belligerents.

SUPPORT FOR NEUTRALITY

Most Americans supported neutrality and were pleased that the United States was not involved in the war. Beyond that, private reaction to the war was mixed. Many people, particularly recent immigrants, maintained strong sentimental ties with the Old World. Some Americans of German and Austrian descent tended to sympathize with their homelands. Irish-Americans, always implacable foes of Great Britain, also sympathized with Germany. But most Americans, influenced by the strong cultural and economic ties between the United States and Great Britain, supported the Allies. As the war progressed support for the British increased, and Germany gradually became the enemy.

OPPOSITION TO NEUTRALITY

Not all Americans approved of neutrality. The people of the United States were not familiar with war. Their most recent experience had been the one-sided and relatively bloodless conflict with Spain twenty years earlier. They were certainly not familiar with the brutal new military technology being used in Europe. Some young men looked upon war as a great adventure and yearned to participate. Many of these men went to Canada, England, and France, where they enlisted in the armed forces of those nations. Others remained at home, where they joined quasi-military organizations. These outfits sent their members to camp and instructed them in military drill. Supporters of this movement, including former president Theodore Roosevelt, argued that the war was a threat to the United States and called for a program of preparedness, including an increase in the size of the army and navy.

THE PEACE MOVEMENT

Other Americans, particularly many of the leaders of the progressive movement, were horrified by the war. For them war was a barbaric act, the antithesis of modern, rational reform. They feared—correctly—that war would interfere with their campaign for reform. These progressives became leaders in a peace movement that worked for two goals: keep the United States out of the war and achieve a mediated settlement of the war in Europe.

Maritime Problems

At the beginning of the war the United States maintained its traditional policy of free trade. Neutral nations, the United States argued, had the right to trade with all nations during time of war without interference from the belligerents. This policy was a great benefit to American business. If American ships were allowed to sail unimpeded while the merchant fleets of the warring nations were confined to port, then American shippers stood to make huge profits. Needless to say, the belligerent nations objected to this, for under this arrangement their enemy could have unrestricted access to supplies. Great Britain declared a total blockade of German ports, and the Germans announced that their U-boats would sink any ships headed for Allied ports.

WARTIME TRADE

Gradually, the United States shifted its support to the Allies. The government objected to the restrictions imposed by the British blockade, but given the strength of the ties between the two countries, the objections were mild. Furthermore, England, recognizing the importance of maintaining America's good will, moderated its policy just enough to ease American concerns. Most important, however, was the huge volume of American war supplies flowing into England. Germany had never been a major trading partner of the United States, and the vast increase in wartime trade with the Allies more than made up for the losses incurred by the blockade. United States trade with Germany and Austria declined from $169 million in 1914 to less than a million dollars in 1916. At the same time, trade with the Allies skyrocketed from $865 million to over $3 billion. In addition, American bankers provided the Allies with loans to finance the war effort. Officially the United States was neutral. There was little doubt, however, that the United States was clearly in the Allied camp.

GERMAN U-BOAT ATTACKS

Equally important to the shift in American policy were the German U-boat attacks. Germany, which could not tolerate this massive flow of material to the Allies, used its new fleet of submarines (called U-boats) to disrupt the supply line. In 1915 the Germans declared a U-boat blockade of Great Britain. Unlike modern submarines, U-boats had to surface before they could attack. Unable to defend themselves from armed vessels, U-boat effectiveness depended on the ability to make surprise attacks and then quickly escape. In traditional blockades warships seized offending vessels and released the crews. U-boats, however, attacked without warning and without giving crews and passengers a chance to escape before the ship was sunk. The United States considered these attacks immoral and unjust, as well as a violation of neutrality. Citizens became outraged in May 1915 when a U-boat sank the British passenger liner *Lusitania* with the loss of 1,200 lives, including 128 Americans. The fact that the ship was carrying war supplies (the British hoped that the presence of so many passengers would shield the ship from attack) was not accepted as an excuse. President Wilson shared the progressives' desire for peace and a mediated end to the war. But when the Germans rebuffed his demand for an end to submarine warfare, he increased the size of the army and the navy and made other preparations for war.

LATIN AMERICAN AFFAIRS

While the United States government grappled with the diplomatic problems presented by the war in Europe, it also exerted itself to keep control over the Caribbean and Central America. Wilson, like Roosevelt, did not hesitate to use military force to protect American interests.

The Caribbean   HAITI AND THE DOMINICAN REPUBLIC

In 1915 revolution erupted in debt-ridden Haiti. Several European nations, including Germany, threatened to intervene in order to insure repayment of their loans. President Wilson sent troops to the island nation, established a protectorate, and arranged for American supervision of the country's finances. When revolution struck the following year in the Dominican Republic (which had been a United States protectorate since 1907) Wilson ordered the military to take control of the government.

THE VIRGIN ISLANDS

As the threat of war with Germany increased, the United States became increasingly concerned about the security of the Caribbean. Fearful that the Germans would gain possession of the Danish-owned Virgin Islands, Wilson renewed American efforts to purchase this chain of over fifty islands. Denmark, which had rejected a previous offer in 1902, agreed to the transfer, and the Virgin Islands became American territory in 1917.

Mexico   THE MEXICAN REVOLUTION

Mexico posed a greater problem. When Wilson became president in 1913, Mexico was in the midst of a rebellion against the dictatorial General Victoriano Huerta. American business interests, which were suffering under the Huerta regime, favored American aid to the insurgents. Wilson, hoping to avoid intervention, urged an armistice between government and rebel forces and offered to mediate. He also called upon Huerta to resign. When Huerta refused, Wilson offered to send troops to aid the rebels. Venustiano Carranza, the leader of the opposition forces, feared American intervention and rejected the proposal. He did, however, accept an offer of arms and equipment. Wilson authorized arms sales to the rebel forces and ordered the navy to patrol the coast of Mexico to prevent the delivery of supplies to Huerta.

VERA CRUZ

Mexican-American relations reached a dangerous level in April 1914 when Mexican troops arrested a group of American sailors in Tampico. The sailors were released, but the commander of the American fleet was dissatisfied with the Mexican apology. With Wilson's permission, he ordered an attack on Vera Cruz, Mexico's leading port, ostensibly to prevent a German ship from landing supplies for Huerta. After a brief but bloody battle American troops occupied the town, a move that prompted Huerta to sever diplomatic relations with the United States and threaten war. An attempt by Argentina, Brazil, and Chile to mediate the dispute failed when Mexico rejected the proposed settlement. The crisis was defused in July 1914 when the revolutionaries forced Huerta from office. The United States withdrew its troops from Vera Cruz and recognized the newly established government under Carranza.

PANCHO VILLA

Tensions between the two countries flared again in early 1916. Some of the rebel forces in Mexico refused to accept the new government. Pancho Villa, a rebel leader in northern Mexico, tried to topple the government by provoking American intervention. He killed Americans working in Mexico, and in March 1917 rebels under his command attacked the town of Columbus, New Mexico, killing seventeen people. President Wilson sent a force of 15,000 men under General John Pershing into Mexico in pursuit of Villa. The Mexican government reluctantly allowed the expedition, but as time passed and the troops remained, the Mexicans began to object. Pershing pursued Villa for almost a year but was unable to capture him. Meanwhile, the trouble with Mexico diminished in importance as the likelihood of war with Germany increased. Wilson finally recalled the troops in February 1917 when a new constitution promised political stability in Mexico.

STEPS TOWARD WAR

Attempts at Mediation

It did not take President Wilson long to realize that neutrality alone would not keep the United States out of the war in Europe. His only hope for peace was that the war would end before the United States became involved. In December 1914 Wilson dispatched his friend and advisor Edward House to Europe in a futile hope to initiate peace talks. A second mission in February 1916 likewise failed. In the early stages of the war both sides thought they could win and neither was willing to negotiate. By the end of the year, however, the war had reached a stalemate, and the German government asked Wilson to act as mediator. Wilson's response was to ask the belligerents to state their war aims. Neither side had ever given any explanations for why they were fighting or what they hoped to achieve at the end of the war. Wilson believed that the first step toward a settlement was for each side to state its position. The Allies responded by presenting a series of demands for reparations and territorial cessions—terms that Germany and its allies would not willingly accept. Germany, locked in an internal power struggle between the civilian government and the military, was unable to offer any terms. Rebuffed once again, Wilson began to formulate a plan of his own, a plan that proposed to bring an end to the fighting and achieve a "peace without victory."

The 1916 Election

The main issues of the 1916 election were progressive reform and the war in Europe. Wilson, who had compiled a credible record on both, stood for reelection as a Democrat. The Republicans, still suffering from the Roosevelt-Taft division, nominated Charles Evans Hughes, a former reform governor of New York and a respected member of the Supreme Court. In some of his campaign statements Hughes sounded more warlike than he was. This false impression, combined with former President Roosevelt's open support for America's entry into the war, cast the Republicans as the prowar party. Wilson's campaign effectively countered this with the slogan, "He kept us out of war." The race was close, and Wilson won by a margin of only half a million votes (see Appendix B).

Renewed U-Boat Attacks

By the time of Wilson's inauguration in March 1917 German-American relations had begun to deteriorate. The Germans, who had agreed in early 1916 to no longer attack ships without warning, announced in January 1917 that they would resume their U-boat attacks on all ships trading with the Allies. The Germans knew that the renewal of unlimited submarine warfare would most likely bring the United States into the war. But the high command in Berlin believed that the disruption of the supply line to England would offset any advantage the Allies would gain from America's entry into the war. When a U-boat sank the *USS Housatonic* on February 3 the United States broke diplomatic relations with Germany.

The Zimmermann Note

Tension increased the following month when the British intercepted "the Zimmermann note." The message, sent by German Foreign Secretary Arthur Zimmermann to the German ambassador in Mexico, proposed that Germany and Mexico form a military alliance and that Mexico, with German assistance, invade the southwestern United States. This message, like the DeLome letter before the Spanish-American War, infuriated the American people and fueled the growing anti-German feeling in the country.

Declaration of War

Wilson, hoping that a show of force would deter the Germans from any further anti-American activity, announced that all American merchant ships sailing for Europe would be armed. This policy failed to have any effect, however; during March 1917 the Germans sank five American freighters. Faced with this increased belligerency the United States declared war on April 6.

THE WAR

When the United States entered the war in 1917 the effort became, like overseas expansion and the progressive reform movement, a crusade. According to Wilson and other proponents of the war, this was not a campaign for territorial expansion or national aggrandizement; it was a campaign for peace. The American goal, they claimed, was to restore order and stability to war-torn Europe. Wilson declared war with the belief that American troops could break the stalemate and force the Europeans to the conference table—where the United States would promote the creation of a new Europe where law and moderation would replace war and aggression.

Public Reaction   SUPPORT FOR THE WAR

Most Americans, agreeing that intervention was necessary, supported the president and rallied in support of the war effort. The government fueled this spirit by launching a massive propaganda campaign that depicted the Germans as barbaric aggressors; Americans, on the other hand, were the defenders of freedom and democracy. The presidentially appointed Committee on Public Information directed this work, employing volunteer speakers, parades, posters, and pamphlets to promote the war cause. An important part of this campaign was the sale of Liberty Bonds. These bonds, along with increased taxation, financed the war. The government conducted four war-bond drives and used every means at its disposal to convince people that it was their patriotic duty to support the war effort by purchasing bonds.

OPPOSITION TO THE WAR

Not all Americans supported the war, however. Many people adhered to the peace movement that had begun before the United States entered the war. These dissidents argued that German provocation did not justify a declaration of war, that the United States should continue the policy of isolation from European conflicts, and that war was not a solution to the world's problems. The government, believing that the country was embarked on a crusade to save the world, had little tolerance for these objections. Opponents of the war were accused of being unpatriotic, were harassed, and, in some cases, were deported from the country. State and local governments contributed to this campaign by passing and fervently enforcing sedition ordinances of their own. These laws were aimed at labor organizations and people of German descent as well as war protesters. Anyone voicing dissent of any kind was libel to prosecution.

Waging the War

MOBILIZATION

This effort to stamp out dissent and rally popular support for the war was part of a vast mobilization plan. The federal government appointed hundreds of wartime commissions to oversee the war effort. These commissions supervised the production of war materials, directed a massive ship-building program, encouraged farmers to produce more crops, regulated prices, settled labor disputes, and managed the railroads. Congress authorized a building program to increase the size of the navy and—despite objections that it was despotic and un-American—instituted a draft. Of the 24 million men who registered, almost 3 million were drafted.

STATE OF THE WAR: JUNE 1917

In all, some 5 million men served in the armed forces during the war; about 2 million served in Europe. The first American troops, under the command of General John Pershing, arrived in France in June 1917, but the American army did not reach full force until the following summer. The United States entered the war at a critical time. After three years of war the opposing sides had fought themselves to a standstill in northwestern France. The arrival of American troops provided necessary reinforcements for the Allies, for a revolution had broken out in Russia and most of the soldiers in the Russian army had mutinied. When the Russians withdrew from the war in the fall of 1917 thousands of German troops were transferred from the Russian front to France. This German military superiority was balanced by the effectiveness of the British blockade and by a deep division within the German government. The military favored continuing the war, but many civilian officials wanted an armistice. The German war effort was also hampered by the eventual failure of its U-boat campaign. When the United States entered the war it established the practice of using American and British warships to accompany the supply convoys crossing the ocean. The U-boats did not dare surface for an attack when warships were present. By the end of the war attacks were almost unknown.

AMERICANS IN COMBAT

American troops saw some combat during the fall and winter of 1917, but fighting in earnest did not begin until the spring of 1918. The Germans, hoping to defeat the Allies before the entire American contingent was ready for battle, launched a massive offensive in March 1918. The Germans broke through the Allied line but were unable to destroy their army. General Pershing, unwilling to commit his army to combat before it was ready, sent detachments forward as reinforcements for the French and British. The Allies, assisted by 85,000 American soldiers, stopped the German advance in July at the second Battle of the Marne. The Allies then launched a counter-offensive, and American troops saw action up and down the line. In

September the Americans were given their own section of the battle line. Pershing pulled most of his troops together and joined the offensive. An advance by 550,000 men quickly captured the German position at St. Mihiel. The massed American army of 1.2 million men then advanced against the Germans in the Argonne Forest. This attack was part of the final Allied offensive that broke the German line. The summer offensive and Allied counter-attack cost the Germans over a million casualties. By early November the German war effort had collapsed. The army was shattered and in retreat, the U-boat campaign against Allied shipping had failed, the navy had mutinied, and Austria had surrendered. When rebellions began in different parts of Germany, Kaiser Wilhelm, the German emperor, abdicated and fled the country. On November 11 German officials admitted defeat and signed an armistice ending the war.

CASUALTIES

American forces were exposed to combat for a relatively short time—only seven months, compared to four years for the French and British. But this was enough to introduce them to a new kind of warfare. Trenches, barbed wire, machine guns, tanks, airplanes, poison gas, and powerful new artillery and rifles put an end to the massive infantry and cavalry charges of an earlier era. Never had the world seen such a brutal war: Altogether, over 10 million soldiers died. American casualties, although light compared to the losses suffered by other nations, were severe: 49,000 killed and 230,000 wounded. Equally deadly were the living conditions of the soldiers, for disease continued to kill more men than enemy bullets did: 63,000 Americans died of disease while in France, most of them struck down by an influenza epidemic that swept through the Allied camps.

THE PEACE

The end of World War I offered the United States an excellent opportunity to assert itself in world affairs. American participation in the war had been instrumental in the Allied victory and, as a result, the United States was guaranteed a principal role in the peace settlement. More important than this, however, was President Wilson's decision to attend the peace conference. Wilson had formulated a plan designed to guarantee long-term peace in Europe and wanted to use his personal influence to assure its acceptance.

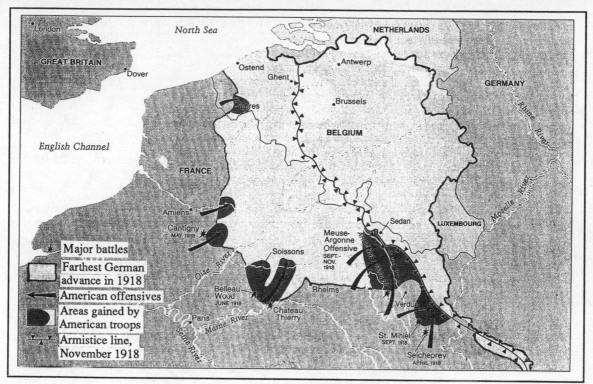

Fig. 4.1 Western Front of the Great War, 1918

Map legend:
* Major battles
* Farthest German advance in 1918
* American offensives
* Areas gained by American troops
* Armistice line, November 1918

Wilson's Peace Plan

THE FOURTEEN POINTS

Wilson the peacemaker was similar to Wilson the progressive reformer. His goal was not just to stop the war. Rather, he proposed to remove the causes of war and promote future peace by establishing order and stability throughout Europe. He presented his program, known as the Fourteen Points, in a message to Congress in January 1918. The first five points called for adjustments in international relations that had contributed to the war: no more secret treaties, freedom of the seas, removal of trade barriers, arms reduction, and an adjustment of colonial claims. The next eight points dealt with the political map of Europe: territory occupied during the war would be restored, the Austrian and Turkish empires would be dissolved and the various nationalities within those empires granted autonomy, and all nations would have the absolute right to determine their own political futures. The last point called for the establishment of an international organization to mediate disputes and guarantee the political and territorial rights of all nations. Notably missing from this proposal were any requirements for the Germans to pay reparations or make territorial concessions.

Table 4.1 The Fourteen Points
1. No secret treaties
2. Freedom of navigation of the seas
3. Removal of all economic trade barriers
4. Arms reduction
5. Adjustment of colonial claims
6. Evacuation of Russian territory; Russia allowed to determine its own political development
7. Evacuation and restoration of Belgium
8. Evacuation and restoration of French territory; Alsace-Lorraine returned to France
9. Adjustment of Italian border
10. Breakup of the Austro-Hungarian empire; autonomy granted to various nationalities
11. Evacuation and restoration of Romania, Serbia, and Montenegro
12. Breakup of the Turkish empire; autonomy granted to various nationalities; Dardenelles opened to free passage of all ships
13. Establishment of independent Poland
14. Establishment of League of Nations

THE LEAGUE OF NATIONS

The League of Nations was the keystone of Wilson's plan. Overseas territorial expansion and increased foreign trade made the United States more vulnerable to war. If nothing else, the disruption of trade caused by war would be contrary to American interests. Wilson realized that the Atlantic Ocean would no longer shield the United States from European conflicts and that any future fighting would be a threat to the United States. America's only hope for future peace, he argued, depended upon the implementation of measures that would prevent the outbreak of war. Like his predecessor Theodore Roosevelt, Wilson favored arbitration as a means of resolving international disputes. Indeed, in 1913 Wilson's first secretary of state, William Jennings Bryan, negotiated treaties with twenty-one nations providing for the referral of international disputes to a permanent board of arbitration. Wilson's proposal for the League of Nations called for the formation of an international assembly of nations that would arbitrate disputes and guarantee the political and territorial independence of all members.

The Treaty of Versailles

Wilson left the United States for Europe on December 4, 1918. At Versailles, where the peace conference met, Wilson encountered opposition from the Allied leaders, who wanted to punish Germany for the war and who were bound by previous treaties. France, for example, wanted reparations and territorial concessions from Germany, and France and England had signed a treaty dividing Turkey's Middle East empire between them. Wilson quickly discovered that national interests were more important to the Europeans than his idealistic peace plan. Faced with these problems, Wilson made concessions on most of his Fourteen Points in order to assure acceptance of the League of Nations.

THE FATE OF THE FOURTEEN POINTS

The first five of Wilson's Fourteen Points were abandoned altogether. The terms of the treaty were negotiated in private by the leaders of the United States, Great Britain, France, Italy, and Japan. Indeed, the principle of no secret treaties was dead long before the conference began, for many issues had already been settled by secret treaties that had been negotiated before or during the war. Great Britain objected to any provisions relating to freedom of navigation, and all the Allies objected to the removal of tariffs and an arms reduction. Japan, France, and England had captured all of Germany's colonies during the war and refused to give them up.

The provisions dealing with European territory were, for the most part, implemented. Occupied territory in Belgium, France, Russia, and the Balkans was evacuated, and the Austrian and Turkish empires were dissolved. Seventeen new countries were created, and borders throughout Europe were redrawn. This redrawing of the map, dictated by the victorious Allies, followed strategic rather than nationalistic lines. Thousands of Germans, for example, found themselves living in the new countries of Poland and Czechoslovakia rather than in Germany.

TERMS FOR GERMANY

Wilson returned home on February 24, 1919, and was back in France on March 13. The Allies finished work on the treaty and presented it to the Germans on May 7. The defeated countries, which had not been allowed to attend the treaty conference, had no choice but to accept the terms dictated by the victors. The final terms of the treaty, which Germany signed on June 28, forced the Germans to accept total blame for the war, forced them to make territorial concessions and pay reparations to the Allies, stripped them of their colonies, and required them to disarm.

LEAGUE OF NATIONS

President Wilson was not happy with the Treaty of Versailles. But he believed that many of the problems not resolved at the peace conference could be handled by the newly formed League of Nations. The League was created at Versailles for the purpose of arbitrating future international conflicts. The basic provisions of the League's covenant closely followed Wilson's ideas for the maintenance of peace. Members agreed to protect the independence and territory of all member nations, they pledged to reduce armaments, and they agreed to submit disputes to the League for arbitration. Any nations refusing arbitration and resorting to war would be subject to League-imposed sanctions.

Table 4.2 Provisions of the Covenant of the League of Nations
1. An assembly in which all member nations had an equal vote
2. A council made up of the United States, Great Britain, France, Italy, Japan, and four nations elected by the assembly
3. An administrative office located in Geneva, Switzerland
4. Members agreed to protect territory and independence of all member nations
5. Members agreed to submit for arbitration all disputes that might lead to war
6. League would apply sanctions against nations going to war
7. Members would reduce armaments
8. An international court of justice

Opposition to the Treaty

ISOLATION

When President Wilson returned to the United States on July 8, he and the treaty received a hostile reception. The greatest concern was that ratification of the treaty would be a major departure from the traditional American policy of isolation from European affairs. Opposition to the proposed League of Nations had surfaced even before Wilson had left for Europe. Many Americans feared that membership in an international assembly would commit the United States to all sorts of foreign treaty obligations. Participation in World War I may have been necessary, critics argued, but there was no need for the United States to commit itself permanently to an international alliance. Rather than maintaining peace, they argued, membership in the League of Nations would result in United States involvement in wars around the globe. Part of the opposition was political: Some Republicans believed that a defeat of the treaty would favor their party in the upcoming presidential election. Most opposition, however, was based on real concerns for the future of the nation and crossed party lines.

Opposition was particularly strong in the Senate, which had to ratify the treaty. A majority of senators favored membership in the League but wanted to amend the treaty to protect certain American interests. Wilson, fearful that any modification of the treaty would destroy the League, pushed for unconditional ratification. Both sides took their cases to the public. Wilson, who had become ill in Europe, embarked on a 9,500-mile nationwide tour to win support for the treaty, delivering thirty-six speeches in twenty-two days. This hectic pace took its toll. In October he suffered a stroke, from which he never fully recovered.

FINAL REJECTION

Between November 6, 1919, and March 19, 1920, the Senate considered a number of resolutions on accepting the treaty with amendments, all of which were defeated. Wilson and the Democrats made ratification a central issue in the presidential campaign of 1920; their candidate, James M. Cox, openly avowed his support for the League. The Republicans were divided on the issue, and their candidate, Warren Harding, refused to take a stand on it. Harding's victory was seen as a repudiation of Wilson's foreign policy and the League of Nations. On July 2, 1921, Congress passed a joint resolution declaring an end to the war. The United States signed separate treaties with Germany, Austria, and Hungary in October 1921. The war was officially over.

THE FATE OF THE LEAGUE OF NATIONS

The League of Nations began to function without American participation. It was moderately successful at arbitrating disputes between small countries and successfully administered occupied territory in Germany. It was powerless to control the large nations, however. Whether the United States could have provided the necessary clout for the League to enforce its provision is a point still open to debate.

When the United States entered World War I it embarked on a new era in foreign affairs. Despite the repudiation of Wilson's attempt to enroll the country in the League of Nations, the United States would no longer be able to remain aloof from international affairs. The military success of the United States in the war and Wilson's participation in the peace conference at Versailles confirmed the country as a world power. The United States had become an indispensable member of the world community whether it desired that distinction or not.

Selected Readings

Burk, Kathleen. *Britain, America and the Sinews of War, 1914–1918* (1985)

Calhoun, Frederick. *Power and Principle: Armed Intervention in Wilsonian Foreign Policy* (1986)

Coffman, Edward. *The War to End All Wars: The American Military Experience in World War I* (1986)

Ferrell, Robert. *Woodrow Wilson and World War I, 1917–1921* (1985)

Haley, Paul. *Revolution and Intervention: The Diplomacy of Taft and Wilson with Mexico, 1910–1917* (1970)

Kennedy, David. *Over Here: The First World War and American Society* (1980)

Levin, N. Gordon. *Woodrow Wilson and World Politics: America's Response to War and Revolution* (1968)

Link, Arthur. *Wilson the Diplomatist: A Look at His Major Foreign Policies* (1957)

Smythe, David. *Pershing: General of the Armies* (1986)

Stone, Ralph. *The Irreconcilables: The Fight Against the League of Nations* (1970)

Walworth, Arthur. *America's Moment, 1918: American Diplomacy at the End of World War I* (1977)

_____. *Wilson and His Peacemakers: American Diplomacy at the Paris Peace Conference, 1919* (1986)

5

Postwar Conservatism: 1919–1929

1919	Volstead Act provides for enforcement of prohibition amendment
1921	Warren Harding becomes president
1921–1922	Washington Naval Conference
1923	Teapot Dome Scandal
	President Harding dies; Calvin Coolidge becomes president
1924	U.S. troops withdrawn from Dominican Republic
	Coolidge reelected to the presidency
1925	Scopes monkey trial
1926–1933	U.S. troops in Nicaragua
1927	Kellogg-Briand Pact outlaws war
	Sacco and Vanzetti executed
	Charles Lindbergh makes nonstop solo flight from New York to Paris
1929	Herbert Hoover becomes president
	Stock market crash; beginning of Great Depression

*W*orld War I, coming hard on the heels of the battles over progressive reform, took a heavy toll on the psyche of the American people. Reform and war seemed to have accomplished little. Social problems, labor unrest, *unprecedented corporate power, political corruption, and international turmoil continued. Disillusionment and apathy replaced the crusading spirit and the social and political activism of the preceding twenty years. Tired of saving the world, Americans turned to the safe conservative politics offered by the Republicans and tried to enjoy the prosperity created by industrial expansion. It was an uneasy rest, however, for problems of great magnitude continued to confront the nation and the wave of prosperity excluded too many people.*

THE REPUBLICAN DECADE

Repudiation of Wilson's Foreign Policy

The long and bitter debate over the League of Nations marked the end of one era and the beginning of another. The American people, shocked by the brutality of World War I, were ready to retreat into isolation from European affairs. They repudiated President Wilson's foreign policy in the election of 1918 when they returned Republican majorities to both houses of Congress and again in 1920 when they elected a Republican president.

Republican Domination

This Republican ascendancy was partly the result of a split in Democratic ranks. The Democratic party has always been a coalition of diverse groups. Wilson's drive for approval of America's membership in the League of Nation overshadowed other issues, and the coalition fell apart. Constituencies as different as rural southern Protestants and urban Catholic immigrants were unable to find a common ground on which they could unite. This division allowed the Republican party, which had dominated national politics since 1861, to regain control of the government. The Republicans occupied the White House from 1921 to 1933 and held majorities in both houses of Congress from 1919 to 1931.

Repudiation of Progressivism

The Republican leadership of the 1920s was an odd mixture. During the first two decades of the century the liberal progressive wing (led by Theodore Roosevelt) dominated the party. The conservatives made a brief resurgence in 1912 with the election of William Howard Taft, but even then progressive reform remained the central issue. In 1920 the conservatives once again took control and, this time, set the party's agenda. The Republican administrations of the 1920s, believing that corporate expansion was the key to national prosperity, took a decidedly probusiness position. They favored less regulation, higher tariff rates, and lower taxes. They abandoned the government activism of the preceding decades and returned to the practice of letting business set its own course. They also rejected the progressive goal of federally legislated social reform. At the same time, however, they retained some vestiges of progressivism. Reform-minded conservatives believed that corporations needed to be responsive to civic needs, but they believed that business should do so voluntarily, without government regulation or interference. They likewise believed that government had no role in social reform—that too was the duty of the private sector. President Warren Harding summed up the conservative position when he said that "all human ills are not curable by legislation."

THE REPUBLICAN PRESIDENTS

Warren Harding

THE 1920 ELECTION

When the Republican convention of 1920 became deadlocked in a battle between the two leading contenders, the party leadership pushed the nomination of Warren Harding, a congressman from Ohio. Harding was a perfect compromise candidate for the Republicans. He was well known, likable, and—beyond his adherence to the pro-business and anti-regulation position of the conservatives—devoid of convictions. On the main issue of the day, the Treaty of Versailles, he had little to say. His victory over his Democratic opponent, James Cox, was more a repudiation of Wilson's foreign policy than an affirmation of Harding's qualifications (see Appendix B).

HARDING'S CABINET

Harding was a compromise candidate and his cabinet reflected the coalition of interests within the Republican party. Secretary of the Treasury Andrew Mellon, a corporate baron from Pittsburgh, ran the Treasury Department for the benefit of corporate interests. Secretary of Agriculture Henry Wallace represented the party's progressive wing. Secretary of State Charles Evans Hughes, a former progressive governor of New York and the Republican presidential candidate of 1916, reflected the views of Republican moderates. Herbert Hoover, the secretary of commerce, represented a new breed of progressive conservative who favored aggressive government action in support of small business. Other appointees included party regulars and friends of the president. Harding had little interest in administration and left the conduct of government affairs to his advisors and cabinet members. Mellon and Hoover soon emerged as the leading figures in the government.

Scandals of the Harding Administration

Mellon, Wallace, Hughes, and Hoover, however diverse their opinions and interests, were honest, capable, and dedicated public servants. This was not true of all of Harding's appointees. Congressional investigations and criminal proceedings found a number of top-level officials guilty of graft, bribery, and theft. Charles Forbes, director of the recently established Veterans Bureau, and Thomas Miller, custodian of the obscure Alien Property Office, were both convicted of defrauding the government. Attorney General Henry Daugherty, a long-time friend and advisor of Harding, barely escaped conviction for receiving bribes. Jesse Smith, another friend of Harding and an assistant to Daugherty who had arranged the bribery payments, committed suicide.

The most notorious scandal of the Harding era concerned naval oil reserves at Teapot Dome, Wyoming, and Elk Hills, California. Secretary of the Interior Albert Fall persuaded the navy to transfer the reserves to his department. After Fall secretly leased the reserves, a congressional investigation revealed that Fall had received several "loans" from the oil executives who had received the leases. Fall was convicted of bribery and became the first cabinet officer to go to jail. Secretary of the Navy Edwin Denby was tried for his role in the affair but was not convicted.

HARDING'S DEATH

Harding learned of the scandal during the spring of 1923 and was devastated by the betrayal of his friends. The president never had to deal with the scandal, for he suffered a heart attack and died in San Francisco on August 2, 1923. News of the corruption did not become public until after his death.

Calvin Coolidge

POLITICAL PHILOSOPHY

Vice-President Calvin Coolidge advanced to the presidency following Harding's death in 1923. Coolidge, a stern and taciturn man, rose to national prominence when, as governor of Massachusetts, he suppressed an unpopular police strike in Boston. Coolidge was the most conservative of the presidents of the 1920s. If Theodore Roosevelt wanted to be the "steward of the public welfare," Coolidge was content to be caretaker of the federal government. He was an absolute believer in private enterprise and adamantly opposed government interference in business affairs. By all accounts Coolidge was not a brilliant or outstanding president. He was, however, an able politician whose quiet ways and willingness to maintain the status quo suited the mood of the nation.

THE 1924 ELECTION

The scandals of the Harding administration did little to harm the Republican party. This was due in part to Coolidge. He had not been involved in the scandals, and when he became president he forced Dougherty, Denby, and the other officials suspected of corruption to resign. When Coolidge stood for nomination as the Republican candidate for president in

1924 he encountered almost no opposition. The Democrats, on the other hand, could not decide on a candidate. It took them 103 ballots to select John W. Davis, a corporate lawyer and former official in the Wilson administration. The most interesting aspect of the 1924 election was an attempted resurgence by the Progressive party which nominated Robert LaFollette for president. LaFollette had earned a national reputation as the reform governor of Wisconsin at the time when that state stood at the forefront of progressivism. Coolidge had little trouble with these challenges and received more votes than Davis and LaFollette combined (see Appendix B).

Herbert Hoover

THE 1928 ELECTION

Coolidge, who later acknowledged that he did not consider himself fit to be president, declined to run for reelection in 1928, even though he was popular and probably could have won another term. The Republican nomination went to Herbert Hoover, the popular and well-known secretary of commerce. Hoover's election was almost a foregone conclusion, for the Republicans could boast eight years of unprecedented prosperity. His Democratic opponent, Governor Alfred Smith of New York, brought a new factor to a presidential election: He was a Catholic. His religion and big-city origins won him support in the cities and among immigrants but aroused hatred among many Protestants. Smith made an impressive showing but could not overcome Hoover, who received 21 million votes to Smith's 15 million (see Appendix B).

HOOVER'S BACKGROUND

Herbert Hoover, the most complex and most able of the three Republican presidents of the 1920s, brought a long history of administrative experience with him when he became president in 1929. He had become a millionaire from his work as a mining engineer; had been the director of the Belgian Relief Program and administrator of food production and distribution in the United States during World War I; and served as secretary of commerce during the administrations of Warren Harding and Calvin Coolidge.

POLITICAL PHILOSOPHY

Hoover, like Coolidge, believed that hard work, thrift, and private initiative were the keys to success and prosperity. Also like Coolidge, he opposed government regulation. But unlike Coolidge, Hoover saw a positive role for government in the national economy. Hoover thought that small businesses, not the great corporations, were the pillars of American prosperity, and he believed that the federal government should formulate policies that would promote economic opportunity for these smaller businesses. And while he eschewed direct federal regulation, he believed that the government should offer moral leadership to the nation. Hoover had directed voluntary relief programs during the war and had concluded that private voluntary action could solve the social and economic problems confronting the nation. According to Hoover, the federal government should help business and civic leaders identify problems and formulate solutions. Implementation of reform and regulation, however, was the duty of private organizations. Hoover was a progressive in the sense that he recognized the need for reform and regulation. But he rejected the progressive belief that federal legislation was the best means of achieving those goals. Even so, Hoover was forced to acknowledge that federal regulation was necessary; as secretary of commerce he administered new legislation regulating radio transmissions and civil air traffic.

REPUBLICAN FOREIGN POLICY

The League of Nations

The Republican administrations of the 1920s retreated from the Wilsonian activism of the previous decade, but all three presidents agreed that the United States should continue to work to secure international peace. The Republicans opposed joining the League of Nations because they believed that membership would commit the United States to decisions and actions that it did not approve of. The greatest fear of opponents of the League was that American participation in collective security would draw the United States into wars that the country did not want to fight. Once in office, the Republicans favored cooperation with the League of Nations as long as that cooperation did not commit the nation to action. Representatives of the United States served on a number of League commissions, and American officials played an important role in implementing the provisions of the Treaty of Versailles. The United States even maintained an agent in Geneva to represent American interests before the League. At the same time, the United States insisted on preserving its diplomatic independence and demanded the right to accept or reject League decisions, a freedom it would not have had if it had been a member.

Naval Disarmament

Of special interest to the Republicans was naval disarmament. The United States, like other nations, believed that competition among the great powers to assemble massive and heavily armed navies increased the likelihood of war. Governments were also distressed by the expense of maintaining these fleets. In November 1921 Secretary of State Charles Evans Hughes convened the Washington Armament Conference. At this meeting the five leading naval powers (the United States, Great Britain,

France, Japan, and Italy) agreed to limit the size of their fleets and the armaments carried by their ships. The treaty established a ten-year moratorium on naval construction and even provided for the destruction of existing ships. A second naval disarmament conference met in Geneva in 1927 but adjourned without producing a treaty. A third conference, held in London in 1930, produced only limited results.

The Kellogg-Briand Pact

An even more ambitious attempt to limit aggression was the Kellogg-Briand Pact (named for American Secretary of State Frank Kellogg and French Foreign Minister Aristide Briand). This international agreement, drafted in 1928 and eventually signed by sixty-two nations, renounced warfare as a means of settling international disputes. The pact was little more than a statement of principle, for the agreement contained no provisions for enforcement.

Latin America

THE GOOD NEIGHBOR POLICY

In the area of Latin American relations, the Republican presidents instituted the Good Neighbor Policy. This too was a repudiation of the foreign policy of preceding administrations. Adherents of the new policy claimed that the aggressive actions of Roosevelt, Taft, and Wilson had alienated the people of Latin America. The Good Neighbor Policy relied primarily on negotiation to protect American interests; military intervention was to be used only when all else failed. Harding made a good start on this policy in 1922 when he convened a conference in Washington and negotiated a settlement of differences among the Central American nations. Coolidge followed up on this by withdrawing American troops from the Dominican Republic in 1924 and from Nicaragua in 1925. But like his predecessors, Coolidge found intervention to be a handy tool, and in 1926 he sent troops to help suppress a revolution in Nicaragua. The United States negotiated a settlement between the two factions and supervised an election in 1928, but fighting continued, and U.S. troops were not withdrawn until 1933. In the main, however, the United States tried to maintain friendly relations with the southern nations. In 1927 the American ambassador to Mexico peacefully resolved a long-standing dispute caused by the Mexican government's attempt to gain control of mines, oil fields, and land owned by foreigners. In 1928 President-elect Herbert Hoover made a good-will tour of eleven Latin American countries in a successful effort to improve relations with those nations.

DOMESTIC ISSUES

*Postwar
Conservative
Reaction*

COMMUNISM

As Americans retreated from the progressive activism of the preceding decades several events occurred that enhanced the conservative mood of the nation. Americans were especially frightened by the Russian Revolution of 1917. Radical labor movements such as socialism were never very strong in the United States, but they did attract a significant number of adherents. There was enough violence and radicalism associated with the socialists to keep mainstream capitalist America uneasy. When the Communists seized control of Russia and announced their intention to spread their revolution throughout the industrial world, many Americans took the threat seriously; for them, the step from socialism to communism was a short one.

Reaction to the Russian Revolution was swift and complete. Patriotic and veterans' associations, worked to a fever pitch by the anti-German hysteria of the war years, became inveterate foes of communism. Federal, state, and local governments used their wartime sedition laws to attack suspected communists. The tone for the country's war against radicalism was set at the beginning of the decade by Woodrow Wilson's attorney general, A. Mitchell Palmer. In the summer of 1919 a small group of radicals made bomb attacks on a number of public officials, including one that damaged Attorney General Palmer's house. These attacks were the work of a few individuals and not the result of an international conspiracy. Even so, they were enough to strike fear into the American people. Beginning in the fall of 1919 Palmer launched a series of raids against suspected communists and arrested some 6,000 people. A number of those arrested were deported and others sent to jail; most, however, were exonerated. By May 1920 the hysteria had passed, and the raids came to an end.

SACCO AND VANZETTI

The most celebrated case concerning radicalism during this period was the trial of Nicola Sacco and Bartolomeo Vanzetti in 1921. The two men, Italian immigrants and avowed anarchists, were arrested in Massachusetts and charged with murder and armed robbery. The evidence against them was weak, and their supporters charged that they were being prosecuted not for the crime but because of their political views. Following their conviction, demonstrations throughout the Western world demanded their release. A review committee examined the evidence and confirmed the verdict. Sacco and Vanzetti were sentenced to death and went to the electric chair in 1927.

LABOR UNREST

One element that contributed to the growing fear of communism was a series of strikes that occurred in 1919. In all, some 4 million workers went on strike in an effort to win wage increases that would keep pace with high postwar prices. Some workers were successful in their demands, but many lost their jobs when employers hired strikebreakers and, with the aid of federal and state governments, violently crushed the strikes. The general public had little sympathy for the strikers, for they accepted the owners' explanations that the strikes were responsible for the higher prices and that the labor leaders were communists.

IMMIGRATION RESTRICTION

Native-born Americans had become increasingly alarmed at the mass immigration of the early years of the twentieth century. They were particularly distressed by the large number of immigrants from eastern and southern Europe, many of whom were Jewish and Catholic. The first attempt at restricting European immigration (there were already laws against Asian immigration) came in 1917 when Congress passed a law over President Wilson's veto that required prospective immigrants to pass a literacy test. This law had little effect, but America's entry into World War I partially stopped the flow. During the war immigration dropped to its lowest level since 1862. When the war ended, the flood of immigration began once more.

Congress made the first serious effort to reduce the number of immigrants entering the country in 1921 when it enacted legislation that set quotas according to nationality. When this law failed to produce satisfactory results Congress passed a second quota law that was more effective: Immigration fell from 707,000 in 1924 to 294,000 in 1925. The most restrictive legislation of the decade, passed in 1927, set a cap of 150,000 European immigrants a year. This law established a quota system that cut off the flow of arrivals from southern and eastern Europe. It also prohibited the entry of

Table 5.1 Immigration to the United States, 1918–1935			
1918	110,610	1927	335,175
1919	141,132	1928	307,255
1920	430,001	1929	279,678
1921	805,228	1930	241,700
1922	309,556	1931	97,139
1923	522,919	1932	35,576
1924	706,896	1933	23,068

Asians into the country. The new quotas reduced immigration to the lowest level since the early 1800s: In 1933 only 23,000 people entered the country. Part of this decline can be attributed to the worldwide depression that began in 1929. It was mainly, however, a result of the quota system.

BLACK MIGRATION TO THE NORTH

The decline of agriculture in the early twentieth century drove many black farmers off the land. Black farmers throughout the South, suffering from falling prices and worn-out soil, gave up farming and moved into towns. Many found jobs in southern cities, but a great number of them headed north. The black population of all the great industrial cities increased dramatically. This migration added to urban tension. Middle-class whites saw blacks as one more element undermining the peace and stability of their world. Immigrants saw them as competitors for jobs and housing. Union members also disliked them, for the newly arrived blacks, desperate for jobs, often worked as strikebreakers. Tension also resulted from the return of black soldiers from the war. These veterans, with their heightened sense of pride and self-worth, resented the discrimination they encountered and were unwilling to accept the abuse they frequently received. As the blacks looked for jobs and tried to establish communities, they met resentment from their white neighbors. In 1919 anti-black riots occurred in twenty-six cities. A riot in Chicago lasted for thirteen days and claimed the lives of twenty-three blacks and fifteen whites.

RELIGIOUS FUNDAMENTALISM

As the American people turned to conservatism, they embraced the more conservative religion of fundamental Christianity. Religious revivals swept the country, and evangelists such as the Reverend Billy Sunday attracted great followings. One highlight of this movement was a campaign against the theory of evolution. Fundamentalists believed in a literal interpretation of the Bible and condemned Darwin's theories as heresy. Their influence was so great, particularly in the South, that they were able to persuade several state legislatures to pass laws against the teaching of evolution in public schools. Both sides in the debate wanted to test the constitutionality of these laws.

In 1925 the famous "Scopes monkey trial" took place, in which John Scopes, a Tennessee schoolteacher, went on trial for teaching evolution. The trial attracted national attention, for William Jennings Bryan, a former leader of the Democratic party and now a stalwart of the fundamentalists, handled the case for the prosecution. Clarence Darrow, the greatest trial lawyer of the time, represented the defense. After much sensationalism—including a muddled attempt by Bryan to explain biblical creation—the trial ended in Scopes's conviction. For all the attention it received, the trial had very little effect on the debate. Believers in modern science held to their position, as did the fundamentalists. Scopes, who had volunteered to be the defendant in the test case, had his conviction overturned in a higher court. The law against teaching evolution remained on the books as a dead letter.

THE KU KLUX KLAN

The reaction to the perceived threats of radicals, immigrants, and blacks, as well as to the many changes taking place in the United States, was embodied in the revival of the Ku Klux Klan. This new version of the Klan, organized in Atlanta in 1915, presented itself as a Christian patriotic organization opposed to groups it considered anti-American: communists, immigrants, Catholics, Jews, and blacks. Lower-middle-class whites from the South, Midwest, and West, feeling threatened by the social and economic changes of the early twentieth century, joined the Klan by the thousands. In the early 1920s membership reached a reported 5 million; in August 1925 40,000 Klansmen participated in a march in Washington. Interest in the Klan was brief, however, for exposure of its violent activities—including the conviction of one of its leaders for murder—led to its rapid decline. By 1930 membership had dwindled to a mere 9,000.

The Resurgence of Corporate Power

GOVERNMENT SUPPORT FOR BUSINESS

The conservative wing of the Republican party had always been friendly to big business, even at the height of the progressive era. The ascendancy of the conservatives to power and the curtailment of progressive regulation abetted the expansion of corporate activity. "The business of America is business," President Coolidge proclaimed. Of special value to the business community was Andrew Mellon's twelve-year reign as secretary of the treasury. Mellon firmly believed that a healthy corporate sector was essential to national prosperity, and he set fiscal policies that benefited big business. The central feature of his program was the reduction of the high tax rates—especially corporate taxes and surtaxes on the rich—that had been enacted during the war. He also favored higher tariff rates that would reduce foreign competition. Congress followed Mellon's lead on these matters and reduced taxes in 1926 and again in 1928. The tariff laws of the decade raised the rates significantly.

MERGERS

The corporations, rebuffed in their attempts to establish monopolies during the progressive era, renewed their drive for consolidation. Corporations grew in size and decreased in number as the larger companies bought out the competition or merged together. Corporations such as General Electric, duPont, and General Motors also increased their size (and their profits) by diversifying their product line and by purchasing companies that produced different types of commodities. These conglomerates brought a large portion of American industrial production under the control of a small number of individuals. In 1920 the 200 largest companies in the United States controlled half the nation's corporate wealth.

ADVERTISING

Businesses also took a more aggressive tack in selling their products. Companies had always advertised their goods, but the 1920s saw the emergence of a new class of advertising executives who specialized in the mass marketing of a company's products. These new admen directed massive advertising campaigns that touted their products in magazines and newspapers, in stores, and on signs. The ads featured pictures of famous and glamorous people using the product—with the inference that if a person bought and used the product, he or she would become glamorous. Products that people had lived without for generations became—in the ads—essential to health and happiness. Advertising became such an important adjunct to marketing that advertising agencies—businesses that specialized in advertising—became common.

LABOR RELATIONS

The 1920s began with a series of violent strikes, and labor unrest persisted throughout the decade. On the whole, however, labor relations began to improve. Despite their anti-union rhetoric, factory owners began to realize that their workers did not desire to overthrow the capitalist system or murder their bosses. American workers were, for the most part, not that radical. Socialism—which never had that many adherents—was on the decline by 1920, and the Communist party had few followers. Factory workers and their unions had no quarrel with the system itself; all they wanted was better pay and better working conditions.

During the 1920s factories came under the control of professional managers. These managers, seeking innovative ways to increase production and profits, discovered that they could woo their workers away from radicalism and the unions by making contract concessions and offering worker incentives. They also realized that by offering higher wages, improving working conditions, and providing pensions, holidays, and paid vacations they could win their employees' loyalty and create a more stable and orderly work force. This stability led to increased efficiency and production and greater profits for the company.

DECLINE OF UNIONS

Union membership, which had risen significantly during the war, fell off again during the 1920s. One reason for this was the willingness of employers to grant concessions. Workers found that they could get improved working conditions without belonging to a union. Another reason was the apparent decline in the power of the unions. The progressive presidents were not pro-union, but they did believe in the arbitration of disputes. Federal arbitrators usually sought a middle ground, a strategy that usually resulted in a settlement beneficial to workers. The positive results of labor action taken to arbitration greatly enhanced the influence of the unions. The conservative government of the 1920s abandoned the policy of arbitration and gave full support to management. Judges readily issued injunctions against the unions to prevent strikes. This government opposition and the brutal suppression of the strikes of 1919 eroded the prestige of the unions. Many workers decided that they could do better without them.

SOCIETY AND CULTURE

Improved Standard of Living

NEW HOUSING AND HOUSEHOLD CONVENIENCES

The many technological and social advances of the preceding years began to take effect in the 1920s. A massive postwar building boom resulted in the construction of thousands of modern houses and apartment buildings. Residents of these and other remodeled homes enjoyed the benefits of electricity, indoor plumbing, and telephones. Those Americans who received higher wages were able to purchase many of the new consumer goods that were available, especially electrical household appliances such as washing machines, vacuum cleaners, refrigerators, and radios.

Advances in Health Care

Americans also enjoyed better health. The success of the progressives' campaign to promote improved diets, personal hygiene, physical fitness, and better health care was apparent across the country. Death rates declined, life expectancy increased, and recovery from illness and injury occurred faster and more often. Progressive reform was instrumental in creating these improved conditions, but so was the widespread availability of modern household conveniences. Indoor plumbing and household appliances such as the refrigerator improved sanitation and reduced the chances of contacting disease and illness.

ADVANCES IN EDUCATION

The campaign for educational reform also began to bear fruit. State and cities spent more money on education, illiteracy dropped, and school attendance increased, as did high-school graduations and college enrollments.

PEOPLE EXCLUDED FROM BENEFITS

Not everyone benefited from this new standard of living. Urban dwellers participated to a greater extent than did people living in the country, but even many city residents were excluded. Despite the higher pay offered by many employers, the wages of a significant number of people did not keep pace with rising prices and the availability of consumer goods. Many workers simply could not afford to buy what they produced. And, of course, poverty excluded many. Inhabitants of urban slums could barely afford the essentials of life, let alone any amenities. Even so, the new standard of living became the norm toward which people aspired.

Agriculture

The farm community was one sector of American society that did not participate in the prosperity of the 1920s. The war had created a great demand for agricultural products, and the government had encouraged farmers to increase their yields. When the war ended, the market for farm produce collapsed under the weight of large harvests for which there was no longer a demand. Farmers who had borrowed heavily to finance expansion found themselves saddled with debts they could not pay. Furthermore, small farmers found themselves in competition with large planters whose mechanized operations could outproduce and undersell them. Many farmers gave up and left the land; for the first time in the country's history, farm population declined. For many of those who remained on the farm, low prices and rural isolation deprived them of the amenities enjoyed by urban dwellers. Electricity, for example, was unavailable in many rural areas.

Impact of the Automobile

By 1920 the automobile was a fact of life in America. The number of automobiles in the United States increased from 468,000 in 1910 to 9,239,000 in 1920 and 26,750,000 in 1930. The impact of the automobile extended well beyond its use as a means of transportation. The rapid and widespread acceptance of the automobile influenced how and where people traveled, it stimulated all sectors of the economy, and it changed the face of the landscape.

INCREASED MOBILITY

Americans have always been a very mobile people. The automobile enabled people to move about with greater freedom and speed than ever before. The automobile proved ideal for both short- and long-distance travel. Short-distance travel became much faster than when people traveled by foot or by wagon. The railroad remained faster for long-distance travel, but Americans quickly discovered that they enjoyed the privacy and independence of traveling on their own. In both short- and long-distance travel motorists enjoyed greater freedom, for they were not bound by railroad and streetcar schedules. They could—within limits—go where they wanted when they wanted. The automobile also made it easier for urban dwellers to leave the city for holidays and vacations. Automobile touring and camping became a popular pastime. Even President Hoover used an automobile to travel from Washington to his fishing camp in the Blue Ridge Mountains.

STIMULATION OF THE ECONOMY

As noted in chapter 1, the automobile was a great stimulant to industry, creating a huge demand for steel, rubber, oil, and other materials needed in its manufacture and operation. It affected the economy in other ways as well. People found employment selling and repairing cars. The transportation of goods became faster and more efficient as motorized trucks replaced horse-drawn wagons. Gasoline-driven farm machinery—particularly the tractor— enabled fewer farmers to produce greater yields. Motorized equipment such as gas-driven bulldozers, excavation machines, and cranes became essential to the building industry. Banks found new customers among the many people who sought loans to buy cars.

IMPACT ON THE LANDSCAPE

The impact of the automobile on the landscape was visible for all to see. States and cities built new roads and streets, paved old ones, and for the first time instituted a numbering system for the country's highways. Parking lots, traffic signals, stop signs, gas stations, garages, diners, and tourist motels became common features of cityscape and countryside alike. These changes also represented part of the automobile's impact on the nation's economy, for the construction of roads, the manufacture of roadway equipment, and the operation of automobile-oriented businesses created thousands of jobs.

INFLUENCE ON URBAN GROWTH

Cities themselves began to grow as a result of the automobile. City size is limited by the distance people are willing to travel to and from work. The physical size of early nineteenth-century cities was determined largely by the distance people were willing to walk. The introduction of the streetcar and the inter-city railway broadened the confines of the city, but it was the widespread adoption of the automobile that did the most to promote the expansion of cities and the growth of distant suburbs. Automobile owners, no longer confined to the city, bought homes in parklike suburbs and drove to work. Some cities, fearful of being overrun by automobiles, tried to discourage commuters from driving to work. Motorists pretty much disregarded this effort and set a pattern for commuting that continues to this day.

Prohibition

Prohibition was one of the defining elements of the 1920s. Prohibition took effect in 1919 when Congress passed the Volstead Act, giving the federal government the authority to enforce the newly enacted constitutional ban on the manufacture and sale of alcoholic beverages. Supporters of temperance and prohibition had campaigned for over a hundred years in their battle against liquor. Their victory was a hollow one, however, for prohibition was never popular and did very little to curb the nation's appetite for drinking. Evasion of the law was widespread, and bootlegging—the illegal manufacture and sale of alcohol—flourished in the countryside and city alike. Anyone who wanted a drink could get it. Illegal alcohol was so popular, in fact, that manufacturers and sellers stood to make large profits. Gangsters such as Al Capone in Chicago took control of the illegal liquor traffic and made it a major source of income for crime organizations. A wave of violence swept the nation as gangsters battled law-enforcement officers and each other for control of the trade. In Chicago alone, gang warfare claimed 250 lives between 1920 and 1927.

Vestiges of Progressivism

For the most part, Americans in the 1920s had abandoned the campaign for reform. The federal government and a majority of the American people simply were no longer interested in confronting the nation's problems. President Calvin Coolidge told humorist Will Rogers that his formula for dealing with problems was to ignore them. Many people developed a negative attitude toward the reform efforts of the preceding decades. Indeed, the one great remaining example of progressive reform—prohibition—was immensely unpopular. The new generation looked upon reformers as meddling do-gooders or as communists.

Despite this attitude, some progressives continued the battle. Labor reformers continued to work for child-labor laws, and women's rights activists began to campaign for an equal rights amendment to the Constitution. In 1924 dissident Republicans resurrected the Progressive party and nominated Robert LaFollette, the veteran progressive from Wisconsin, for president. Their platform called for an end to monopoly, government ownership of the railroads, an end to the use of injunctions against unions, child-labor laws, and other traditional progressive goals. Needless to say, this program was not very popular, and LaFollette received less than 5 million votes (16 percent of the votes cast).

The Jazz Age

The prosperity of the 1920s was especially evident in the nation's cities. Middle-class urbanites found themselves with more money and more leisure time than ever before. Young adults, in particular, benefited from the prosperity of the age. Many of them pursued leisure with a carefree abandon.

The jazz age took its name from the new musical form that had been developed by black musicians in the lower Mississippi Valley. A free-form, improvisational style of music, jazz reflected the attitudes of the musicians and their audiences. It also became associated with the underworld of the prohibition era, for jazz musicians performed, for the most part, in speak-easies and at parties where illegal alcohol was consumed.

The youth culture of the jazz age contrasted with the more dour conservatism of older Americans. Automobiles, fast dances, illegal drinking, new clothing styles, a looser attitude toward sexuality, the glamour of the motion pictures, and Charles Lindbergh's daring solo flight across the Atlantic became hallmarks of the era. But these young people, in their headlong pursuit of pleasure, shared their elders' rejection of progressivism. World War I made a profound impression on this generation, and their disillusionment ran deep. The novels of F. Scott Fitzgerald and Sinclair Lewis and the plays of Eugene O'Neill expressed the disillusionment of this generation and its attempt to escape the realities of life in the world of leisure.

*P*rosperity and a weariness with the social activism of the preceding two decades dominated American society in the 1920s. Business profits and expansion were seen as being good for the country, and the government was willing to let the corporations take their own course. Social and economic problems continued to exist but were considered inconsequential. Americans sat back and enjoyed their prosperity as if it would last forever.

Selected Readings

Carter, Paul. *The Twenties in America* (1975)

Chandler, Alfred. *The Visible Hand: The Managerial Revolution in American Business* (1977)

Fausold, Martin. *The Presidency of Herbert Hoover* (1984)

Fitzgerald, F. Scott. *The Great Gatsby* (1925).

Flink, James. *The Car Culture* (1975)

Hemingway, Ernest. *The Sun Also Rises* (1926)

Hicks, John. *The Republican Ascendancy, 1921–1933* (1960)

Leuchtenburg, William. *The Perils of Prosperity, 1914–1932* (1958)

Lewis, Sinclair. *Elmer Gantry* (1927)

_____. *Main Street* (1920)

McCoy, Donald. *Calvin Coolidge, The Quiet President* (1967)

Marchand, Roland. *Advertising the American Dream: Making Way for Modernity, 1920–1940* (1985)

Marsden, George. *Fundamentalism and American Culture: The Shaping of Twentieth Century Evangelicalism, 1870–1925* (1980)

Murray, Robert. *The Red Scare: A Study of National Hysteria, 1919–1920* (1955)

Schuller, Gunther. *Early Jazz: Its Roots and Musical Development* (1968)

Sinclair, Andrew. *Prohibition: The Era of Excess* (1962)

Trani, Eugene, and David Wilson. *The Presidency of Warren G. Harding* (1977)

Wilson, Joan Hoff. *Herbert Hoover, Forgotten Progressive* (1975)

Wolfe, Thomas. *You Can't Go Home Again* (1940)

6

The Great Depression and the New Deal: 1929–1939

1929	Great Depression begins
1931	Federal government loans money to states for unemployment relief
1932	Reconstruction Finance Corporation established
	President Hoover defeated in bid for reelection
1933	Franklin Roosevelt begins first term as president
	New Deal legislation introduced
	National Recovery Administration (NRA) established
	Tennessee Valley Authority (TVA) established
	Eighteenth Amendment (prohibition) repealed
1935	Second New Deal legislation introduced
	Social Security Act
1937	Roosevelt begins his second term as president
	Third New Deal legislation introduced
1939	Germany invades Poland; World War II begins
1941	Japan attacks Pearl Harbor; United States enters World War II

The Great Depression began with the collapse of the stock market in October 1929. The country had experienced economic depressions before: Most recently, there had been an economic downturn in 1921 and 1922 following the demobilization after World War I. Most economists and public officials saw depressions as a regular part of a cycle in which the economy suffered periodic reverses followed by rising prosperity. President Herbert Hoover, assuming that this depression was like all the others, relied upon the private sector to make the adjustments necessary for a return to prosperity. The Great Depression, however, was unlike any previous depression. Never had the nation's economy fallen so far. The measures used by business to revive the economy had little effect, and many people began to call upon the federal government to take a more active role in promoting recovery. By the end of 1930 even Hoover admitted that federal action was required. His response was too little and too late, however.

In 1932 the Democrats, under the leadership of Franklin D. Roosevelt, regained control of the federal government. Roosevelt believed that direct federal intervention was necessary. His program—known as the New Deal— called for massive government spending to stimulate the economy and spur recovery. Conditions began to improve under Roosevelt, but it took the complete mobilization of the nation for World War II to pull the country out of the depression.

THE GREAT DEPRESSION

Economic Problems Contributing to the Collapse

The prosperity of the 1920s originated in the unprecedented industrial output of the decade: Between 1920 and 1929 the country's gross national product (GNP) increased 40 percent. This prosperity lulled the public into ignoring a number of economic problems confronting the nation. Conservative national leaders viewed the decade's prosperity as a vindication of their anti-regulatory policies; they also chose to ignore these problems.

REAL ESTATE SPECULATION

The industrial expansion and the construction boom of the 1920s caused real estate values to escalate rapidly, and astute investors earned healthy profits on their speculations. As the real estate boom continued, however, land derived its value from its potential for future development rather than from its actual use. The easy credit terms of the period abetted this speculation. Bankers and brokers readily made loans or extended credit on real estate transactions. As a result, much of the wealth of the period was based upon property that was not paid for and whose real value was considerably lower than the market price. When the crash came, these speculators found themselves deeply in debt and owning assets of little or no value. They suffered, as did the bankers and brokers who had extended them credit.

STOCK MARKET SPECULATION

A similar pattern evolved in the stock market. As industrial production increased, so did stock values. But as stock values increased, investors looked not at the profits of the company to determine the value of stock, but at the rising price of shares. As a result, the value of stock was based upon the willingness of someone to buy it, not on the income of the company. In other words, the great value of stock was in its market value rather than its dividends. And as in the real estate market, stock could be bought on credit—for as little as 10 percent down. Once again, investors owned property that was not paid for and that had less value than they thought.

Another problem relating to sale of stock was corporate investment policy. As companies expanded they issued more stock to generate revenue to finance their enlarged operations. The proceeds from the stock went into the construction of factories, the purchase of machinery, and other forms of capital expansion. Dividend payments and wage increases did not keep pace with this expansion.

OVERPRODUCTION

The increasing industrial capacity of the nation's factories led to a rapid increase in industrial output. A demand for consumer goods in the early years of the decade led factories to increase their production. This increase led to more jobs, which spurred the demand for more goods. As the boom continued manufacturers concentrated on building more factories and increasing production capability rather than raising wages. Production soon outran demand, however, as high prices limited the buying power of the consumer. Even when sales were brisk, production outran consumption. By the end of the decade manufacturers had huge factories operating well below their capacity and warehouses full of unsold products. When the depression began, factories laid off workers and tried to sell their excess inventories.

HIGH PRICES, LOW WAGES

The prosperity of the 1920s was widespread, and wages for many workers increased. The wage increase was somewhat illusory, however. Earnings for many people had been very low, and the increase merely raised them to the subsistence level. Furthermore, the increase in pay did not keep pace with rising prices. Too many people simply could not afford the many new products coming out of the nation's factories.

AGRICULTURE

Agriculture was the weakest part of the American economy. Prices plunged at the close of World War I and remained low throughout the 1920s. Farmers who had borrowed heavily during the war to increase production found themselves saddled with debts they could not pay. Throughout the twenties the Republicans steadfastly refused to enact legislation that would bolster farm prices. In 1929 Congress passed a law that sought to stabilize prices by providing low-interest loans that would allow farmers to hold their produce off the market until prices improved. This, however, did little to alleviate the problem.

INTERNATIONAL FINANCE

During World War I American bankers lent the European Allies over $10 billion. Repayment of this loan (including interest) came to over $22 billion. At the end of the war, Europe's economy was in a shambles. In addition to the war damage, Germany—whose economy had been destroyed—owed the Allies $56 billion in reparations. France, Belgium, and other Allied nations owed England $10 billion. The United States, untouched by the war, had little sympathy for the European nations and repeatedly rejected proposals to cancel the Allied debt. By 1925, however, the United States admitted that debt relief was necessary and canceled part of the Allied debt. The United States also participated in a plan that restructured German reparation payments. The dollar amount was reduced, and the Allies arranged loans for the Germans. This arrangement led to circular payments: The United States lent money to Germany; Germany used the money to pay its reparations to the Allies; and the Allies used the reparation payments to pay their debt to the United States. When the depression hit, this scheme came undone, and in 1931 President Hoover declared a moratorium on war-debt payments.

THE PROTECTIVE TARIFF

Allied payments were hampered by Germany's inability to pay the reparations. Repayment was also restricted by American tariff policy. The Republican-led Congress, in an effort to boost American industrial profits, passed a protective tariff that greatly reduced foreign imports. The tariff was successful in promoting industrial profits, but it also had three side effects: It drove up consumer prices, thereby limiting consumer sales; it led to retaliatory tariffs by foreign nations, which reduced American exports; and it reduced European exports and impaired the ability of the Europeans to pay their war debts.

Extent of the Depression

THE STOCK MARKET CRASH

By 1927 industrial expansion began to slow as inventories built up. Trading and prices on the stock exchange reached new highs, however, as speculation continued regardless of the downward trend in industrial production. This speculation came to an end in late October 1929 when a wave of panic selling set in. By mid-November losses totaled $30 billion; by spring 1933—the low point of the depression—losses in the stock market exceeded

$75 billion. Under normal circumstances, a panic on the stock market would not have incurred such huge losses. The facade of prosperity covered a structurally weak economy, however. When the stock market collapsed, the rest of the economy toppled with it.

BUSINESS LOSSES

When the stock market collapsed many businesses sharply curtailed operations, a move that accelerated the downward spiral of the economy. Between 1929 and 1932 industrial production fell by half, corporate profits declined from over $8 billion to just over $3 billion, and over 100,000 businesses closed. The banking industry, already in bad shape from speculative operations during the twenties, declined rapidly. Unable to collect on their loans, banks across the nation began to close. By early 1933 over 5,500 banks had failed, with losses in excess of $3 billion. When panicked depositors began to withdraw their money, state governments across the nation stepped in and closed the banks in an effort to prevent the complete collapse of the banking system.

FARM LOSSES

The depression brought an abrupt end to a period of prosperity for urban dwellers. Farmers, however, had been living in a depression since 1919; the collapse of 1929 was, for them, the worsening of an already bad situation. Bankruptcies and foreclosures more than doubled, the number of rented farms increased, and the farming population continued to decline. Conditions grew even worse in the early 1930s when a severe drought hit the Great Plains. Without water, the topsoil of the denuded prairies lay like dust and blew away in the great windstorms that swept the plains. Farmers from Texas to North Dakota gave up and moved away—many of them to California, where they became migrant farm workers, living in camps and barely surviving.

UNEMPLOYMENT

The reduction of industrial production led to increased unemployment. The number of people out of work skyrocketed from 5 percent of the work force at the end of 1929 to nearly 40 percent at the beginning of 1933—almost 15 million workers. Unemployment decreased after that but still remained severe. The unemployment rate exceeded 20 percent until the outbreak of World War II. Factory workers suffered the most, but people in all walks of life lost their jobs as the depression spread through the whole economy.

As bad as the depression was, the economy did not come to a complete standstill. Even at the worst point of the depression over 60 percent of the labor force remained on the job. But continued employment came at a price.

Factories and businesses cut wages as much as 60 percent in order to stay open. Laid-off workers who found other jobs usually worked at a reduced salary. The national income declined from $81 billion in 1929 to $49 billion in 1932. The country's standard of living, which had risen to such heights during the 1920s, declined considerably, as families struggled to keep food on the table and a roof over their heads.

Hoover's Recovery Programs

VOLUNTARY ACTION

No one recognized the severity of the depression when it began in 1929. Government and business leaders assumed that it was just another periodic downturn in the economy and that after a year or two prosperity would return. President Hoover assured the public that the nation's economy was healthy. He met with business leaders and urged them to maintain wage and price levels and to conduct their business as usual. In keeping with his political philosophy, he urged private groups and local governments to provide assistance to those suffering from the depression.

FEDERAL AID

As the depression deepened, Hoover held to his belief that private and local action was the correct method of ending the depression and providing relief to the unemployed. He insisted that the role of the federal government was to provide moral leadership and to stimulate the economy without direct intervention. He opposed increased expenditures, for he believed that a federal deficit would destroy faith in the government and worsen the economy. In 1930 Congress enacted a new tariff law and reduced income taxes, measures designed to encourage increased manufacturing and more investment.

The unremitting severity of the depression eventually persuaded the president that some federal action was necessary. Opposed to direct federal intervention, Hoover instituted a number of loan and public-works programs that funneled federal money to local and state governments. This federal money was not intended for direct relief but rather to stimulate the economy and assist the private sector and local governments in their resolution of the problem.

In December 1930 Hoover asked Congress to appropriate $150 million for public-works projects. This money was given to local and state governments to administer. This was the only program that gave money for relief efforts. Hoover's other programs, in keeping with his belief in private responsibility, provided loans. The centerpiece of his relief efforts was the Reconstruction Finance Corporation (RFC). Established in 1932, the RFC was authorized to lend money to banks and other lending institutions. Later that same year the RFC received further authorization to lend money to state and local governments to fund public-works projects and to provide unemployment relief if local funding was inadequate. The Federal Home Loan Bank Act, also passed in 1932, provided loans to pay off mortgages and to purchase new homes.

The Election of 1932

HOOVER'S DECLINING POPULARITY

Herbert Hoover was a very talented man who sincerely wanted what was best for the country. Unfortunately, he was by temperament and political philosophy unfit to deal with the crisis confronting the nation. A quiet and aloof man, he was unable to communicate well with the public. He worked hard to end the depression but was unable to convey any sense of concern or optimism to the American people. Hoover personified the conservative belief that hard work and frugality resulted in success. In 1932, however, people who had worked hard and saved their money found themselves unemployed and penniless. Bewildered at this, they considered themselves failures and blamed the president for leading them astray. Depression-era shantytowns were called Hoovervilles in his honor.

FRANKLIN ROOSEVELT

Franklin Roosevelt, the Democratic candidate for president, presented an entirely different image. Roosevelt was a very personable man who conveyed an air of confidence and optimism. Particularly inspiring was his victory over personal tragedy. In 1921, at the age of 39, he was paralyzed by an attack of polio. Despite this handicap he continued his rising political career: He served two terms as governor of New York and in 1932 won his party's nomination for president. During the campaign he stressed his sympathy for the plight of the people and his hope for the future.

THE BONUS ARMY

A good example of the difference between Hoover and Roosevelt was their dealings with the Bonus Army that camped in Washington in 1932. In 1922 Congress passed—over President Coolidge's veto—legislation that provided for the payment of a bonus to World War I veterans. The bonus was in the form of an annuity payable in twenty years and against which veterans could borrow. As the depression worsened many veterans asked Congress to amend the law to provide for immediate payment of the bonus.

During the summer of 1932 some 15,000 unemployed veterans and their families journeyed to Washington to demand a cash payment of their bonuses. This Bonus Army built a camp on the outskirts of Washington and vowed to stay until the bonus was paid. Congress failed to pass a bonus law but did vote money that would allow the veterans to pay their way home. All but two thousand left. President Hoover, who considered the veterans a lawless group of rabble rousers, refused to meet with their leaders. In late July officials decided to clear the camp. When a raid by the Washington police failed to remove the veterans, Hoover sent in federal troops who were successful in driving the remnants of the Bonus Army from Washington.

After Roosevelt became president, a group of veterans returned to Washington to press once again for immediate payment of the bonus. President and Mrs. Roosevelt went out to their camp, met the leaders, and assured them of his interest in their problems. Satisfied that someone had finally listened to them, the veterans went home.

THE ELECTION

The 1932 election was held as the depression approached its lowest point. In his campaign, Roosevelt advocated a program of federal legislation to combat the depression. He was careful, however, to say that such a program should be used only as a measure of last resort. Hoover, who stood for re-election, defended his conservative policies and warned voters that Roosevelt's radical proposals would ruin the nation. A number of Americans supported Hoover's conservative approach, for he received almost 16 million votes. This was only 40 percent of the total cast, however, and Roosevelt easily won, with 23 million votes (57percent). The Democrats, who had won a majority in the House of Representatives in 1930, won huge majorities in both the House and the Senate. If nothing else, this election confirmed the faith of the American people in capitalism. Even in this worst year of the worst depression, the socialists, communists, and other radical critics did poorly, with six candidates sharing just over a million votes (see Appendix B).

THE NEW DEAL

When Roosevelt delivered his acceptance speech at the Democratic National Convention, he pledged to offer "a new deal for the American people." This phrase caught on and became the title for the recovery legislation that Roosevelt sponsored. The new president, despite Hoover's charges, was not intent on introducing radical changes into the American economy. He firmly believed in private enterprise and had no intention of introducing socialism into the United States. He did, however, believe that the federal government should take action when local government and private efforts proved unable to solve problems. He was convinced that some degree of national economic planning was necessary to spur recovery. Roosevelt was certainly more radical than Hoover in his use of federal power, but he approached the problem cautiously. Indeed, his first proposals, although providing for more federal action, sought the same end as Hoover's—to stimulate the private sector into recovery. The first New Deal programs were designed to assist business and industry on the road to recovery; direct relief for the poor and unemployed was only a small part of this initial program.

Opening Steps

BANK HOLIDAY

Roosevelt took office on March 4, 1933, and immediately demonstrated his willingness to take action. On March 5 he declared a four-day national bank holiday and placed a ban on the export of gold, silver, and currency. This proclamation, coming on the heels of the state bank holidays, stopped the drainage of currency from the banks. This temporary closure stabilized the banking industry and restored public confidence. When the banks reopened, depositors who had made withdrawals began to return the money.

SPECIAL SESSION OF CONGRESS

Roosevelt's next move was to call Congress into a special session known as "the One Hundred Days." Congress met on March 9 and over the next hundred days put together a package of relief and recovery programs.

FIRESIDE CHATS

Shortly after his inauguration Roosevelt gave the first of his "fireside chats." In these informal talks, which were broadcast nationwide on the radio, the president discussed the problems facing the country and what he was trying to do to solve them. These talks were very popular and helped restore the confidence of the nation.

Banking Reform

RELIEF MEASURES

The first law passed by Congress during the special session was the Emergency Banking Relief Act. This legislation brought all gold, silver, and currency under the control of the federal government, required banks in the Federal Reserve System to be inspected before they could reopen, and broadened the activities of Federal Reserve banks. The Home Owners Loan Corporation, created later in the session, provided money for refinancing mortgages. Another law, the Banking Act of 1933, tightened the regulation of banks, enlarged the Federal Reserve System, and created the Federal Deposit Insurance Corporation. The FDIC, an innovative measure designed to protect people with small bank accounts, insured individual deposits up to $5,000.

MONETARY REFORM

In April 1933 the United States went off the gold standard. This meant that the value of the dollar would no longer be determined by the price of gold. Roosevelt hoped that this change would stimulate business by raising prices and increasing American exports.

Relief Programs

THE FEDERAL EMERGENCY RELIEF ACT

The Federal Emergency Relief Act provided money to the states for unemployment relief and for public-works projects. This program differed from Hoover's in that under Hoover the federal government loaned the money to the states; this new legislation gave the money to the states. The Emergency Relief Act had a twofold purpose: It sought to provide assistance to individuals by giving money to the states for relief programs, and it sought to stimulate the economy by increasing the amount of money in circulation.

THE CIVILIAN CONSERVATION CORPS

The Civilian Conservation Corps was the first public-works project operated by the federal government. The CCC employed young men in a number of conservation programs, such as the construction of reservoirs, work in the national forests and parks, and reforestation. Originally authorized to employ 250,000 men, at times it provided as many 500,000 jobs. Between 1933 and 1941 over 2 million men served in the CCC.

FARM RELIEF

The Agricultural Adjustment Act was the first serious attempt to stop the decline of American agriculture. The act created a system of parity pricing designed to prevent the violent fluctuation in the price of farm commodities. Another provision of the law offered direct cash subsidies to farmers in exchange for reduced production. This measure was an effort to bolster farm prices by reducing overproduction. The Agricultural Adjustment Act also allocated money for the refinancing of farm mortgages.

Recovery Programs

The primary goal of the New Deal was to enact measures that would stimulate the economy and end the depression. During the One Hundred Days Congress enacted several pieces of important legislation designed to promote economic recovery.

THE NATIONAL RECOVERY ADMINISTRATION

The National Industrial Recovery Act (NIRA) was the centerpiece of the New Deal. Under this plan trade groups were allowed to draw up price and production guidelines for their business or industry. If the schedules met the approval of the National Recovery Administration (NRA), they became law. If an industry was unable to arrive at a workable arrangement, the NRA had the authority to provide one. The law also recognized the right of workers to organize unions and bargain collectively for their contracts.

The NIRA established the Public Works Administration. Workers for the PWA built roads, bridges, public buildings, and other projects. Like the other relief programs it had the dual purpose of providing jobs and stimulating the economy by placing more money into circulation.

When business groups proved to be too slow in adopting industry guidelines, the NRA drafted a code of regulations that was broad enough to be applied to most industries. This code won widespread acceptance. The NRA seemed to work at first. Business stabilized, wages increased, and, without the fierce price wars of the preceding years, prices rose. Gradually, however, the NRA began to lose its effectiveness. Businesses began to neglect the guidelines, and the NRA administrators became bogged down in minor details. Critics of the program argued that the law did nothing but sanction monopoly and price fixing. In 1935 the Supreme Court ruled the NRA unconstitutional.

THE TENNESSEE VALLEY AUTHORITY

The Tennessee Valley Authority (TVA) encompassed a broad-based plan for the economic development of the Tennessee River Valley. The main component of the TVA was a series of government-built and government-operated hydroelectric dams. These dams provided a number of benefits to the region. They created a system of flood control for an area plagued by regular flooding, stopped the erosion of valuable topsoil, and produced electricity for residential use and industrial development.

The TVA, like other New Deal programs, is usually considered to be the work of Franklin Roosevelt. But like other New Deal programs, the TVA owed its inception to the men who worked along with Roosevelt. Senator George Norris of Nebraska had campaigned unsuccessfully throughout the 1920s for a federally operated water-power system in the Tennessee Valley. When Roosevelt became president, Norris found a powerful ally. Roosevelt, also an advocate of government-controlled water-power projects, embraced Norris's plan and gave it the necessary presidential endorsement.

Subsequent New Deal Legislation

RELIEF PROGRAMS

When Congress reconvened in October 1933 it continued the work of the One Hundred Days. Much of this new legislation focused on relief for farmers. A series of laws extended price supports for a number of commodities and set production limits. Other laws increased the amount of money available for farm loans and mortgage refinancing. More money was also voted for the Federal Emergency Relief Administration to employ more people on federal, state, and local public-works projects. In an attempt to stimulate residential construction, Congress created the Federal Housing Administration, which insured homeowners' loans made by banks and other lending institutions.

REGULATORY AGENCIES

In a major shift from the policy of the preceding Republican administrations, Congress established several new regulatory agencies. It created the Securities and Exchange Commission to regulate the stock market and the Federal Communications Commission to regulate the communications industry. The National Labor Relations Board, another new agency had the authority to settle disputes between management and labor.

Reaction to the New Deal

APPROVAL

The programs of the New Deal did not always work as planned. Indeed, they failed in their avowed purpose of hastening recovery. Conditions did improve—employment and wages increased, prices rose, and business stabilized—but the country was still in the grasp of the depression. Even so, the New Deal programs tended to be popular, for they instilled a sense of faith in the people and showed that the government was trying to end the depression. The electorate signaled its approval of the New Deal by increasing the Democratic majorities in both the House and the Senate in the 1934 congressional elections.

CRITICISM

The New Deal was not without its critics, however. Conservatives claimed that Roosevelt was investing the federal government with too much power, that the New Deal was leading to socialism, and that it was too expensive. Communists and socialists, on the other hand, continued to argue that the depression was the result of the iniquities of capitalism. They saw the New Deal as a futile attempt to save a dying economic system. The chief complaint against Roosevelt's program—one raised by supporters as well as critics—was that it concentrated too much on economic recovery and not enough on relief for the unemployed.

HUEY LONG

A number of groups and individuals attracted national followings for their attacks on the New Deal and for their proposals for recovery, but they never coalesced into a single movement. The best known of the New Deal critics was Senator Huey Long of Louisiana. Long had become popular as governor of Louisiana because of his public-works programs and his assaults on business. A corrupt, demagogic, and tyrannical politician, Long used these measures to increase his popularity and his political power. His control of Louisiana was absolute, and he ruled the state single-handedly. In 1934 he organized the Share Our Wealth Society, which advocated heavy taxation of the rich and a guaranteed minimum income for all American families. Long harbored presidential ambitions, but his career was cut short when he was assassinated in 1935.

THE SUPREME COURT

The New Deal created a number of new agencies with broad powers. A number of these programs were challenged in the Supreme Court and a number of provisions were declared unconstitutional. The most serious victims of the Court's rulings were the National Recovery Administration (struck down in 1935) and the Agricultural Adjustment Administration (invalidated in 1936). In both cases, the Court ruled that the laws gave the executive branch too much power and that they regulated economic matters outside the authority of the federal government.

The Second New Deal

In January 1935 President Roosevelt announced his intention of launching a new round of relief legislation. Referred to as the Second New Deal, this new program shifted the emphasis from recovery to social reform. In part, Roosevelt was responding to the critics who claimed that he was not doing enough to provide relief and jobs for people suffering from the depression. But he was also facing up to the realization that his programs of national planning were not working. He abandoned his efforts to stimulate the economy from above and instituted a campaign to stimulate it from below by creating jobs and providing direct relief payments.

WORK RELIEF PROGRAMS

The Emergency Relief Appropriations Act of 1935 put an end to direct federal unemployment relief. Thereafter, state and local governments resumed sole responsibility for relief payments. Instead, federal money went into the Works Progress Administration (later the Works Projects Administration), a large-scale public-works employment program. WPA workers constructed highways, bridges, airports, parks, and public buildings. Artists, writers, musicians, actors, and scholars participated in WPA-sponsored artistic and scholastic programs. Between 1935 and 1943 over 8.5 million people worked on WPA projects. The National Youth Administration, another work relief program established in 1935, provided employment for teenagers and college-age people.

HOUSING ASSISTANCE PROGRAMS

The Emergency Relief Appropriations Act, which had established the WPA, granted the president authority to enact other unspecified relief measures. Roosevelt used this authority to establish the Resettlement Administration and the Rural Electrification Administration. The Resettlement Administration provided money for farmers living on worn-out farms or farmers who rented to buy new farms. It also financed the construction of low-cost suburban housing for low-income families. The Rural Electrification Administration provided low-interest loans to utility companies to finance the extension of electrical service into rural areas.

LABOR RELATIONS

In contrast to his predecessors, President Roosevelt took a clear pro-labor stance. The NRA, which was declared unconstitutional in 1935, had included provisions for the right of workers to organize and join unions. In July 1935 Congress passed the National Labor Relations Act. This law reconfirmed the right of labor to organize and strengthened the authority of the National Labor Relations Board to mediate disputes. The Government Contracts Act of 1936 required companies working under government contracts to pay their employees a minimum wage set by the secretary of labor, operate on a forty-hour work week, and not use child labor.

In labor matters, as in other areas, President Roosevelt relied upon the wisdom of his advisors. Secretary of Labor Frances Perkins (the first woman to hold a cabinet appointment) and Senator Robert Wagner of New York were both strong advocates of labor, and both figured prominently in the administration's pro-labor policy. Wagner was the author of much of the labor legislation passed during the New Deal.

THE UNIONS

During the 1920s union membership declined as workers lost faith in the ability of the unions to represent their needs. During the 1930s this trend reversed itself and membership increased dramatically—3 million in 1933, 4 million in 1937, 7 million in 1938, and 9 million in 1939. This increase resulted from the pro-labor policies of the New Deal and from the aggressive tactics of union organizers. Prior to the 1930s unions had been organized by crafts, an arrangement that left many factory workers unrepresented. In the 1930s the new Congress of Industrial Organizations launched a campaign to unionize workers by industry. This new method of organization extended union membership to millions of new workers. Corporate response to unionization was mixed. Some companies violently resisted, while others accepted it and negotiated contracts.

BUSINESS REGULATION

Congress passed a number of laws widening federal regulation of business. Congress granted the Interstate Commerce Commission power to regulate interstate truck and bus traffic, created the National Bituminous Coal Commission to regulate coal mining, and broadened the authority of the Federal Reserve Board in its regulation of banks. Other legislation increased federal regulation of the public utilities industry.

TAX REFORM

Throughout the 1920s, the Republicans had reduced taxes for the wealthy and for business. The Revenue Act of 1935 reversed that trend. The new tax law raised the tax rate for people with high incomes and for large corporations. The tax law of 1936 increased the tax rate for corporations, and the 1937 law closed a number of loopholes that had allowed wealthy taxpayers to avoid payment.

SOCIAL SECURITY

A criticism of the progressive reform legislation at the beginning of the century was that it had not provided a comprehensive plan for unemployment relief or for the support of the elderly. This same criticism had been leveled against the New Deal. In August 1935 Congress responded to this criticism by passing the Social Security Act. This act established a nationwide system in which employers paid a federal unemployment tax. This money was given to the states to distribute as unemployment compensation. A second tax, levied equally on employers and employees, provided a fund for the payment of old-age pensions. The law also provided for federal aid to the states for a number of social service and public health programs.

THE 1936 ELECTION

President Roosevelt encountered stiff opposition in his bid for re-election in 1936. Conservatives—Republicans and Democrats alike—accused him of destroying free enterprise and increasing federal power to a dangerous level. Populist and left-wing critics attacked him for his failure to institute radical relief programs. His greatest problem, however, was the continuing depression. The economy had improved steadily since he took office in 1933, but the country was still far from recovery. This was particularly obvious to the 7 million workers who remained unemployed. Roosevelt met this challenge with his characteristic energy and cheerfulness. His sense of confidence and his openness to the American public—he made frequent radio broadcasts and held press conferences twice a week—were his greatest weapons.

Despite the continued problems of the depression, the Democratic victory was complete. They increased their majority in both houses of Congress, and Roosevelt easily outpolled his Republican opponent, Governor Alf Landon of Kansas. Roosevelt received 27.7 million votes to Landon's 16.7 million and carried every state except Vermont and Maine. Once again third parties did poorly. A field of five candidates polled just over a million votes among them (see Appendix B).

THE SUPREME COURT CONTROVERSY

Disheartened by the Supreme Court's invalidation of a number of key pieces of New Deal legislation, Roosevelt submitted a bill to Congress in February 1937 that called for a reorganization of the federal judiciary. The key feature of this plan was to increase the number of justices on the Supreme Court from nine to as many as fifteen. This proposal quickly encountered severe opposition, with critics charging that the president wanted to pack the Supreme Court with supporters who would endorse the New Deal. Roosevelt responded by launching a public campaign in which he argued that reform of the Court was needed to protect important legislation passed by Congress. The proposal to increase the number of judges died in Congress, but the debate over the bill had an effect on the Court. Public expression of support for Roosevelt and the New Deal was strong, and the justices, responding to this sentiment, upheld the constitutionality of a number of important New Deal programs during the spring and summer of 1937. Ironically, Roosevelt was able to make important changes on the Supreme Court. Between 1937 and 1941 seven vacancies occurred on the Court, and Roosevelt made the new appointments. Several of these appointees—most notably Felix Frankfurter, Hugo Black, and William Douglas— were among the most distinguished justices to serve on the Supreme Court.

RECOVERY AND RECESSION

Roosevelt's New Deal programs, particularly the public-works projects, stimulated the economy and pushed along a gradual recovery. Recovery came at a price, however, for support of these programs required deficit spending by the federal government. Roosevelt was uncomfortable with the huge federal deficits and saw recovery as an opportunity to end deficit spending. During the summer of 1937 the government severely cut its spending and reduced the number of workers employed by the WPA. The private sector was not yet strong enough to make up the difference, and the economy plummeted. The government once again increased its spending, and by 1939 the economy revived to its 1937 level.

The Third New Deal

The slow rate of recovery and the recession of 1937 prompted President Roosevelt to initiate a third round of relief measures. This new legislation extended the relief policies of the second New Deal and attempted to fill the gaps left by earlier programs.

FARM RELIEF

Despite the gains of the preceding five years many problems still plagued the nation's farmers. In 1937 Congress created the Farm Security Administration, which provided loans that would enable tenant farmers and sharecroppers to buy their own farms. The FSA also sought to aid migrant farm workers by regulating wages and working hours, establishing camps where they could live, and providing basic social and health services. In 1938 Congress passed a new Agricultural Adjustment Act to meet the objections raised by the Supreme Court when it struck down the original law. This new law renewed the parity payments and subsidies for limited production.

CONSUMER AND LABOR LEGISLATION

Two major pieces of New Deal legislation passed during 1938 were the National Housing Act and the Fair Labor Standards Act. The Housing Act provided low-cost loans for slum clearance and the construction of low-rent public housing. It also granted rent subsidies. The Fair Labor Act introduced a plan for the gradual implementation of a minimum wage and a forty-hour work week for all businesses engaged in interstate trade. It also prohibited child labor. In 1939 the government introduced a food-stamp program. Recipients of the stamps could use them to buy surplus food supplies. The program had the dual purpose of assisting low-income families and of selling surplus farm produce.

The New Deal and Minorities

Franklin Roosevelt had little interest in minority problems and made little effort to end racial discrimination during his presidency. Even so, the 1930s was a time of improvement for minorities. Blacks were at the bottom of the economic scale, and when the depression struck they suffered more than most Americans. Black factory workers were among the first laid off, blacks everywhere received the least assistance from local relief agencies, and black farmers suffered severely from the collapse of agriculture. Many New Deal programs, by their very nature, aided blacks and Mexican-Americans. Relief payments assisted all poor and unemployed people. Many blacks and Mexican-Americans found work in the WPA. Farm relief programs benefited black tenant farmers and sharecroppers and Mexican-American migrant farm workers. Furthermore, many of Roosevelt's advisors, including his wife, Eleanor, were advocates of civil rights. These upper-level administrators took an interest in minority problems, and many of them appointed blacks to important management posts in the government. These efforts were comparatively small, but they were enough to convince blacks that someone in the government finally cared about them. During the 1930s the great majority of black voters abandoned the party of Lincoln and switched their allegiance to the party that gave them jobs and unemployment relief.

The Close of the New Deal

GROWING DISENCHANTMENT

When President Roosevelt delivered his annual message to Congress in January 1939 he did not propose any new relief measures. The depression was not over, by any means, but Roosevelt felt that the necessary legislation was in place and that it was only a matter of time before it took effect. Furthermore, by 1939 the mood of the country was beginning to shift. The unity of the Democratic party, which had expedited the passage of New Deal legislation, was beginning to unravel as conservative Democrats, particularly from the South, began to rebel against the social implications of New Deal legislation. Many voters began to show their dissatisfaction as well.

Roosevelt's efforts to defeat conservative Democrats in the 1938 congressional elections failed, and for the first time since 1928, the Republicans increased their representation in both houses of Congress. Attitudes also began to change within the administration.

Table 6.1 Principal New Deal Legislation and Programs	
1933	Emergency Banking Relief Act
	Civilian Conservation Corps Act
	Federal Emergency Relief Act
	Agricultural Adjustment Act
	Tennessee Valley Authority
	Federal Securities Act
	National Employment System Act
	Home Owners Refinancing Act
	Banking Act of 1933
	Farm Credit Act
	National Industrial Recovery Act
	Civil Works Administration
1934	Farm Mortgage Refinancing Act
	Civil Works Emergency Relief Act
	Home Owners Loan Act
	Securities Exchange Act
	Federal Communications Commission Act
	Federal Farm Bankruptcy Act
	National Housing Act
1935	Emergency Relief Appropriations Act
	Resettlement Administration
	Rural Electrification Administration
	National Youth Administration
	National Labor Relations Act
	Social Security Act
	Banking Act of 1935

	Table 6.1 Principal New Deal Legislation and Programs
	Public Utilities Holding Company Act
	Revenue Act of 1935
	Bituminous Coal Conservation Act
1936	Revenue Act of 1936
	Government Contracts Act
	Farm Tenant Act
1937	Revenue Act of 1937
	National Housing Act
1938	Agricultural Adjustment Act
	Food, Drug, and Cosmetics Act
	Fair Labor Standards Act
1939	Food Stamp Plan

INFLUENCE OF WORLD WAR II

As war clouds gathered in Europe and Asia interest began to shift from domestic programs to international matters. When Roosevelt addressed Congress in January 1939 he talked not of recovery measures but of defense. The slide toward war had begun, and Roosevelt suspected that once again the United States would not be able to remain aloof from the conflict.

The New Deal put the United States on the road to recovery, but it did not end the Great Depression. Rapid recovery began in September 1939 when war broke out in Europe, and the United States once again became the arsenal for the European nations fighting Germany. When the United States entered the war in 1941, total mobilization projected the country out of the depression and onto a new level of prosperity.

The depression, which had proven the ineffectiveness of the Republicans' passive approach and even Roosevelt's initial conservative program, had been brought under control by the massive federal spending and employment programs of the second New Deal. Federal public assistance increased from $218 million in 1932 to almost $5 billion in 1939. When Roosevelt became president, his main goal was to end the suffering caused by the depression and bring a return to prosperity. By 1939 he had effected a revolution in government. As president he had committed the federal government to the maintenance of the social and economic welfare of the nation. Programs such as Social Security and the TVA confirmed that the federal government would *continue to have a strong and active role in social and economic affairs. No longer would a retreat such as the one undertaken by the Republican presidents of the 1920s be possible.*

Selected Readings

Agee, James, and Walker Evans. *Let Us Now Praise Famous Men* (1941)

Conkin, Paul. *The New Deal* (1967)

Daniel, Pete, Mary Foresta, Maren Stange, Sally Stein. *Official Images: New Deal Photography* (1987)

Fausold, Martin. *The Presidency of Herbert C. Hoover* (1984)

Leuchtenburg, William. *Franklin Roosevelt and the New Deal, 1932–1940* (1963)

McElvaine, Robert. *The Great Depression: America, 1929–1941 (1984)*

Sitkoff, Harvard. *A New Deal for Blacks: The Emergence of Civil Rights as a National Issue* (1975)

Steinbeck, John. *The Grapes of Wrath* (1939)

Worster, David. *Dust Bowl: The Southern Plains in the 1930s* (1979)

7

World War II: 1939–1945

1939 Germany invades Poland; World War II begins; U.S. declares neutrality

Neutrality Act of 1939 authorizes the sale of arms and munitions to the Allies

1940 President Roosevelt urges Congress to increase appropriations for defense

U.S. begins sending military aid to England

President Roosevelt approves expansion of the navy

U.S. establishes first peacetime draft

1941 Roosevelt begins his third term as president

Japan invades Indochina; Japanese-American relations worsen

Japanese forces attack Pearl Harbor and other military installations in the Pacific and southern Asia; U.S. declares war on Japan

Germany and Italy declare war on the U.S.

1942 American bombers attack Tokyo

U.S. forces in the Philippines surrender to the Japanese

Allies begin air raids on Germany

American naval victory at Midway stops Japanese advance

U.S. offensive in the Pacific begins with attack on Guadalcanal

U.S. troops join Allied offensive in North Africa

1943 German forces in North Africa surrender

Allied conquest of Sicily

Allies invade Italy; Italian government surrenders

1944 Germans driven out of Rome

Allied forces land in Normandy

U.S. begins regular air attacks on Japan

U.S. troops begin reconquest of Philippines

Allied forces land in southern France

Allied forces liberate Paris

Allied forces enter Germany

1945 Roosevelt begins his fourth term as president

U.S. troops complete reconquest of Philippines

President Roosevelt dies; Harry Truman becomes president

United Nations founded

Russians occupy Berlin

Germany surrenders

U.S. drops atomic bombs on Hiroshima and Nagasaki

Japan surrenders

During the mid-1930s Americans watched in horror as once again Europe moved toward war. A majority of the people, haunted by memories of World War I, had no desire to engage in another European war. But once again American interests abroad made the country vulnerable to the emerging crisis in Europe. Equally dangerous were the territorial ambitions of the Japanese in Asia and the Pacific. The dual threats of Germany and Japan promised that the coming conflict would indeed be a world war.

PRELUDE TO WAR

The Rise of Fascism

PROBLEMS IN GERMANY

Germany suffered greatly after World War I. The Treaty of Versailles, which had been drafted by the Allied leaders and forced upon Germany, crippled the German economy. The treaty stripped Germany of some of its most valuable industrial territory and saddled the country with heavy reparation payments. The Germans were required to surrender material goods such as railroad stock, trucks, farm equipment, and ships, as well as to make cash payments. Germany's great industrial capacity and a reduction of the reparation payments helped speed recovery, but the depression hit Germany hard, as it did all the Western industrial nations. Even worse than the economic effects of the treaty was its impact on the German psyche. Humiliated by their defeat in the war and expecting moderate terms based upon Wilson's Fourteen Points, the German people were outraged at the harshness of the dictated treaty.

THE RISE OF ADOLF HITLER

Adolf Hitler, the charismatic and fanatical leader of the fascist National Socialist Party (Nazis), manipulated the anger and humiliation of the Germans to fuel his party's ruthless rise to power. Hitler played upon the strong sense of German nationalistic pride by attacking the Allies for the harsh terms of the Treaty of Versailles and by blaming postwar German leaders for accepting the terms of the treaty. He also exploited a long-standing racial hatred of the Jews by blaming them for many of Germany's economic problems. By 1933 the Nazis had become the dominant party in Germany, and Hitler became chancellor (or prime minister). The Nazis soon had control of the entire country and named Hitler fuhrer, giving him dictatorial power to govern the nation.

THE RISE OF BENITO MUSSOLINI

In the immediate aftermath of World War I Italy sank into chaos. Strikes and disorder were widespread as socialists and communists battled for control of the country. The majority of Italians, weary of war and strife, turned to the Fascist party and its leader, Benito Mussolini, who promised to defeat the communists, restore peace and prosperity to the country, and raise Italy to new heights of national greatness. When the Fascists threatened to march on Rome and seize the government in 1922, the king appointed Mussolini prime minister. From this post it was easy for Mussolini to make himself dictator.

German and Italian Aggression

GERMAN REARMAMENT

One of the provisions of the Treaty of Versailles was that Germany was to be disarmed. In 1934 Hitler asked the League of Nations to make several revisions in the treaty, including the right to rearm. When the League refused, Germany withdrew from the League and, in defiance of the Allies, began to rearm in 1935. In 1936 the German army occupied and began to fortify the demilitarized Rhine Valley in violation of the Versailles Treaty.

GERMAN EXPANSION

The Treaty of Versailles, in its creation of new states in eastern Europe, reduced the borders of Germany and broke up the Austro-Hungarian empire. As a result, over 13.5 million Germans lived outside Germany and Austria.

One of Hitler's goals in his drive for power was to expand Germany's borders and repatriate these people. In 1938 he arranged the union of Germany and Austria and annexed the Sudetenland, a portion of Czechoslovakia with a predominantly German population. Not yet ready to challenge Great Britain and France, Hitler proceeded cautiously with his program of expansion. The British, hoping to avoid another war with Germany, acquiesced in this expansion. Prime Minister Neville Chamberlain, believing that these limited territorial gains would satisfy Germany, met with Hitler at Munich in 1938 and approved the annexation of the Sudetenland.

ITALIAN AGGRESSION

Italy also had territorial ambitions. In 1935 the Italians invaded Ethiopia, the only country in Africa not under European control. The poorly armed Ethiopian forces were no match for the well-equipped Italian army. In less than a year the Italians subdued the Ethiopians and established a colonial government.

THE SPANISH CIVIL WAR

In 1936 a bloody civil war broke out in Spain between the democratically elected left-wing government and fascist insurgents. Both Germany and Italy sent troops to aid the Spanish fascists. The Western nations, hoping to prevent a widening of the conflict, remained neutral. After three years of bloody fighting, the fascists gained control of the country, and their leader, General Francisco Franco, became dictator.

THE LEAGUE OF NATIONS

The League of Nations, established in 1918 as a means of preventing aggression and war, proved totally ineffective in the growing crisis. It was unable to prevent German rearmament, and its sanctions against Italy for the invasion of Ethiopia were meaningless. Great Britain and France were the only nations capable of enforcing League decisions, and they were unwilling to confront Germany and Italy.

Japanese Expansion

During the 1930s the military government of Japan launched a campaign to establish dominance over Asia and the Pacific. In 1931 Japan seized the Chinese province of Manchuria and created the Japanese-controlled state of Manchukuo. The Chinese Nationalist government of Chiang Kai-shek, engaged in a civil war with Communist forces led by Mao Tse-tung, was unable to prevent the conquest. Six years later, in 1937, Japan launched a full-scale invasion of China. The Nationalists and the Communists suspended their civil war and turned their forces against the invaders. The Japanese drove the Chinese government from power in a brutal campaign but were unable to subdue the country.

American Reaction

The people and the government of the United States watched this spreading aggression with increasing alarm. Some Americans favored action, and a number of them fought in Spain against the fascists. But most people, even though they condemned the aggression and ruthless totalitarianism of the Germans, Italians, and Japanese, opposed any involvement in the growing conflict. The government, reflecting this mood, passed neutrality laws in 1935, 1936, and 1937 forbidding Americans to provide aid to any belligerent nation. Between 1934 and 1936 Senator Gerald Nye of North Dakota chaired a Senate committee that investigated the wartime profits of bankers and military contractors. These investigations, which revealed the huge profits earned during World War I, implied that wars were fought for the benefit of big business and helped to increase the antiwar feeling in the nation.

The Beginning of the War

By 1939 Hitler felt strong enough to defy France and Great Britain and began his campaign for continental domination. In March 1939 he made his first move and annexed Czechoslovakia. Mussolini, following Hitler's lead, sent Italian troops into neighboring Albania. The Allies condemned this aggression but refused to take any definite action. On September 1 Hitler invaded Poland. France and Great Britain, no longer able to tolerate German aggression, declared war on September 3. In April 1940 Germany launched an offensive in western Europe and quickly overran Norway, Denmark, Belgium, Luxembourg, and the Netherlands. By June France had surrendered, and the British army had been driven from the continent.

THE UNITED STATES AND THE WAR

American Preparation for War

The outbreak of war produced a mixed reaction in the United States. A majority of Americans supported the British but had no interest in going to war. At the same time, they realized that the spreading war threatened the United States and that eventual American involvement in the conflict was a very real possibility.

AID TO THE ALLIES

President Roosevelt reacted immediately to the crisis in Europe and issued a proclamation of neutrality. He then asked Congress to enact a new neutrality law that would reaffirm America's intention of staying out of the war but that would also allow the United States to provide arms and munitions to the Allies. When Congress complied, the president ordered the military to supply the British with surplus equipment.

DEFENSE MEASURES

The government also began to prepare the nation for war. Congress tripled the defense budget, and the president authorized a stepped-up program of aircraft and ship construction. Representatives of the United States, Canada, and the Latin American nations met on several occasions to make arrangements for the mutual defense of the western hemisphere. In the summer of 1940 the National Guard was called into federal service, and in October the government began the nation's first peacetime draft.

PUBLIC OPINION

Roosevelt's efforts to prepare the nation for war drew a divided response from the American people. As the war in Europe and Asia broadened, a portion of the American people began to favor American involvement. Others, however, became increasingly alarmed at the preparations for war and became more adamant that the United States should stay out of the fighting.

THE 1940 ELECTION

Despite this division of opinion, the war was not much of an issue in the 1940 presidential election. The New Deal and Roosevelt's unprecedented bid for a third term received more attention than defense preparations did. Republican candidate Wendell Willkie was an avid opponent of the New Deal but agreed almost completely with Roosevelt's defense measures. Like Roosevelt, he vowed to keep the country out of the war. Roosevelt won easily, winning 55 percent of the vote and carrying thirty-eight states. Support for third parties continued to decline; the four other candidates received only 240,000 votes among them (see Appendix B).

Expansion of the War in Europe

Both Germany and England opened new fronts in the war. Germany launched a series of air raids against the British Isles, escalated the naval war, sent troops into the Balkans, and in June 1941 invaded Russia. The British, for their part, opened an offensive in North Africa.

AMERICAN-BRITISH RELATIONS

This expansion of the conflict drew the United States closer to war. President Roosevelt increased American aid to the Allies and vowed to offer all the assistance he could, "short of war." But even as the president renewed his pledge to try to keep the country out of the fighting, he recognized the growing danger, and the United States and Great Britain began to plan for the contingency of America's entry into the war. British and American military leaders met in Washington to formulate strategy, and in August 1941 Roosevelt met with British Prime Minister Winston Churchill to discuss war aims. Together they drafted the Atlantic Charter, which outlined the principles of a postwar settlement.

Table 7.1
The Atlantic Charter
1. Renounced any territorial gains from the war
2. Opposed territorial changes without the consent of the people affected
3. Supported the right of nations to choose their own form of government
4. Supported the relaxation of international trade restrictions
5. Supported cooperative efforts to improve economic and social conditions worldwide
6. Supported freedom from want and fear
7. Supported freedom of the seas
8. Called for disarmament of aggressor nations after the war

NAVAL WARFARE

As the United States increased the flow of supplies to the Allies and as the Germans increased their naval activity in the Atlantic, the likelihood of conflict between the two increased. After a German submarine attacked an American warship off the coast of Iceland in September 1941, Roosevelt authorized the navy to engage German warships in defensive action. In November Congress authorized the arming of American merchant ships.

Japan

DECLINING JAPANESE-AMERICAN RELATIONS

Relations between the United States and Japan had been declining for a number of years as Japan tried to extend its influence in Asia and the Pacific. The invasion of China and the formation of a military alliance with Germany and Italy worsened the situation. In 1940 the United States warned Japan that it opposed any expansion into southeast Asia. When the Japanese occupied French Indochina in July 1941, the United States and Great Britain declared a trade embargo with Japan and threatened military action if any additional Japanese expansion occurred.

PEARL HARBOR

The exchanges between the United States and Japan were, in a way, a dangerous game of bluff. Both nations had massive naval construction programs under way, but neither was ready to go to war with the other. In November the two countries began a round of fruitless negotiations in Washington. Neither the United States nor Great Britain had any faith in these talks. Both expected war and began to prepare for a Japanese attack on the Philippines or the British colonies on the Asian mainland. The

Japanese, hoping to cripple the American navy, launched a devastating surprise air attack on the fleet anchored at Pearl Harbor in Hawaii on December 7. This unexpected attack was a great victory for the Japanese. The United States lost nineteen warships, 150 airplanes, and suffered 3,500 casualties, including 2,400 dead. Japanese forces also attacked the Philippines, Guam, Midway, Hong Kong, and the Malay Peninsula. The United States declared war on Japan on December 8. Three days later Germany and Italy declared war on the United States.

MOBILIZATION AND THE HOME FRONT

Government Agencies

When the war broke out the federal government turned the vast organizational capabilities of the New Deal toward mobilization for the war. Dozens of new government agencies directed the war effort and maintained peace and stability at home. The War Production Board had the central task of marshaling the nation's industrial forces for the production of military equipment. The War Manpower Commission, the Office of Scientific Research and Development, the National War Labor Board, and a host of other agencies managed the many activities involved in fighting a large-scale global war. On the home front, the Office of Price Administration (OPA) fought war-time inflation by setting prices for consumer goods. The OPA also supervised the rationing of scarce and valuable commodities.

Popular Support

The attack on Pearl Harbor galvanized the American people in their support of the war. Some opposition to the war continued, but compared to the bitter animosity provoked during World War I, it was relatively mild. Most people rallied to the war effort and did what they could to support it. Evidence of the war was everywhere. Taxes rose, the government urged people to buy bonds to help finance the war, and communities collected scrap iron, old tires, and other material needed to produce military equipment. A constant reminder of the war were the ration coupons needed to purchase food, oil products, tires, and shoes.

In order to stimulate continued support for the war the Office of War Information directed a propaganda campaign in which the entertainment business played a crucial part. The movie industry made films and newsreels that portrayed the war as a crusade to save the world from tyranny. Radio broadcasts focused on war-related themes. Celebrities reminded the American people of their patriotic duty to support the war.

The End of the Depression

The most immediate positive result of the war was an end to the depression. The great demand for war materials created millions of jobs and pumped billions of dollars into the economy. The country's GNP rose from $100 billion in 1940 to $212 billion in 1945. Unemployment dropped from 15 percent in 1940 to less than 10 percent in 1942 and stood at just under 2 percent at the end of the war. Indeed, the increased production and the reduction in the work force due to enlistments and the draft (over 12 million Americans served in the armed forces during the war) created a labor shortage. Much of this shortage was filled by women, who went to work in unprecedented numbers and in industrial jobs previously forbidden to them. In 1945 over 19 million women were working outside the home.

This surge in employment meant that people who had been living on relief or in reduced circumstances now had money to spend. Unfortunately, there was little to buy, for the production of consumer goods had almost ceased, and rationing limited what was available. At first the government feared that this surplus of money would lead to runaway inflation, but the Office of Price Administration's policy of price fixing held inflation to a moderate rate. The American people pocketed their money and dreamed of what they would buy when the war ended.

Wartime Race Relations

BLACKS

Discrimination and animosity toward blacks continued during the war. The armed forces remained segregated, and many black soldiers were relegated to menial tasks. When activists led by A. Philip Randolph threatened to organize 100,000 blacks for a march on Washington to protest discrimination, President Roosevelt issued an executive order banning discrimination in the government and in defense industries. This order had only limited success, for segregation and racial hatred were too deeply ingrained. The thousands of blacks who migrated to northern cities were able to find jobs, but they encountered discrimination in the workplace and anger from their new white neighbors. Racial tension continued throughout the war years, and race riots occurred in several northern cities.

JAPANESE-AMERICANS

When the war broke out Americans turned their racial hatred toward Japanese-Americans. By 1941 most German-Americans had become part of the mainstream white population. Racial differences, however, made the Japanese easily identifiable. In California, where there were large concentrations of Asian-Americans, discrimination against them was as great as it was against blacks. The attack on Pearl Harbor intensified this feeling. When the war began, 110,000 Japanese-Americans—most of them American citizens—were removed from their homes and sent to camps in the western deserts. When fears of subversion subsided, many of the internees were allowed to leave the camps and resettle in the Midwest. Many of the men enlisted in the army where they more than proved their loyalty and patriotism.

The 1944 Election

The presidential election of 1944 was more a referendum on Franklin Roosevelt than a debate on national policy. Although much of Roosevelt's support had evaporated over the years, the Democratic party showed little hesitation in nominating him for a fourth term. The Republicans and their candidate, Governor Thomas Dewey of New York, continued to criticize the New Deal but had little to say about the war, which was the main issue of the day. Roosevelt, who received 25 million votes to Dewey's 22 million and carried thirty-six states, won easily (see Appendix B).

Roosevelt's Death

Franklin Roosevelt, worn out by his long battle with polio and the trials of being president for twelve years of depression and war, suffered a stroke and died on April 12, 1945. Newly elected Vice-President Harry Truman inherited the responsibility of prosecuting the war to its end.

THE WAR

The United States and Great Britain, confronted with a global war, decided to concentrate on defeating Germany, the stronger and more dangerous of their two enemies. They planned an offensive against the Japanese, but the European campaign was given priority for resources and manpower. In a way, the Germans were also the most vulnerable. Their early successes left them in control of all of Europe and part of North Africa. This was an immense amount of territory to defend, particularly since the Allies were able to launch attacks on several fronts at once.

Hemispheric Defense

LATIN AMERICAN RELATIONS

Even before the war began, Roosevelt worked to improve relations with the Latin American nations. When revolution erupted in Cuba Roosevelt refused to send troops. When peace was finally restored in 1934 the United States negotiated a new treaty with Cuba and abrogated the Platt Amendment, which had given the United States the right to intervene in Cuban affairs. Roosevelt also withdrew American troops from Haiti in 1934. Negotiations led to improved relations with Brazil, Panama, and Mexico.

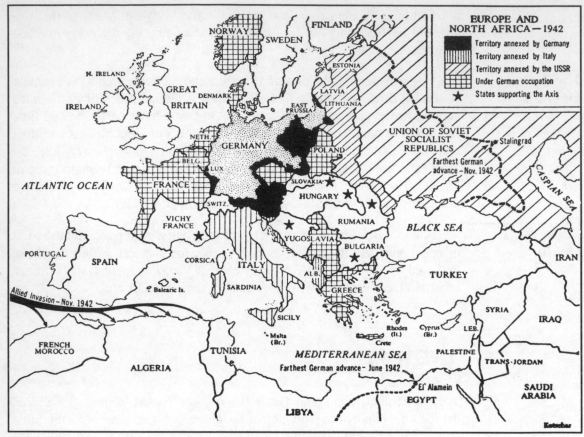

Fig. 7.1 Europe and North Africa, 1942

MUTUAL DEFENSE PACTS

Increasing unrest in Europe and Asia led the countries of the Americas to unite for common defense. Leaders of the various nations met in a series of conferences (the earliest held in 1933) to agree upon mutual defense and plan the protection of the western hemisphere. When the war broke out the United States established air and naval bases from Greenland to Brazil and began to supply the Latin American nations with arms and munitions. In 1942 all the Latin American countries except Chile and Argentina joined the war against Germany.

Allied Diplomacy

World War II was the first truly global war. Needless to say, a war of such magnitude required close cooperation among wartime leaders. Luckily for the Allies, President Franklin Roosevelt and British Prime Minister Winston Churchill respected each other and generally agreed on the goals of the war and the peace. The two leaders met repeatedly during the war to plan strategy and discuss goals. These meetings were held in such diverse places as Washington, Casablanca, Quebec, Cairo, and Teheran. In November 1944 Roosevelt and Churchill met for the first time with Premier Josef Stalin of the Soviet Union. The United States and Great Britain welcomed the powerful Soviet Union as an ally against Germany, but they remained suspicious of the communist country and its dictatorial leader. During the course of the war Roosevelt and Churchill conferred with other Allied leaders, including General Chiang Kai-shek of China. Roosevelt, Churchill, and Stalin met for a second time at Yalta, in the Soviet Union, in February 1945. At this meeting they discussed the final phase of the war in Europe, agreed to certain Russian territorial claims, and laid the groundwork for the formation of the United Nations. The final conference of the war was held in July 1945 at Potsdam, Germany, where Truman, Churchill, and Stalin discussed the postwar occupation of Germany and demanded the immediate surrender of Japan.

The War in Europe

THE ALLIED COUNTERATTACK

The Germans continued their advances during the spring and summer of 1942, pressing to the gates of Moscow and Leningrad and subduing a strip of North Africa along the Mediterranean. This marked the high tide of their advance, however, for during the summer the Allies launched a counteroffensive. The Russians stopped the German advance and by early 1943 had them in retreat. The British flew massive air raids over Germany and began a counterattack in Africa. The first American troops arrived in the British Isles in January 1942, and American bombers joined the attack on Germany in August of that year.

The African and Italian Campaigns

The first American ground offensive began in November 1942 when troops under General Dwight Eisenhower joined the British offensive in North Africa. The combined British and American force made steady progress, and the last German forces in North Africa surrendered in May 1943. The Allies then turned their eyes toward Europe. British and American troops overran Sicily in July and August. In September they landed in Italy. The Italian government, disheartened after eight years of fruitless warfare, deposed Mussolini and surrendered to the Allies shortly after the invasion. This has little impact on the fighting, however, for the German army occupied most of Italy. Allied forces did not capture Rome until June 1944.

ALLIED ADVANCES

The Allies kept up the pressure on Germany during late 1943 and early 1944. The bombing of Germany continued, and British and American troops advanced slowly in Italy. On the Eastern Front the Soviet army continued its drive against the Germans and entered Poland in January 1944. Partisans in Greece, Yugoslavia, and other occupied countries stepped up their guerrilla war against the Nazis.

THE INVASION OF FRANCE AND GERMANY

On June 6, 1944—D-Day—Allied forces under General Eisenhower made the largest amphibious assault in history. Allied troops poured ashore on the coast of Normandy in France and began to fight their way inland. By the beginning of July over a million Allied soldiers were in France. Another Allied force landed in southern France in mid-August. The Allies liberated Paris on August 28 and entered Germany on September 12. In December the Germans launched a surprise counteroffensive against the British and Americans in the Battle of the Bulge—so called because of the shape of the Allied lines. The German attack drove the Allies back but failed to break the line. The Allies renewed their attack on Germany and crossed the Rhine River in March 1945. The Russians continued their advance from the east and captured Berlin on May 2. Mussolini, who had fled when the Italians surrendered, was captured and executed, Hitler committed suicide, and German troops all across Europe began to surrender. What was left of the German government and army officially capitulated on May 9.

SOVIET RELATIONS

Throughout the war the Western leaders, particularly Winston Churchill, remained suspicious of the Soviet Union. The United States and Great Britain, the world's leading capitalist nations, were natural enemies of the communist state. Germany's great might, however, made the alliance a marriage of necessity. The three countries generally agreed on wartime strategy, but as the war drew to a close and the Allies began to concentrate on postwar arrangements in Europe, differences in goals became evident.

Russia, which had been invaded by Germany twice in the twentieth century, had little faith in collective security. For the Soviet Union, military might and control of neighboring countries offered the best protection against aggression. Soviet leader Josef Stalin agreed to participate in the United Nations, but he put very little faith in its ability to maintain peace. The League of Nations, after all, had failed miserably. He also agreed that the nations of Europe should be free to determine their own political future.

As the Allies closed in on Germany, distrust of the Russians increased. The Russian army occupied a large portion of eastern Europe, and communist-led partisans dominated the resistance movement in that region. When anticommunist partisans in Poland rebelled against the Germans, the Russians refused to help them, even though their army was only a few miles away. Churchill, afraid that the Soviets would not withdraw their army from eastern Europe after the war, wanted the British and American armies to push as far east as possible. This may have been good politics, but General Eisenhower, the commander of the Allied army in Europe, considered it an unwise military move and refused to alter his strategy of defeating the German army.

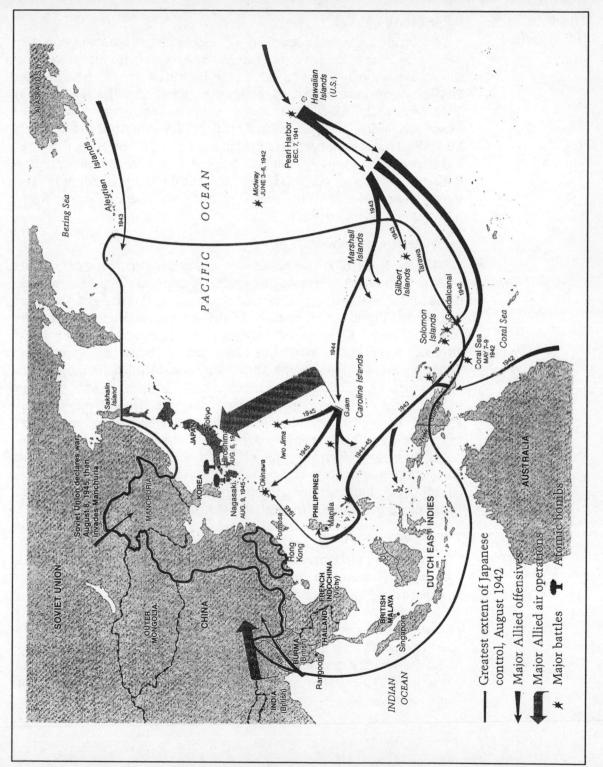

Fig. 7.2 World War II: Pacific Theater

The War in the Pacific

JAPANESE ADVANCES

Following the surprise attacks of December 7, the Japanese stepped up the war in China, occupied most of southeast Asia, invaded the Philippines, and occupied a number of islands in the Pacific. American troops in the Philippines, unable to withstand the Japanese advance, surrendered in May 1942. Meanwhile, Allied naval and air forces were organizing to stop the advance. American bombers began air raids on Tokyo in April 1942. In early May Allied naval forces defeated the Japanese in the Battle of the Coral Sea and stopped their advance toward Australia. In early June an American fleet inflicted heavy losses on the Japanese navy at the Battle of Midway. This victory destroyed Japan's offensive capability and opened the way for an American counteroffensive.

THE AMERICAN ADVANCE

The American offensive began with an attack on the island of Guadalcanal in the south Pacific in August 1942. Fighting was hard and slow—the battle for the small island of Guadalcanal lasted six months—but American forces gradually advanced island by island and approached the Philippines from the south. A second offensive, which began in November 1943, advanced across the island chains of the central Pacific and approached Japan. A third offensive, mounted by American and British troops, attacked the Japanese in southeast Asia. In June 1944 American bombers began regular attacks on Japan, and American forces under General Douglas MacArthur landed in the Philippines. In early 1945 the Allies began preparing for their attack on Japan. The Japanese fleet was all but destroyed, the Allies stepped up their air raids on Japan, and in February MacArthur completed his reconquest of the Philippines. American forces captured the islands of Iwo Jima and Okinawa after bloody fighting, and in April Allied forces drove the Japanese from southeast Asia.

THE ATTACK ON JAPAN

The capture of Okinawa in June 1945 placed American troops within 350 miles of Japan. On July 26 the Allied leaders meeting in Potsdam demanded that Japan surrender, an ultimatum that the Japanese rejected. The Allies hoped to end the war without invading Japan, for although the Japanese military was severely battered, millions of Japanese remained ready to sacrifice their lives to defend their homeland. To avoid such a costly invasion—military planners estimated that at least a million American soldiers would die in the invasion—President Truman decided to drop the atomic bomb.

THE ATOMIC BOMB

American interest in building an atomic bomb began in 1939 when the brilliant scientist Albert Einstein, a German refugee, informed President Roosevelt that Hitler's scientists were working on such a weapon. The United States started its own atomic bomb project—named the Manhattan Project—in 1941. After four years of work, scientists successfully exploded a bomb in New Mexico on July 16, 1945. Thirteen days later, on August 6, the United States dropped an atomic bomb on the Japanese city of Hiroshima, destroying most of the city and causing 160,000 casualties. The Americans dropped another bomb on Nagasaki on August 9. The Japanese surrendered on August 10.

Casualties

Figures on the losses suffered in World War II challenge the imagination. Fifty-seven nations took part in the war with combined armies of 90 million men. In all, 12.5 million Americans served in the armed forces during the war; 322,000 died, and another 800,000 were wounded. The casualty rate was considerably lower than in World War I thanks to improved sanitation and better medical care. As in World War I, American casualties were comparatively light: Current estimates place Russian losses at 30 million dead. Altogether, 15 million soldiers died in the war. Civilian losses are estimated at over 25 million, including the 6 million Jews who died in Hitler's concentration camps.

The United Nations

When Roosevelt and Churchill first met in August 1940 and drafted the Atlantic Charter, they discussed the need for an international organization to maintain the peace after the end of the war. The countries fighting Germany and Japan organized themselves as the United Nations and adopted the Atlantic Charter as a statement of their war aims. The name "United Nations" was used in the various cooperative activities of the Allies during the war, and it followed that the peacetime successor to the Allies would also bear that name. In September 1944 representatives of the United States, Great Britain, the Soviet Union, and China met in Washington to create a framework for this peacekeeping body. In April 1945 delegates from fifty nations met in San Francisco and organized the United Nations. The new organization consisted of a general assembly in which each member nation had a single vote; a security council comprised of eleven members, including five permanent members (the United States, Great Britain, France, the Soviet Union, and China); an international court of justice; and a full-time administrative secretariat directed by a secretary-general.

*W*orld War II, fought to end the aggression of Germany, Italy, and Japan, had a long-term impact on the United States. At home it ended the worst depression the country ever suffered and projected the nation to a level of unprecedented prosperity. Abroad the United States, with its tremendous military and industrial might, became the predominant country in the postwar world. The war also signaled the beginning of a dangerous rivalry between the United States and the Soviet Union.

Selected Readings

Ambrose, Stephen. *The Supreme Commander: The War Years of General Dwight D. Eisenhower* (1970)

Blum, John M. *V Was for Victory: Politics and American Culture During World War II* (1976)

Buchanan, A. Russell. *The United States and World War II*, 2 vols. (1964)

Churchill, Winston. *The Second World War*, 6 vols. (1948–1953)

Dallek, Robert. *Franklin D. Roosevelt and American Foreign Policy, 1932–1945* (1979)

Divine, Robert. *The Reluctant Belligerent: American Entry into World War II* (1965)

Groves, Leslie. *Now It Can Be Told: The Story of the Manhattan Project* (1962)

Heller, Joseph. *Catch-22* (1961)

Hersey, John. *Hiroshima* (1985)

Iriye, Akira. *The Origins of the Second World War in Asia and the Pacific* (1987)

_____. *Power and Culture: The Japanese-American War, 1941–1945* (1981)

Prange, Gordon. *At Dawn We Slept* (1981)

Wouk, Herman. *War and Remembrance* (1978)

_____. *The Winds of War* (1971)

8

The Postwar Era: 1945–1960

1945 Harry Truman begins first term as president

World War II ends; Allied troops occupy Germany and Japan

1946 Philippines become independent

Federal government seizes control of coal mines to prevent nationwide strike

1947 Truman Doctrine announced

Taft-Hartley Act restricts certain union practices

National Security Act creates the Department of Defense, the National Security Council, the Central Intelligence Agency

1948 Marshall Plan initiated

Organization of American States established

Israel becomes a nation

Berlin airlift

1949 Truman begins second term as president

North Atlantic Treaty Organization (NATO) established

Communists gain control of China

Alger Hiss convicted of perjury

1950 Korean War begins

McCarthy hearings begin in the Senate

1951 U.S. occupation of Japan ends

1952 Federal government seizes control of steel mills in order to prevent nationwide strike

1953 Dwight Eisenhower begins first term as president

Korean war ends

Julius and Ethel Rosenberg executed for espionage

1954 Joseph McCarthy censured by the Senate

1955 U.S. sends military advisors to South Vietnam

Allies end occupation of West Germany

1956 Highways Act creates interstate highway system

1957 Eisenhower begins second term as president

1959 Communists gain control of Cuba

1960 American U-2 spy plane shot down over Soviet Union

*W*orld War II left the United States strong and prosperous, but it did not
bring peace to the country or the world. When the war ended, the United
States found itself facing a powerful new enemy—the Soviet Union. The
Russians had suffered terribly in the two world wars. Intent on protecting
themselves from future invasion, the Soviets annexed territory along their
borders and seized control of Eastern Europe. The Soviets also sought to
expand their influence in other parts of the world. During the 1940s and
1950s Asia and Africa erupted in revolution as people in those regions
sought to end colonial rule. Russia, exploiting the fact that the Western
nations were the leading colonial powers, extended aid to the
revolutionaries. The United States, as leader of the Western alliance, assumed the duty of containing Soviet expansion and maintaining the power
and prestige of the Western nations. The result was a protracted war, fought
with words and proxies, as the United States and the Soviet Union
maneuvered to expand their own influence while checking the power of the
other.

On the home front, Americans found themselves enjoying the feast after
the famine. People who had suffered through over fifteen years of depression
and war suddenly found themselves with money to spend and plenty to buy.
The great wartime industrial machine shifted to the production of consumer
goods and filled the nation's stores with a vast array of merchandise.
Americans, tired of the years of deprivation, reveled in their great prosperity.
At the same time, a great uneasiness permeated the country. The great

propaganda war with the Soviets was waged at home as well as abroad, and Americans lived in fear of Soviet attack and communist subversion.

THE BEGINNING OF THE COLD WAR

Soviet-American Relations

The United States considered the communist government of the Soviet Union an adversary from the moment of its rise to power in 1917. Karl Marx, the founder of communism, argued that capitalism was an exploitative economic system that profited the few at the expense of the masses. He envisioned a state in which the workers controlled the government and the economy. The communists in Russia took control of the country in the revolution of 1917 and established an absolute dictatorship in the name of the working class.

IDEOLOGICAL DIFFERENCES

There were two issues that put the Soviet Union at odds with the United States. One was ideological. The Soviet Union became the bastion of communism and directed an international campaign for the spread of communism and Soviet influence. This placed Russia in direct opposition to the United States, which was committed to the dissemination of democracy and capitalism and the expansion of American economic and diplomatic influence. The Soviet threat seemed particularly insidious since the Russians claimed the loyalty of American communists. Middle-class and upper-class Americans, always suspicious of any semblance of foreign influence within the United States, became particularly hostile to what they considered a subversive force.

SOVIET TERRITORIAL SECURITY

The second factor in American-Soviet relations had more to do with Russian national security than with the spread of communism. Russia's vast sprawling empire had always been subject to foreign invasion. Most recently, the German invasions of 1914 and 1942 had cost millions of lives. The communists, like the czars before them, were committed to the establishment of buffer states, particularly in Eastern Europe, to protect their boundaries.

SOVIET EXPANSION

In prewar Europe communists became a growing and, in places, an influential political faction. This spreading influence scared many people; indeed, the fascist leaders Hitler, Mussolini, and Franco owed much of their popularity to their anticommunist rhetoric. When the war started, the United

States and Great Britain formed a reluctant alliance with the Soviet Union. Neither Churchill nor Roosevelt trusted the Soviets, but there was no denying that the Soviets were a valuable ally.

Prior to the war the Soviet Union had been beset by internal problems and posed only a minor threat to the West. Russia was nowhere near as dangerous as Japan or Nazi Germany. But like the United States, the Soviet Union emerged from the war as one of the great powers and possessed the means to pursue its international goals.

When the war ended the Allies found themselves at odds over the disposition of postwar Europe. The United States and Great Britain wanted to reestablish prewar boundaries and guarantee peace through the collective security of the United Nations. The Soviet Union had no faith in collective security and sought to protect itself from future invasion. The Russians refused to withdraw from Eastern Europe, and in the several years following the end of the war Soviet-backed communists took control of the countries occupied by the Russian army.

CONTAINMENT

American policymakers looked with dismay on the spread of communism in Europe. Convinced that the Soviets were intent on world domination, the United States embarked on a campaign to counteract Soviet measures. This policy of containment committed the United States to the use of its diplomatic, economic, and military power to limit Soviet influence and stop the spread of communism.

The belief in a Soviet drive for world domination led to a flawed American foreign policy. American planners saw communism as a monolithic institution controlled from Moscow. This restricted world view obscured an already complex situation in which the Soviets tried to exploit anticolonial nationalist uprisings around the globe. Leaders of the nationalist movements, although attracted to communism, owed no allegiance to Moscow. Unfortunately, American opposition to any hint of communism drove some nationalists into the Soviet camp.

Tension in Europe

TURKEY AND GREECE

The first confrontation between the United States and the Soviet Union in postwar Europe came in Turkey and Greece in 1946 and 1947. The Soviet Union demanded territorial concessions from neighboring Turkey and put pressure on the Turks to enter the Soviet sphere of influence. In Greece, a communist-led rebellion threatened to topple the government. President Harry Truman, intent on stopping Soviet expansion, raised the possibility of American military intervention. The Truman Doctrine, announced in March 1947, codified his position. The United States, Truman stated, would provide aid to any nation threatened by "attempted subjugation by armed minorities or outside pressures." Congress supported Truman's policy and approved financial aid for both Greece and Turkey. By 1949 Truman was able to proclaim the Truman Doctrine a success: The Greek communists had been defeated, and Turkey had not only rejected the Soviet demands but had entered the Western alliance.

THE MARSHALL PLAN

In 1947 Secretary of State George Marshall proposed that the European nations draw up a comprehensive plan for the economic recovery of war-battered Europe based upon extensive American aid. The Soviet Union and its satellites, condemning the action as an act of American imperialism, refused to participate. Sixteen other nations accepted the offer and designed a master plan for American-funded reconstruction. The program went into operation in 1948 and was a tremendous success. Between 1947—when Congress first approved funding—and 1951 the United States funneled $13 billion into Europe. Rebuilding moved rapidly, and by 1951 Western Europe was in better economic shape than it had been before the war began in 1939. The Marshall Plan was also a diplomatic success, for it strengthened the Western alliance and limited communist influence in Western Europe.

GERMANY

When the war ended, the Allies divided Germany into four zones, with the United States, Great Britain, France, and the Soviet Union each occupying a zone. When the Allied leaders met at Potsdam in 1945 they agreed to administer the country jointly, but cooperation ended when the Soviets and the Western nations were unable to agree on the rehabilitation of Germany. In 1948 the United States, Great Britain, and France consolidated their zones in western Germany and allowed the Germans to establish a new government: the Federated Republic of Germany (West Germany). The Russians, in an effort to solidify their control of eastern Germany, blocked Western access to Berlin, which was under joint occupation but lay entirely within the Russian zone. The Americans and British, who had control of West Berlin, stopped all communication between their sector and Soviet-controlled East Berlin and commenced an airlift to bring food and other supplies into the city. The Berlin blockade, which began in June 1948 and lasted until May 1949, convinced the Western nations that cooperation with the Soviet Union was fruitless and intensified the hostility between the East and the West.

THE NORTH ATLANTIC TREATY ORGANIZATION (NATO)

As tension with the Soviet Union increased, the Western nations began to consider the need for a new military alliance. In 1948 Great Britain, France, and three other European nations signed a mutual defense treaty and hoped that the United States would join as well. The Warsaw Pact—a mutual defense treaty signed by the Soviet Union and its Eastern European satellites in 1948—and the Berlin blockade persuaded the United States to enter into the Western European alliance. In April 1949 the United States, Canada, and ten European nations signed the North Atlantic Treaty, which called for mutual defense in case of an attack on any member nation. NATO, which eventually included fifteen members, became the bulwark of defense against Soviet aggression in Europe. The United States had become—for the first time—a member of a peacetime European military alliance.

Tension in Asia

CHINA

When the war against Japan ended in 1945 the Nationalists and communists in China renewed their civil war. The United States extended aid to the Nationalist government of Chiang Kai-shek, who had been an ally during the war. The United States was very cautious in this, however, for it did not wish to be drawn into the conflict. Furthermore, there was considerable disenchantment in Washington with the inefficiency and corruption of the Nationalist government. The communists under Mao Tse-tung rolled to victory, and in December 1949 Chiang and his supporters fled to the island of Formosa. President Truman considered recognizing the communist government, but political pressure at home and the outbreak of war in Korea persuaded him to abandon this position. The United States continued to support the exiled Nationalists as the legitimate government of China.

JAPAN

American troops occupied Japan when the war ended in August 1945. The civilian Japanese government remained in place, but American forces under the command of General Douglas MacArthur exercised considerable authority in the country. In 1947 Japanese officials approved a new constitution, which had been drafted by the Americans. This constitution introduced numerous political, economic, and social reforms and placed severe limits on Japan's ability to militarize. When China fell to the communists in 1949 Japan, well on its way to becoming a westernized nation, became an important bastion against communist expansion in Asia. American occupation ended in 1951, but a new treaty between the United States and Japan allowed American troops to remain.

KOREA

When World War II ended Allied troops occupied Korea, which had been part of the Japanese empire. American troops occupied the southern half of the country, and Russian troops moved into the north. In 1947 the United States asked the United Nations to supervise the establishment of a civilian government in Korea. The Soviets refused to participate in any U.N. program and in 1948 established a new government in North Korea. Shortly thereafter the U.N. oversaw the creation of another government in South Korea. Both claimed to be the legitimate government for all of Korea, and both vowed to use force to achieve unification. American troops withdrew from Korea in 1949.

In June 1950 North Korean forces invaded the South and quickly overran the country. The United Nations, taking advantage of the absence of the Soviet representative (who was boycotting the U.N. because of its failure to seat the representative of Communist China), called upon its members to defend South Korea. President Truman immediately ordered American forces into action. General Douglas MacArthur, the commander of the American troops in the Pacific, was placed at the head of the U.N. forces.

In August and September allied forces landed in South Korea and began to push northward. In October they captured the capital of North Korea and advanced toward the Chinese border. The Chinese then came to the aid of the North Koreans and drove the U.N. forces back into South Korea. General MacArthur, who advocated an all-out attack on China, disagreed with the policy of President Truman and the United Nations, both of whom favored a negotiated settlement to reestablish prewar boundaries. When MacArthur appealed directly to Congress for support in April 1951, Truman removed him from command. The Soviets called for a cease-fire in July 1951; peace talks, interspersed with periods of combat, continued until July 1953. The final armistice established a demilitarized zone between the North and the South and gave de facto recognition to the existence of two separate countries. The United States, which bore the brunt of the fighting for the allies, ended the war with 56,000 dead and 103,000 wounded. The South Koreans lost 50,000 dead, and the other U.N. members 3,000.

The Atomic Bomb

The invention of the atomic bomb and its great destructive capability introduced an entirely new element into warfare. So frightening was this weapon that people began to demand its regulation as soon as its existence became known. In early 1946 the United States proposed that the United Nations assume control of all atomic technology. According to this proposal, the U.N. would regulate the peaceful use of atomic power and enforce a ban on atomic weapons. Once the U.N. had created the proper agencies and established an effective means of preventing the production and use of atomic weapons, the United States would destroy its atomic arsenal. The Soviet Union opposed this plan and demanded that the United States destroy its atomic bombs immediately. The Soviets also blocked efforts to give the U.N. effective control of atomic weapons.

Meanwhile, the great powers embarked on a nuclear arms race. The United States established the Atomic Energy Commission to supervise atomic technology and continued its program of creating bigger and better bombs. The Soviet Union exploded its first atomic bomb in 1949, and the British did likewise in 1952. The United States, maintaining its superiority, increased its nuclear capability by exploding a hydrogen bomb in 1952.

THE COLD WAR

The Arms Race

The United States exploded its first hydrogen bomb in 1952, and the Russians followed with one of their own the following year. This nuclear parity led both sides to amass huge nuclear arsenals and to develop new types of bombs that could be dropped from airplanes or carried on missiles launched from land or from ships. Both countries adopted the strategy of massive retaliation—the ability to launch a massive nuclear counterattack should the enemy attack—as a means of deterrence. Since both countries possessed the means of destroying the other, open war between the two became unlikely, even though their armies faced each other in Europe. Instead, they fought each other in small proxy wars such as the Greek civil war, in which the Americans and the Russians provided support to opposing sides, or the Korean war, in which the United States fought a Soviet client state but not the Soviet Union itself. This deadly game required both countries to maintain large military establishments which led to a massive buildup of conventional weapons as both sides tried to win military superiority.

Colonial Revolutions

In the 1930s independence movements began in a number of colonies in Asia and Africa. World War II interrupted this development, but when the war ended anticolonialism resurfaced and swept the Third World. The response of the ruling nations varied. In some cases the imperial powers granted independence without question, and in others they used military force to suppress colonial uprisings. This vast independence movement complicated the Cold War, for both the Western nations and the communists used the emerging nations and the colonial wars as pawns in their international struggle for power. In most cases, the insurgents were revolting against a Western nation; it was natural for them to turn to the West's enemy—the Soviet Union—for assistance. Many of the insurgents were communists, but others simply sought independence for their nations. American policymakers refused to differentiate between nationalist-minded revolutionaries and Soviet proxies. In their eyes, all revolution was communist inspired. They refused to admit that any colony could have a legitimate complaint against a member of the Western alliance.

Vietnam REVOLT AGAINST THE FRENCH

During World War II the Japanese occupied the French colony of Vietnam and established an independent government under Japanese control. When the Japanese withdrew at the end of the war this government collapsed. The resistance movement—which, like the resistance movements in Europe, included both communists and non-communists—declared independence and established its own government. The French returned in 1945, established a colonial government, and set out to crush the independence movement. Ho Chi Minh, the leader of the insurgents, appealed to the United States and the United Nations to intervene and supervise the creation of an independent Vietnam. President Truman, unwilling to offend the French, refused to respond. Rebuffed by the United States, the insurgents turned to the Soviet Union and China for assistance. The French colonial government had little popular support, and Ho Chi Minh, although fighting a guerrilla war against the French, controlled much of the country.

AMERICAN INVOLVEMENT

The United States was unsure how to proceed and refused to support either side. Finally, in 1950, the United States decided to support the French and began to supply military aid; in all, the United States paid three-quarters of the cost of the French war effort. By 1954 the French were ready to seek a negotiated settlement. The United States opposed this move, arguing that if the French pulled out, Vietnam would fall to the communists, and the other nations of southeast Asia would follow like "a row of falling dominoes." The United States even considered direct military intervention, but the French refused assistance. When the Vietnamese rebels captured the French stronghold at Dien Bien Phu in northern Vietnam in June 1954 France gave up.

CIVIL WAR

A postwar settlement, agreed upon during the summer of 1954, provided for the temporary partition of Vietnam, with the insurgents in control of the North and the French colonial party in control of the south. The agreement also called for a nationwide election in 1956 to determine the future of the country. Fighting began almost immediately between the North and the South. The United States gave its support to the government of Ngo Dinh Diem in the South and sent CIA operatives and military advisors to assist and train his army. Meanwhile, the Viet Cong, the communist faction within the independence movement, took control of the government of the North, with Ho Chi Minh as their leader. In 1955 Diem declared himself president of the Republic of South Vietnam and announced that the South would not participate in the election scheduled for 1956. The United States continued to support Diem, sending money, supplies, and advisors to assist the South in its war against the North.

Germany

In 1955 the United States, Great Britain, and France ended their occupation of Germany, and the West German government was given complete sovereignty, including the right to rearm itself. Allied troops continued to be stationed in West Germany, which had become a member of NATO.

The division of Germany remained a point of contention between the Western nations and the Soviet Union. Reunification of the country remained a stated goal for both sides, but the likelihood of a united Germany seemed bleak. East and West Germany each had their own governments, and the Soviets had sealed the border between the two sections in order to stop the flow of millions of East Germans to the West. In 1955 President Eisenhower met in Geneva with the leaders of France, Britain, and the Soviet Union to discuss future arrangements for Germany. Nothing concrete came out of this meeting, but it did establish a framework for ongoing talks between the Western nations and the Soviet Union.

The occupation of Berlin remained a continual sore point. In 1958 the Soviets threatened to establish another blockade of West Berlin unless the allies recognized the government of East Germany. The Western nations refused and reaffirmed their commitment to protect their part of the city. The crisis dissipated later that year when President Eisenhower met with Soviet Premier Nikita Khrushchev at Camp David, Maryland, and agreed to hold a summit meeting in Paris to once again consider unification. This meeting never occurred, however. In 1959 the Soviets shot down an American spy plane over Russia and forced Eisenhower to admit that he had authorized an ongoing program of aerial surveillance of the Soviet Union. Khrushchev canceled the Paris summit and withdrew an invitation to Eisenhower to visit Russia.

The Middle East

SOVIET INCURSIONS

During World War II Russian troops moved into neighboring Iran in order to forestall efforts by Germany to increase its influence in the Persian Gulf area. When the war ended, the Soviets sponsored separatist revolts in northern Iran and annexed several Iranian provinces. This episode, along with Soviet attempts to annex portions of Turkey, drew American attention to the Middle East and the Russian threat to its valuable oil fields.

ISRAEL

American interest in the Middle East increased in 1948 when the United Nations, under the leadership of the United States, created a new Jewish state in Palestine. Thousands of American and European Jews, devastated by the horrible persecutions of the Nazis during World War II, eagerly returned to their traditional homeland and established the nation of Israel. The Arab nations, themselves only recently independent, were outraged at what they considered the European usurpation of Palestinian territory. They refused to recognize Israel and attacked Jewish settlers. The United States mediated an armistice between the Arabs and Israel in 1949, but animosity between the two remained. Arab nationalists, already hostile toward the French and British for refusing to grant them independence after World War I, added the United States—the sponsor of Israel—to their list of enemies.

AMERICAN INVOLVEMENT

As the Middle East increased in importance during the 1950s the United States began a policy of trying to balance different interests that were often contradictory. The United States tried to maintain friendly relations with the moderate governments in the region, prevent the expansion of Soviet influence, guarantee the existence of Israel, and avoid alienating the more radically nationalist Arab leaders. The creation of Israel and the Soviet-American rivalry added to the tension that already existed among the various religious and national groups in the region.

These various rivalries led to an atmosphere of instability. In 1953 the CIA sponsored a coup in Iran that put a pro-American government in power. Two years later, the Soviets backed a revolt that overthrew the pro-Western government of Iraq. Internal tensions threatened to erupt into revolts in other countries as well; in 1958 American troops landed in Lebanon and British forces went to Jordan to insure the safety of the governments of those countries.

THE SUEZ CRISIS

The greatest crisis in the region was the ongoing war between Israel and its Arab neighbors. A larger war in Egypt in 1956 was narrowly averted. Egyptian President Gamal Abdel Nasser, the strongest figure in the region and the leader of the Arab nationalist movement, had become increasingly friendly with the Soviets. In order to counter Soviet influence, the United States and Great Britain offered to finance the construction of the Aswan Dam, an important irrigation and electrification project. They then withdrew the offer, hinting that financing would become available if Egypt distanced itself from Russia. Angered at this manipulation, Nasser seized the Suez Canal, an important link between the Mediterranean Sea and the Indian Ocean. Great Britain, France, and Israel, fearful that Nasser would close the waterway to their ships, invaded Egypt and captured the canal.

The United States, desirous of stability in the Middle East, condemned the invasion and, working through the United Nations, arranged a settlement of the dispute.

Latin America   RESENTMENT TOWARD THE UNITED STATES

Relations with South America, which had improved during the 1930s and 1940s, declined in the 1950s. Latin America continued to suffer from severe economic problems, most notably widespread poverty and heavy foreign debts. People throughout the region resented American economic dominance and American support for the corrupt dictatorial regimes that had risen to power during the 1930s and 1940s. They watched in anger as the United States grew richer while their own countries sank deeper into poverty. The Organization of American States, created in 1949 to promote hemispheric cooperation, did little to solve the region's economic problems or to stem the widespread hatred of the United States. The extent of hostility became obvious in 1958 when demonstrators throughout South America stoned the car of Vice-President Richard Nixon during an official tour of the continent.

GUATEMALA

The United States was in part responsible for this resentment, for it continued to use a heavy hand in Latin America. In 1954 the democratic government of Guatemala, in an effort to gain some control over the resources of its country, nationalized the banana groves. American fruit companies, seeing this as a threat to profits, complained to the American government. Shortly thereafter, a CIA-backed revolution overthrew the Guatemalan government and replaced it with a pro-American military junta.

CUBA

In the late 1950s a wave of revolution swept Latin America. In 1957 the Cuban people, no longer able to tolerate the corrupt regime of dictator Fulgencio Batista, rose up in revolt. Batista was friendly with the foreign business interests that controlled the Cuban economy; he also had close ties to organized crime, which did a lucrative business in the hotels and casinos of Havana. Batista was driven from Cuba in 1959, and the revolutionaries, under the leadership of Fidel Castro, took control. Castro's campaign for Cuban nationalism was clearly anti-American. As relations between the United States and Cuba deteriorated, Castro increased his ties to the Soviet Union. When Castro began to nationalize foreign business interests, the United States invoked a trade embargo on the island. If Castro was not already fully committed to communism, the hostility of the United States assured his alliance with the Russians. Over the next several years the United States, Cuba, and the Soviet Union engaged in a bitter war of words and threats. In 1961 President Eisenhower severed diplomatic relations with Cuba.

Internal Security

ANTICOMMUNISM

As the nation battled Soviet expansion abroad it also worried about communist subversion at home. A wave of anti-communist hysteria swept the nation, as government officials, business leaders, and patriotic organizations sought to rid the country of communists. Communism became the national bogeyman. Problems facing the nation were believed to be the work of communist conspirators, dissidents were accused of being communists or at least communist sympathizers, and an accusation of being a communist was enough to besmirch anyone's character. These accusations were particularly sinister because they were made in secret. Suspects were denied the right to confront their accusers or even learn their identity.

The federal government took the lead in the suppression of communism. In 1946 a presidential order required federal employees to sign loyalty oaths and to submit to background checks. In 1950 Congress passed—over the president's veto—the McCarran Act, which ordered the attorney general to compile a list of all organizations suspected of being communist and placing severe restrictions on members of those organizations.

Local governments, businesses, and public institutions followed suit and purged themselves of employees accused of having ties to the communists. The purge was particularly bad in the entertainment business, where hundreds of actors, directors, technicians, and musicians were blacklisted and kept from working because of supposed links to the communists. No one was safe from these accusations. Robert Oppenheimer, one of America's most brilliant scientists and a leader of the team that built the atomic bomb, lost his security clearance when an informant claimed he was a communist sympathizer.

CONGRESSIONAL HEARINGS

As communism continued to spread through Europe and Asia, Americans began to wonder at the inability of the United States to stop it. Critics of the government, particularly conservatives in Congress, placed the blame on communist infiltration of the Truman administration. The Un-American Activities Committee of the House of Representatives began to conduct hearings on the matter, and one member of the committee, Republican Richard Nixon, built his political reputation on his attacks on supposed communists and communist sympathizers within the administration. The committee hearings attracted special attention in 1948 when Whittaker Chambers, a confessed former communist, claimed that Alger Hiss, a high official in the State Department, was a Soviet spy. The accusation was never proved, but when Hiss was convicted of perjury in 1949 everyone assumed his guilt. This "conviction" of a high government official seemed to confirm fears of communist infiltration.

THE McCARTHY HEARINGS

In the Senate, Republican Joseph McCarthy began to hold similar hearings in 1950. During the four years in which he conducted hearings, McCarthy played upon the anticommunist hysteria of the time and made numerous—and usually false—accusations against government officials. By 1954 McCarthy had become so irresponsible in his actions that he was an embarrassment to the Senate and the Republican party. His downfall came when he conducted hearings on communist infiltration of the army. These hearings were televised, and millions of Americans watched McCarthy make a fool of himself. No longer able to tolerate him, the Senate voted to condemn his actions. The Republicans, now in control of the White House and no longer in need of McCarthy's attacks on the executive branch, likewise repudiated him.

THE ROSENBERG TRIAL

One of the most noteworthy cases involving suspected communist infiltration was the trial and execution of Julius and Ethel Rosenberg. When the Soviets exploded their first atomic bomb in 1949 Americans within the government and without suspected that the Russians had somehow been able to steal information from the United States. Several people were arrested for espionage, and two of them, husband and wife Julius and Ethel Rosenberg, were convicted and sentenced to death. Some people believed at the time that anticommunist hysteria had more to do with the conviction than the evidence did, and the debate over their guilt or innocence continues still.

POSTWAR POLITICS

The Democratic party under the leadership of Franklin Roosevelt led the country out of the depression and to victory in World War II. But even this was not enough to guarantee continued Democratic dominance in the federal government. A brief period of economic instability during the summer of 1946 unsettled the public. The Republicans, attacking President Harry Truman's ability to govern, captured both houses of Congress in the 1946 elections.

Truman's Domestic Policies: First Term

Harry Truman had been vice-president for a scant three months before he took on the duties of the president in April 1945. He faced the enormous task of ending the war, overseeing demobilization, and directing American foreign policy as the country assumed its new role as leader of the Western nations. During his first two years in office Truman devoted most of his time to the transition from a wartime to a peacetime economy and to foreign affairs.

Truman was a great believer in social reform, and during his years in the Senate he had been a strong advocate of the New Deal. When the Republicans challenged his leadership in 1946, Truman responded by presenting Congress a vigorous program of social reform. The centerpiece of this package was a number of new civil rights bills. Truman asked Congress to establish a civil rights commission, to pass antilynching and anti-poll tax laws, and to provide for the enforcement of civil rights laws. These proposals met with hostility in the conservative Republican Congress. They also alienated southern Democrats.

1948 Election

When the Democrats met for their annual convention in 1948 opposition to Truman was strong. Many Democrats were dissatisfied with his leadership. His ascendancy to the presidency after Roosevelt's death was a twist of fate, for Truman had been a compromise candidate for vice-president in 1944. He had been a senator for over ten years, but he was not an insider with the party leadership. When he became president he made new enemies. Southern Democrats disliked him because of his proposed civil rights legislation, and many New Dealers resented his dismissal of a number of Roosevelt's appointees. Despite this opposition, Truman managed to secure the nomination and set out to win the election. His nomination, however, split the party. Disgruntled southerners formed the States Rights Democratic party (Dixiecrats) and nominated Governor Strom Thurmond of South Carolina for president. New Dealer Henry Wallace was the standard-bearer for the leftist-oriented Progressive party.

The Republicans once again nominated Governor Thomas Dewey for president and had little doubt that they could defeat the badly divided Democrats. Even most Democrats assumed that Truman would lose. Truman conducted a vigorous cross-country campaign tour and rallied mainstream Democrats to his cause. By comparison, Dewey was lackluster and almost complacent. To everyone's surprise Truman beat Dewey, winning 24 million votes to Dewey's 22 million. Thurmond and Wallace received just over a million votes each (see Appendix B). The Democrats also regained control of Congress.

Truman's Domestic Policies: Second Term

Truman spent most of his second term dealing with foreign affairs. Even so, he retained his interest in domestic matters and continued to push his reform program. The return of the Democrats to Congress did little to help Truman, for the national mood remained conservative and his proposals for agricultural reform, national health insurance, aid to education, and civil rights were defeated. When Congress rejected his civil rights program, Truman acted on his own and used his power as chief executive to desegregate the federal government and the armed services.

1952 Election

Foreign affairs, particularly the containment of communism, dominated Truman's second term. Many Americans questioned the wisdom of his policies. By 1952 successes such as the Marshall Plan and the formation of NATO had been forgotten. What lingered in the American mind was that Eastern Europe and China had gone communist, American troops were fighting a seesaw battle to stop the spread of communism in Korea, and the United States seemed to be infiltrated by thousands of communist spies. The United States, the great victor in World War II, seemed unable to defeat this new enemy. The Republicans, once again sensing victory, nominated the immensely popular war hero General Dwight Eisenhower for president. The Democrats nominated Adlai Stevenson, the able but little-known governor of Illinois. The Republican campaign centered on the failure of Truman's foreign policy, but it was Eisenhower's personal appeal that clinched the victory (see Appendix B). Control of Congress continued to fluctuate, as the Republicans once again won majorities in both the Senate and the House.

The 1956 Election

Dwight Eisenhower enjoyed great popularity throughout his presidency. The United States remained in a quiet, conservative mood, and Eisenhower's image as a friendly, grandfatherly type proved attractive to the voters. Eisenhower's image as a quiet man more interested in golf than politics was a facade, however, for the president had a strong character and kept firm control of the affairs of his administration. Eisenhower won a resounding victory in the 1956 election, beating his old adversary Adlai Stevenson by over 9 million votes. This victory was a triumph for Eisenhower, but not for the Republican party. The Democrats recaptured control of Congress in 1954 and increased their majority in the congressional elections of 1956 and 1958.

POSTWAR PROSPERITY

Economic Readjustment

When World War II ended the country faced the task of demobilizing the war effort. Soldiers returned home, and the factories stopped their massive production of war material.

Americans were not sure how demobilization would affect the nation's economy. Government spending for the war had brought an end to the depression, and many people feared that the reduction in government expenditures would plunge the country into a postwar recession. They also worried that unemployment would increase as millions of soldiers returned to the work force. The most immediate concern was inflation. Federal price controls had held inflation to a minimum during the war, but people wondered what would happen when consumer demand increased after the troops came home. The government planned to prevent rapid inflation by continuing the wartime Office of Price Administration (OPA) and allowing it to regulate prices.

Inflation and unemployment did rise, but only slightly and only for a brief period during the summer of 1946. Industry reconverted to the production of consumer goods much faster than anyone expected. The process, which began in 1945, was completed by 1947. An unprecedented demand for these products and the industrial capability to meet the demand limited both inflation and unemployment. Government policy also helped. The OPA held the line on prices for the brief period necessary for the factories to retool. Low interest home loans to returning soldiers contributed to a great housing boom. Most important, however, was federal military spending. The growing tension between the United States and the Soviet Union resulted in the maintenance of a large peacetime army. Modern warfare required sophisticated and expensive equipment, and the manufacture of these armaments contributed significantly to the postwar industrial boom.

Consumer Spending

The late 1940s marked the end of the long consumer-spending drought of the depression and the war. For the first time in almost twenty years there was money to spend and merchandise to buy. The high employment rate and the high wages of the war years continued into the early 1950s, and the nation's factories began to turn out consumer goods that had been unavailable during the war. Food rationing ended, and the production of automobiles—which had stopped completely during the war—began again. Greatly improved electrical appliances and newly invented items—most notably the television—also became available. People who had been forced to save their money during the war because there was nothing to buy now spent freely. The great amount of money in circulation and the high employment rate led to easy credit, and banks and stores introduced a new method of lending: the credit card.

This postwar economic boom differed from that of the 1920s. Manufacturers, bankers, and other businessmen had learned their lesson and took care to avoid the excesses that led to the Great Depression. The federal government had learned its lesson as well. The spirit of the New Deal remained alive, and the many federal regulatory agencies that had been rejuvenated or created during the depression provided a buffer against economic collapse that had not existed in the 1920s.

Government Spending

The massive military buildup of the 1950s required a program of government spending that pumped billions of dollars into the nation's economy. This defense spending, although key to the prosperity of the era, was only one way in which the government stimulated the economy. Federal money also went into road construction. The Highway Act of 1956 allocated $32 billion for the construction of the interstate highway system and for aid to the states for road work. The economic benefits of this program extended well beyond the money spent on construction. The automotive and trucking industries, in particular, profited from improved roadways. The housing industry likewise profited from federal programs. The Veterans Administration and the Federal Housing Administration provided low-cost loans for the purchase of homes, and in 1954 the government initiated a program for the construction of low-cost public housing.

The Business Sector

CORPORATE GROWTH

During the 1950s American corporations continued to grow. The conglomerates continued their pursuit of diversification by purchasing other companies that manufactured a variety of goods and provided a variety of services. They also built factories and purchased subsidiaries in foreign countries and began to operate on a multinational level. This expansion increased their ability to exploit markets and resources abroad, particularly the cheap, nonunionized labor markets of poorer countries.

As the demand for consumer goods increased, manufacturers produced a more varied line of products and offered merchandise that challenged their competitors. A shopper for a washing machine, for example, could choose from machines made by several different manufacturers; furthermore, each manufacturer offered several models with different features and price tags. Retailers were forced to expand in order to handle the great array and volume of merchandise turned out by the manufacturers. This continued expansion led to a new level of standardization of products. A shopper in California could choose from the exact same merchandise that was available in Missouri or Massachusetts.

THE SERVICE SECTOR

A new development of the postwar era was the emerging dominance of the service sector. Throughout most of the nineteenth century most Americans worked in agriculture, and during the first fifty years of the twentieth century a majority worked in manufacturing. Beginning in the 1950s, however, the number of people employed in the service sector—offices, stores, schools, and assorted small businesses—surpassed the number employed in manufacturing. This development had a direct influence on the composition of the work force. Many of the millions of women who went to work during the war preferred to keep working. The great increase in the service sector created many openings for women; the work did not entail the heavy labor common to manufacturing, and many of the jobs—office worker, retail clerk—were positions that traditionally were held by women.

LABOR

Labor unions, which made considerable gains in membership and power during the 1930s and 1940s, continued to increase their authority during the postwar period. Labor had a friend in President Truman. Truman twice threatened to seize the railroads and actually ordered federal control of the nation's coal mines in 1946 and the steel mills in 1952 when management refused to accept federally mediated contracts. Conservatives in Congress tried to curtail union power by passing—over President Truman's veto—the Taft-Hartley Act in 1947. This piece of legislation placed restrictions on certain union activities but did nothing to reduce the power and influence of the unions. Indeed, employers tried to improve their relations with their workers in order to insure a more stable and productive work force. Industrial leaders such as the automakers and the steel companies agreed to contracts that provided guaranteed annual wages, cost-of-living increases, better pension plans, and assorted fringe benefits. These concessions gave workers a new sense of security and helped reduce tension between workers and owners. Union power increased significantly in 1955 when the American Federation of Labor merged with its rival, the Congress of Industrial Organizations. The AFL-CIO represented 90 percent of all union members and gave new strength to an already thriving labor movement.

Social Impact of Prosperity

POPULATION GROWTH

The postwar period witnessed a great increase in the population of the United States. The country's population growth rate had dropped to an all-time low during the depression and the war, but when the fighting ended and prosperity returned, the figures skyrocketed. The number of Americans increased from 151 million in 1950 to 179 million in 1960 (an 18.5 percent increase), the greatest rate of growth since the first decade of the century. The main factor in this change was the birth rate, which rose from 19 per

1000 during the depression to 25 per 1000 in the 1950s. The high point of the "baby boom" came in 1957, when 4.3 million babies were born. Accompanying the increase in the birth rate was a decrease in the mortality rate. Improved health care and the discovery of new medicines—particularly penicillin, antibiotics, antihistamines, and polio vaccine—allowed doctors to reduce the number of deaths from disease. The death rate fell from 11.6 per 1000 in 1936 to 9.5 per 1000 in 1960. Immigration also contributed to growth. The quota system of the 1920s remained in place, but several changes in policy increased the flow of immigrants into the country. The government lifted the ban on immigration from Asia, it increased the number of persons allowed to enter from elsewhere in the western hemisphere, and it allowed political refugees and displaced persons from Europe to enter the country. Altogether, 2.5 million immigrants entered the United States during the 1950s.

SUBURBAN GROWTH

American urban areas continued their rapid growth during the 1950s, but growth occurred not in the cities themselves (where population actually declined) but in the suburbs. Suburbs had been an important part of the urban landscape since the late nineteenth century, but several developments of the postwar era catapulted suburban growth to unprecedented levels. One was the great housing boom of the 1950s. Real estate developers built huge suburban tracts on the outskirts of urban areas where land was cheaper. These new suburbs were larger than anything imagined before. Levittown, New York—the prototypical postwar suburb—contained 17,000 houses. The other main factor in suburban growth was the automobile. The automobile had begun to stimulate suburban growth in the 1920s, but once again, the sheer volume of automobiles—in 1960 Americans owned over 61 million cars—made the difference. Widespread ownership of cars and improved roadways made it easier for commuters to travel to and from the city.

Another facet of suburban growth was the development of the shopping center. As people moved out of the city, retailers followed and set up business in suburban shopping enclaves. Shopping centers were conveniently located along the many new highways near suburban housing. They featured huge parking lots where their customers could park for free, and they stayed open in the evenings so that commuters would have time to shop after they returned home from the city. Once again, numbers tell the story. There were eight shopping centers in the United States in 1945 and over 3,800 in 1960. Another hallmark of suburban shopping was the supermarket. These food emporiums offered a vast array of food products and replaced the small grocery stores, butcher shops, and bakeries of the city.

LEISURE TIME

Americans of the postwar era not only had money to spend, they had free time in which to enjoy it. By the 1950s the forty-hour work week had become standard, and most workers enjoyed an annual paid vacation. This combination of affluence and free time created a demand for recreation, a demand that made entertainment, tourism, and the manufacture of leisure goods important industries in themselves. Manufacturers flooded the market with games, toys, and sporting goods. Tourist attractions such as amusement parks, beaches, and historic monuments attracted millions of visitors, as did movies, live entertainment, and sporting events.

TELEVISION

The great entertainment innovation of the era was television. Developed in the 1920s, television did not become readily available to the public until the late 1940s; by 1960 three-fourths of all American households owned a television set. Television, more than any other single influence, shaped a uniform national culture in the United States. Viewers across the nation watched the same programs, heard the same news, and saw the same advertisements for the same products. Network television, with its access to a massive nationwide viewing audience, delivered the exact same material to people of all economic backgrounds in every part of the country, binding the people of the United States together in a way they had never been before.

The American victory in World War II and the great prosperity of the postwar years created a great sense of optimism in the American people. The United States had become the wealthiest and most powerful nation in history. And yet a feeling of uneasiness permeated American society, for the fear of communism was always present. This fear led to inexcusable repression at home and a patchwork foreign policy abroad. The policy of containment engendered a series of responses to individual crises, not a comprehensive plan for the pursuit of American interests overseas. The absolute opposition to even a hint of communism forestalled the flexibility needed in a rapidly changing world— particularly among the emerging independent nations—and backed the United States into some dangerous corners.

Selected Readings

Divine, Robert. *Eisenhower and the Cold War* (1981)
Donovan, Robert. *Conflict and Crisis: The Presidency of Harry S Truman, 1945– 1948* (1977)
_____. *Tumultuous Years: The Presidency of Harry S Truman, 1949–1953* (1982)
Gaddis, John. *Strategies of Containment: A Critical Appraisal of Postwar American National Security Policies* (1981)
_____. *The United States and the Origins of the Cold War, 1941–1947* (1972)

Galbraith, John Kenneth. *The Affluent Society*, 3rd ed. (1976)

Greenstein, Fred. *The Hidden-Hand Presidency: Eisenhower as Leader* (1982)

Griffith, Robert. *The Politics of Fear: Joseph R. McCarthy and the Senate (1970)*

Hamby, Alonzo. *Beyond the New Deal: Harry S Truman and American Liberalism* (1973)

Kutler, Stanley. *The American Inquisition: Justice and Injustice in the Cold War* (1982)

Leuchtenburg, William. *A Troubled Feast: American Society Since 1945* (1973)

Rees, David. *Korea: The Limited War* (1964)

Stookey, Robert. *America and the Arab States: An Uneasy Encounter* (1975)

9

The Civil Rights Movement: 1954–1972

1948 President Truman orders desegregation of armed services and federal government

1954 *Brown* v. *Board of Education*: Supreme Court outlaws racial segregation in public schools

1955 Montgomery, Alabama, bus boycott

1957 Federal troops help desegregate schools in Little Rock, Arkansas

Civil Rights Act establishes Civil Rights Commission and Civil Rights Division in Justice Department

1960 Sit-in protests against discrimination begin

Civil Rights Act strengthens enforcement of voting rights

1961 John Kennedy becomes president

1962 James Meredith admitted to the University of Mississippi

1963 Civil rights march on Washington

President Kennedy assassinated; Lyndon Johnson becomes president

1964 Twenty-fourth Amendment bans poll tax as requirement for voting in federal elections

Economic Opportunity Act creates Job Corps, VISTA, other work programs

Civil Rights Act outlaws discrimination in public accommodations, schools, employment

1964–1968   Riots in cities across the nation

1965   Johnson begins second term as president

Johnson introduces the Great Society

Voting Rights Act provides for federal supervision of voter registration

Malcolm X assassinated

1968   Martin Luther King assassinated; riots in 125 cities

Open Housing Law prohibits discrimination in sale or rental of housing

1969   Richard Nixon becomes president

1971   Federal courts order the busing of students for racial integration of schools

Not all Americans shared in the great prosperity of the postwar era. As the United States grew wealthier and fought against tyranny and oppression in other countries, a glaring inconsistency began to trouble the American people: Racism excluded black Americans from the prosperity and liberty enjoyed by most white Americans. When blacks began to campaign in the 1950s for an end to segregation, many whites recognized the justice of their cause and gave it their support. In the 1960s the federal government increased its involvement in civil rights matters and launched a major attempt to eliminate poverty as well.

THE BEGINNINGS OF THE CIVIL RIGHTS MOVEMENT

The New Deal and World War II

The impetus for the civil rights movement came from the New Deal and World War II. New Deal programs were not designed to fight racism or aid blacks specifically, but the relief programs benefited blacks as well as whites. Discrimination and segregation continued, and as recovery progressed blacks tended to get the lowest paid jobs. There was, however, a sense of progress, as blacks shared in the general optimism and confidence of the period.

CHANGES IN ATTITUDE

An important part of this progress was a change in attitude. During the 1930s and 1940s a great number of blacks gave up farming and moved to towns and cities in the North and in the South. Rural blacks worked mostly as tenant farmers and sharecroppers and were, therefore, among the poorest of the poor. A move to town, even if it meant a move to a poor section of town and a menial job, was usually an improvement. For those who remained on the farm, New Deal programs such as agricultural relief and rural electrification brought a sense of improvement. The biggest change came for those who moved north. These migrants settled in large cities where they found thriving black communities. They also discovered that they would be allowed to vote. Together, these improvements gave blacks a sense that things could change and that they could change for the better.

BLACKS IN THE MILITARY

Also contributing to this sense of progress was black enlistment during the war. Service in the military increased the sense of self-worth for many blacks. Those who went to Europe encountered an entirely new experience: Europeans looked upon all American soldiers as liberators. For the first time, blacks found themselves treated as equals by whites. When they returned home they were less willing to accept discrimination and segregation.

FEDERAL POLICY

Federal policy was another influential factor in changing attitudes. President Roosevelt's wartime ban on racial discrimination in the federal government and in defense industries (although lightly enforced) showed blacks that the federal government could work on their behalf. Even more important was President Truman's civil rights program of the late 1940s. In 1948 Truman asked Congress for a package of laws designed to combat discrimination and segregation. When the conservative Congress refused, the president used his executive authority to desegregate the military and ban discrimination in the federal government. He also ordered the Justice Department to step up its investigation and prosecution of civil rights cases. For the first time since the 1870s, the federal government showed some willingness to aid blacks.

These changes engendered a sense of optimism that conflicted with the realities of black life. Despite recent economic and social gains, blacks still occupied the bottom of the social and economic scale. Most blacks held menial jobs and lived in substandard housing. They were denied service by segregated businesses, and their children were unable to receive an adequate education or health care. Most blacks looked on in dismay as the prosperity of the 1950s passed them by.

School Desegregation

BROWN v. BOARD OF EDUCATION

In the early 1950s the NAACP launched a campaign to battle segregation in the public schools. Their strategy of filing lawsuits bore fruit in 1954 when the Supreme Court agreed to hear a case involving the public-school system of Topeka, Kansas. In the landmark case of *Brown* v. *the Board of Education of Topeka* the Supreme Court, comprised entirely of Roosevelt and Truman appointees who were friendly toward civil rights reform, ruled unanimously that the old judicial principle of "separate but equal" facilities for whites and blacks was unequal and unfair. The Court ordered school districts across the country to work with local federal judges to implement desegregation.

LITTLE ROCK

President Eisenhower disagreed with the Court, but he accepted his responsibility to enforce the decision. He desegregated the schools in Washington, D.C., and ordered an end to segregation in government facilities. The southern states, with their system of entrenched and legislated segregation, refused to accept the verdict. Some school districts refused to integrate; in those that did, black students were subject to harassment and abuse. The real test came in 1957 in Little Rock, Arkansas. Governor Orval Faubus, arguing that the admission of black students to a Little Rock high school would lead to disorder and violence, used National Guard troops to keep them out. The local federal court ordered the troops to leave, but harassment of the students continued. When local authorities failed to guarantee the safety of the black children, President Eisenhower placed the Arkansas National Guard under command of the army and ordered military protection for the students.

The Montgomery Bus Boycott

Black grass-roots resistance to segregation began in 1955 in Montgomery, Alabama, when Rosa Parks, a black seamstress, sat on a seat in the front of a bus instead of one of the seats assigned to blacks in the back. Parks's arrest galvanized black feeling, and local leaders organized a boycott of the Montgomery transit system. Thousands of blacks supported the boycott despite the hardship of having to walk to and from work. The boycott lasted almost a year, and bus revenues fell 65 percent, but Montgomery officials refused to yield. The boycott ended in 1956 when the Supreme Court ruled that the segregation of transit facilities was unconstitutional.

Martin Luther King

Black ministers played important leadership roles in the black community, and when the bus boycott began they were among the leaders of the protest. As the boycott progressed, Martin Luther King, Jr., a twenty-seven-year-old Baptist minister, emerged as the primary leader of the movement. King was an eloquent and persuasive speaker who could stir great numbers of people to action. His role in the boycott received national attention and confirmed him as the foremost leader in the fight for black equality.

Civil Rights Bills

Supporters of the civil rights movement recognized that voting would be an important weapon in the campaign. Many southern states had literacy and tax requirements that effectively excluded blacks from voting. In 1957 Senator Lyndon Johnson of Texas introduced a civil rights bill that authorized the Justice Department to file suit to enforce black voting rights. Johnson was an ambitious and at times unscrupulous politician, but he deeply sympathized with the plight of the poor and disadvantaged. Johnson ushered his bill through Congress and in 1960 supervised passage of a second civil rights law that attempted to strengthen the 1957 bill.

THE 1960s

The Kennedy Administration

THE 1960 ELECTION

The 1960 presidential contest pitted Republican Vice-President Richard Nixon against John Kennedy, a Democratic senator from Massachusetts. Nixon, who had built his political reputation in the early 1950s as an avid anticommunist, served two terms as vice-president under Eisenhower and ran on the record of the Eisenhower administration. Kennedy, an energetic and scholarly young man from a prominent Boston family, was the rising star of the Democratic party. He narrowly missed the nomination for vice-president in 1956 and in 1958 won reelection to the Senate with a landslide 860,000-vote margin. Both parties endorsed a strong civil rights program.

The 1960 election was one of the closest in history. Kennedy received a mere 100,000 more votes than Nixon (34,226,731 to 34,108,157) although the margin in the electoral college was greater (303 to 219) (see Appendix B). The election was significant in several ways. It was the first presidential election in which television played a crucial role. Kennedy and Nixon engaged in a series of nationally broadcast debates, and although both did well in their remarks, Kennedy's youthful good looks gave him an edge over the coarser-looking Nixon. The other important feature of the election was Kennedy himself. He was the youngest man ever elected president, and he was a Catholic—the first ever to be occupy the presidency.

DOMESTIC PROGRAMS

Kennedy's youthful vigor contrasted sharply with Eisenhower's quiet grandfatherly image. Like Wilson and the two Roosevelts, Kennedy believed that government should be used to promote the general welfare— that it was a force for progressive change. He and his advisors assembled a program of urban redevelopment, aid to schools, and improved medical care for the poor and elderly, but they had only moderate success in winning congressional approval. Kennedy's great strength was his ability to inspire young people to commit themselves to public service. The president challenged them to become active in government and to work for the betterment of society. His presidency was a time of great optimism, a time when

Americans believed that they could overcome the problems confronting the nation.

Kennedy's response to the civil rights movement was mixed. The greatest advocate of civil rights in the administration was the president's brother, Attorney General Robert Kennedy. The president, although committed in principle to the enforcement of civil rights legislation, had to move cautiously in order to maintain the support of the important southern wing of the Democratic party. The attorney general was an influential voice in favor of civil rights, and he frequently urged his brother to disregard the political risks. When President Kennedy finally acted, he used every weapon at his disposal—court action, federal marshals, the FBI, and the National Guard—to enforce federal statutes.

Protest in the Early 1960s

NEW TACTICS

The early successes of the civil rights movement rallied thousands of blacks across the nation to the cause and set off a massive campaign for an end to segregation and discrimination. The movement continued to rely on lawsuits, but the success of the Montgomery bus boycott had illustrated the power of mass protest. Blacks discovered that peaceful, nonviolent protest was a powerful weapon. They knew that whites would use violence to suppress the movement, but as Martin Luther King argued, an orderly, nonviolent protest would underline the moral aspect of the movement, particularly if met by violent resistance.

The boycott worked well as an instrument of protest, as did a new tactic: the sit-in. In 1960 a group of blacks in Greensboro, North Carolina, staged the first sit-in when they occupied seats at a whites-only lunch counter. Civil rights activists across the South followed their lead and organized sit-ins to force segregated businesses to serve them and to draw attention to the widespread extent of segregation. Martin Luther King became a leading advocate of the sit-in and other forms of civil disobedience. King and his followers openly violated segregation laws in an effort to force their repeal. Black leaders also staged massed demonstrations and marches to protest segregation. The first of these campaigns occurred in Birmingham, Alabama, in 1963, where demonstrators protested the entire racist structure of government, society, and the economy.

Many whites gave their support to the movement, and a number of northern whites—particularly college students—inspired by the struggle for equality and by Kennedy's exhortation to public service, went south to offer their assistance. Their main activity was to participate in a massive voter-registration drive. Blacks comprised the majority of people in many areas, and civil rights leaders hoped to mobilize a vast voting block by registering all eligible black voters and getting them to the polls on election day.

OPPOSITION

The civil rights movement threatened to topple an entire social, political, and economic system based upon racial segregation. Needless to say, resistance was extensive and violent. State and local officials defied court orders and dared the federal government to enforce integration. Mobs attacked civil rights activists; police used clubs, dogs, and fire hoses to break up demonstrations; and protesters were sent to jail. Worst of all was the campaign of violence and murder. Civil rights workers, both black and white, were beaten and occasionally killed. Black churches were bombed, sometimes with loss of life. Medgar Evers, a prominent civil rights leader in Mississippi, was shot and killed outside his home.

FEDERAL RESPONSE

John Kennedy took little action on civil rights during the first two years of his presidency. His narrow margin of victory in the 1960 election made him hesitant to offend southern Democrats. Black voters, who had supported him in great numbers, were disappointed in his performance. In the end, it was southern Democrats who forced his hand. In 1962 Governor Ross Barnett of Mississippi personally blocked the admission of James Meredith, a black student, to the University of Mississippi. When the governor's actions precipitated anti-black riots at the university, President Kennedy sent federal troops to restore order and assure the integration of the campus. The following year the president sent troops to Alabama when Governor George Wallace tried to prevent the integration of the University of Alabama. This resistance, coupled with the violence in Birmingham, convinced Kennedy that comprehensive federal action was needed. In June 1963 the president asked Congress to pass a law that would ban discrimination in public places and in employment. In August 200,000 people gathered in Washington to demonstrate in favor of the bill. The high point of the event came when Martin Luther King delivered his famous "I have a dream" speech. Despite this and other evidence of widespread public support for the bill, opponents in Congress succeeded in blocking its passage.

The Johnson Administration

CIVIL RIGHTS LEGISLATION

In November 1963 John Kennedy was shot and killed while riding in a motorcade in Dallas, Texas. Kennedy's political support had been declining, but this tragedy traumatized the nation and made him a hero. The new president, Lyndon Johnson, took advantage of this sentiment in his effort to win passage of the civil rights bill. Johnson was a strong-arm politician who had been Senate majority leader before becoming vice-president. The new president was firmly committed to civil rights, and in 1964 he persuaded Congress to pass the civil rights bill. One of was arguments was that the bill would be a monument to the martyred Kennedy. The following year he won passage of a voting rights act that allowed federal officials to supervise voter registration.

THE GREAT SOCIETY

In 1964 President Johnson announced that he was declaring "war on poverty" and the following year presented a comprehensive program called the Great Society aimed at eradicating poverty in America. The Economic Opportunity Act created VISTA (a volunteer program of community service), the Job Corps, and a variety of other work-training programs. Two new Social Security programs—Medicare and Medicaid—provided federally supported medical care for the poor and the aged. Congress also passed laws that provided federal aid for education and housing for low-income families. New legislation created the Department of Housing and Urban Development, the National Endowment for the Arts, and the National Endowment for the Humanities. Other laws established water and air quality standards. Congress also tried to stimulate the economy by voting a massive tax cut. These programs, although not aimed specifically at blacks, complemented the civil rights legislation, for Johnson and his advisors recognized the close relationship between racism and poverty. This first package of legislation was passed in the first two years of Johnson's presidency. Reform measures approved later in his administration included urban renewal and low-cost housing legislation, an anticrime bill, and several conservation laws. In 1968 Congress passed the Open Housing Law, which banned discrimination in the sale or rental of housing.

Table 9.1	
War on Poverty and Great Society Legislation and Programs	
1964	Civil Rights Act
	Urban Mass Transportation Act
	Economic Opportunity Act (included Job Corps, VISTA)
	Wilderness Preservation Act
1965	Elementary and Secondary School Act
	Medicare
	Voting Rights Act
	Omnibus Housing Act
	Department of Housing and Urban Development
	National Endowment for the Arts
	National Endowment for the Humanities

	Table 9.1 **War on Poverty and Great Society Legislation and Programs**	
	Water Quality Act
	Air Quality Act
	Higher Education Act
1966	National Traffic Safety Act
	Minimum Wage Increase
	Department of Transportation
	Clean Water Restoration Act
	Model Cities Act
1967	Public Broadcasting Corporation
1968	Open Housing Law
	Omnibus Crime Act
	Federal Housing Act
	Scenic Rivers Act

Disenchant- ment with Reform

OPPOSITION

Racism formed the root of opposition to the civil rights movement, but other issues figured in as well. Closely tied to racism was a fear that the gains made by blacks would come at the expense of whites. Lower-middle-class whites feared job competition from blacks, politicians saw blacks as a voting block they did not control, and whites in general saw equality as a threat to the privileges they enjoyed in a segregated society. Opposition also came on a philosophical level. Conservatives, who tended to be suspicious of any liberal reform program, were horrified by the extensive federal legislation of the period. They believed that the federal government had become too powerful as it exercised more authority over state and local affairs. Elections and schools, for example, which had always been controlled by local and state governments, had now become subject to federal legislation. The cost of these programs also alarmed them. The federal government, conservatives claimed, had become an all-powerful national institution that was spending billions of dollars on programs for which it had no constitutional or traditional right.

BLACK POWER

As the civil rights movement progressed, divisions began to occur among the different constituencies within the movement. The NAACP, the Congress of Racial Equality (CORE), and Martin Luther King's Southern

Christian Leadership Conference (SCLC) directed their efforts toward an end to the entrenched and legally mandated segregation in the South. They advocated the use of lawsuits, voter registration drives, federal legislation, and non-violent demonstrations to achieve integration. By the mid-1960s some blacks began to question these tactics. Some argued that these methods were too slow, and others called for a more radical approach. An increasing number of blacks began to question the ultimate goal of integration. They argued that racism was so entrenched in the United States that whites would never accept blacks as equal, that racism was so ingrained in the American character and worked in such subtle and intricate ways that it could never be ended. The dissenters also rejected the concept of nonviolence. Whites would never allow blacks to be free, they argued; the only way to win freedom was to fight for it. These radicals favored the creation of a separate black society in the United States and black control of the social, economic, and political institutions in the black community. "Black Power" became their watchword.

NORTHERN DE FACTO SEGREGATION

The tactics advocated by Martin Luther King worked well in the South, where segregation was legally mandated. Blacks residing in northern cities faced a different sort of discrimination. Segregation and discrimination were not legislated as they were in the South, but they existed nevertheless. Housing discrimination confined blacks to substandard ghettos. Hiring discrimination kept blacks in the lowest paying jobs and created a high level of unemployment. Inadequate schooling contributed to limited job opportunities. Poor health facilities created a mortality rate that was higher than that for whites and a life-expectancy rate that was lower. Poverty, crime, ignorance, unemployment, alcoholism, and drug abuse were common ingredients of ghetto life. A thriving black middle class existed in most northern cities, but even well-educated blacks found their professional options limited. Rich and poor alike lived in a white-controlled world. Most stores, businesses, and housing in black neighborhoods were owned by whites. Employers, government officials, and policemen were white. Opportunities for advancement were better in the North than in the South, but most urban blacks were condemned to a life of poverty in the ghetto. The promise of a better life that had drawn thousands of blacks to the northern cities during the depression and World War II had failed to materialize.

Urban blacks, confronted by this more subtle form of racism, had little patience for the methods used to achieve integration in the South. The structured segregation of the South gave blacks a target to attack. The de facto segregation of the North was more frustrating. Legally, blacks had equal opportunity with whites. In reality, they were confined to the poorest neighborhoods, the worst schools, and the lowest paying jobs. Northern blacks were not satisfied with equality. They wanted to stop the economic exploitation of their neighborhoods, they wanted better public services, and they wanted access to better jobs.

RADICAL ORGANIZATIONS AND LEADERS

Given the problems facing urban blacks, it is not surprising that a more radical style of protest evolved. The Nation of Islam (or Black Muslims) were among the earliest advocates of black separatism. Driven by the belief that black integration into American society on an equal footing with whites was impossible, the Black Muslims campaigned for self-sufficiency and self-determination for the black community. Malcolm X, a leader of the Black Muslims in New York, matched Martin Luther King as a charismatic leader and eloquent speaker. Malcolm preached that blacks were at war with white America and that violence against the oppressor was justified. Malcolm was assassinated by the Black Muslims in 1965 after he broke with the group and embarked upon a more moderate course. Despite his change of heart—he came to believe that racial harmony was possible—Malcolm X remained a hero to the radical wing of the civil rights movement.

Disenchantment with the civil rights movement was particularly strong among young black men. By the mid-1960s they began to doubt the value of nonviolence and integration. City dwellers especially, faced with bleak prospects for the future, abandoned the nonviolent road to integration advocated by Martin Luther King and converted to the more radical methods of Malcolm X. The Student Nonviolent Coordinating Committee (SNCC) began in 1960 as a youth wing of King's Southern Christian Leadership Conference. By 1965 SNCC members had despaired of peaceful integration and began to espouse more violent action. When students occupied campus buildings in the late 1960s to protest war and racism, SNCC members showed up carrying guns.

The most openly violent and revolutionary of the black activists were the Black Panthers. Organized in Oakland, California, in 1966, the Black Panthers, led by Huey Newton and Eldridge Cleaver, condemned racism as an integral part of capitalist American society. The Panthers organized community activities such as school breakfast and lunch programs and conducted a campaign against self-destructive pursuits such as prostitution, alcoholism, and drug abuse. But they also condemned the government, the courts, and the police as the enemy of all black people. They openly espoused armed resistance, and their frequent confrontations with the police led to many Panthers being killed or imprisoned.

Urban Riots

The pent-up frustrations of ghetto life erupted in 1964 as riots broke out across the nation. Between 1964 and 1968 the United States witnessed the worst domestic violence since the Civil War. The first major riot occurred in August 1965 in the Watts section of Los Angeles following a minor confrontation between a black motorist and a white policeman. When the riot ended five days later thirty-four people were dead, over a thousand injured, and $35 million worth of property destroyed. The following summer there were riots in forty-three cities. In 1967 there were only eight, but the violence of the Detroit riot surpassed anything that had occurred before. Thirty-three blacks and ten whites died, and the looting, burning, and fighting did not end until President Johnson sent federal troops to restore order. A commission appointed by Johnson to investigate the wave of disorder delivered the grim report that, despite almost fifteen years of civil rights protest and legislation, "our nation is moving toward two societies, one black, one white—separate but unequal." The report concluded that "only a commitment to national action on an unprecedented scale can shape a future compatible with the historic ideals of American society."

King's Assassination

The worst riots occurred in April 1968 following the assassination of Martin Luther King in Memphis, Tennessee. By 1968 King had lost much of his following, and the more radical black leaders openly scoffed at his nonviolent tactics. Despite this rift in the movement, blacks continued to admire King for his dedication to civil rights. His murder outraged people across the nation and galvanized blacks in their anger at years of oppression. Riots erupted in 125 cities and lasted almost a week. Some 75,000 National Guardsmen and federal troops were called out to assist local and state police in suppressing the disorder. The most destructive rioting occurred in Washington, where burning and looting occurred within a few blocks of the White House and the Capitol.

National Retreat on Civil Rights

THE NIXON ADMINISTRATION

By the end of 1968 the legacy of the civil rights movement and the Great Society was mixed. Black activism and federal intervention had ended segregation in many places, and blacks had begun to make some headway in their campaign for better jobs, better education, better housing, and better public services. But a horrible gap between white and black still existed. Racism and discrimination continued, and most of the country's blacks lived in poverty. Blacks scored much worse than whites on any scale that measured standard of living.

Despite these prevailing conditions, the federal government all but ceased its active campaign in support of civil rights. Agencies created during the Great Society and charged with anti-poverty programs continued to function, but the commitment of John Kennedy and Lyndon Johnson to ending segregation evaporated when Richard Nixon became president. Nixon had little interest in domestic affairs and even less in civil rights matters. He believed that there was nothing left for the federal government to do. Nixon's attitude on civil rights was shaped in part by politics. The new president received little support from blacks—only 5 percent of the black electorate voted Republican in the 1968 election. Writing off this voting block, Nixon decided to court the southern white conservative vote. This "southern strategy," as it was called, sacrificed support of civil rights in an effort to gain more white votes in the traditionally Democratic South.

Nixon's political interests encouraged him to diminish federal efforts on behalf of civil rights. He could not, however, neglect the continuing problem of poverty. New legislation allowed for cost-of-living increases for welfare payments, an expansion of the food-stamp program begun by President Kennedy, the creation of a new job training program, and a general increase in welfare payments. By the time Nixon left office in 1974, the federal government was spending 60 percent more on social programs than it had in 1968. As was the case with the Great Society, these reforms were not directed at blacks alone. The great number of blacks on welfare, however, were the primary recipients of these benefits.

The Busing Controversy

The court decisions and federal laws of the 1950s and 1960s struck down state and local laws that mandated racial segregation of schools, but they did not end segregation. The racial composition of students in a school reflected the racial characteristics of the school's neighborhood. The de facto residential segregation that existed across the nation resulted in schools that were predominantly white and predominantly black. Furthermore, schools also reflected the economic background of their neighborhoods. The economic disparity between whites and blacks necessarily meant that schools in white neighborhoods were better than those in black areas. In 1971 federal judges began to order school districts to bus students to schools in other neighborhoods to achieve integration, their argument being that a dispersal of students would guarantee quality education at all the schools in a district.

This decision infuriated white parents, for local control of neighborhood schools was a time-honored American tradition. Black parents disliked sending their children a long distance to school, but since it usually meant that they would receive a better education they seldom complained. The de facto segregation of the suburbs insulated middle-class whites from the poverty of inner-city blacks. When busing forced them together deep-seated racial tensions came to the surface. White students boycotted classes, mobs stoned buses carrying black students, and parents transferred their children to private schools.

*B*y the 1970s Americans had, for the most part, accepted the goals of the civil rights movements. Segregated restrooms, transit facilities, and restaurants became things of the past. Blacks found opportunity for advancement in business, government, the military, sports, and entertainment as the old discriminatory barriers fell. An increasing number of blacks moved into the middle class as better jobs and better education became available. By 1972 the framework of institutionalized segregation had been dismantled.

And yet, despite the gains of the 1950s and 1960s—which were real and many—racism and discrimination remained. The public manifestations of racism were gone, but racial attitudes that had been accepted for hundreds of years were not so easily overcome. Nor was economic segregation. As long as blacks continued to constitute a majority of the poor—as they did in the United States—they would remain second-class citizens, and there would be no end to a separation of the races.

Selected Readings

Brown, Claude. *Manchild in the Promised Land* (1965)

Ellison, Ralph. *Invisible Man* (1952)

Garrow, David. *Bearing the Cross: Martin Luther King, Jr., and the Southern Christian Leadership Conference* (1986)

Harrington, Michael. *The Other America: Poverty in the United States* (1962)

Kearns, Doris. *Lyndon Johnson and the American Dream* (1976)

Malcolm X and Alex Haley. *The Autobiography of Malcolm X* (1965)

Parmet, Herbert. *JFK: The Presidency of John F. Kennedy* (1983)

Patterson, James. *America's Struggle Against Poverty, 1900–1980* (1981)

Sitkoff, Harvard. *The Struggle for Black Equality, 1954–1980* (1980)

Wright, Richard. *Native Son* (1940)

10

War and Protest: 1961–1975

1957 Soviets launch first satellite

1958 National Aeronautics and Space Administration established

1961 John Kennedy becomes president

U.S. launches its first manned space flight

Peace Corps established

Bay of Pigs invasion

Berlin Wall built

U.S. troops authorized to enter combat in Vietnam

1962 Cuban missile crisis

1963 U.S. and U.S.S.R. sign multinational limited nuclear test ban treaty

U.S. sponsors coup in South Vietnam

President Kennedy assassinated; Lyndon Johnson becomes president

1964 Gulf of Tonkin Resolutions authorize president to increase military activity in Vietnam

1965 Johnson begins second term as president

U.S. sends troops to the Dominican Republic

U.S. begins air raids on North Vietnam; U.S. ground troops begin major combat operations in South Vietnam

Student antiwar demonstrations begin

1966 National Organization of Women founded

1967 President Johnson and Soviet Premier Kosygin meet at Glassboro, New Jersey

1968 U.S. troop strength in Vietnam exceeds 500,000

Robert Kennedy assassinated

U.S. and North Vietnam begin peace talks in Paris; U.S. halts attacks on North Vietnam

1969 Richard Nixon begins first term as president

U.S. lands man on the moon

U.S. begins bombing of Cambodia and Laos

U.S. begins withdrawal of troops from Vietnam

1970 Pro-American faction in Cambodia stages successful coup

U.S. troops invade Cambodia

Huge antiwar demonstrations protest attack into Cambodia; student demonstrators killed at Kent State University and at Jackson State College

1972 U.S. resumes attacks on North Vietnam

President Nixon visits China; U.S. and China take steps toward normalizing relations

President Nixon visits Moscow; signs several treaties, including one on nuclear arms reduction

Women's Rights Amendment approved by Congress

Watergate scandal begins

1973 Nixon begins second term as president

Soviet General Secretary Brezhnev visits Washington

U.S. negotiates a cease-fire between Israel and Egypt

U.S. and North Vietnam sign peace agreement; last U.S. troops leave Vietnam; fighting continues between North Vietnam and South Vietnam

Vice-President Spiro Agnew resigns after conviction for income-tax evasion; President Nixon appoints Gerald Ford vice-president

1974 Soviet General Secretary Brezhnev visits Washington

President Nixon resigns to avoid impeachment; Gerald Ford becomes president

Ford grants presidential pardon to Nixon

1975   South Vietnamese government surrenders

Pro-American government in Cambodia surrenders

The reform impulse that propelled the civil rights movement influenced American foreign relations as well. In the early 1960s the battle against communism expanded into a crusade to end poverty, tyranny, and oppression the world over, for Americans believed that their might and wealth could accomplish anything. This changed quickly as the United States became bogged down in the war in Vietnam. In 1961 most Americans approved of the nation's foreign policy and saw it as a moralistic campaign for positive change. Ten years later many people viewed that same policy as an arrogant attempt to dictate American terms to the rest of the world. America's involvement in Vietnam began as only a minor part of the country's global strategy. But as that involvement increased, it achieved new importance and soon dominated the politics of the nation.

Even with its overriding importance, the war in Vietnam was only one facet of American foreign affairs at that time. Relations with the Soviet Union remained a paramount concern, and the war against communism that blossomed in Vietnam almost broke out in Europe and in Cuba. Overwhelmed by the war in Vietnam the United States employed a number of measures to prevent the outbreak of war elsewhere in the Third World. The threat of nuclear warfare diffused any direct confrontation with the Soviets and, in the early 1970s, even led to improved relations.

Ironically, the reform impulse that justified American foreign policy also shaped the movement that protested that policy. Young Americans, schooled in the tactics and ideology of the civil rights campaign, organized a nationwide movement to end the war. Indeed, the civil rights movement had an extensive influence on the 1960s and served as the inspiration for a number of reform movements. The antiwar movement was the most prominent of the reform campaigns of the late 1960s, but they were all interrelated, for protesters believed racism, poverty, sexism, and the war to be different parts of the same pattern of injustice and intolerance. A severe reaction by conservative groups and by the government seemed to confirm the impression that the United States was not as liberal and fair-minded as it liked to believe. The war divided the nation and engendered some of the most bitter feelings ever witnessed in the United States. This divisiveness and bitterness extended to the White House and resulted in one of the greatest moral and political crises ever faced by the nation.

KENNEDY AND THE COLD WAR

When John Kennedy became president he continued the anticommunist policies of Truman and Eisenhower. But—as in domestic matters—Kennedy brought a new enthusiasm to foreign affairs. The fight against communism was no longer simply an effort to stop Soviet expansion. Under Kennedy it became a crusade to eradicate evil and injustice. Communism, like racism at home, was a social ill that needed to be cured. "We shall," the new president proclaimed in his inaugural address, "pay any price, bear any burden, meet any hardship, support any friend, oppose any foe, in order to assure the survival and the success of liberty." The fight against communism and the fight against segregation were part of the same reform impulse. While Kennedy was wise enough to understand that—as he said in a speech in 1961—"there cannot be an American solution to every world problem," he believed that the United States had a moral imperative to exercise its power and influence wherever possible.

The United States and the Third World

THE END OF COLONIALISM

Kennedy became president at a time of great global change. The old European empires were breaking up as their former colonies struggled to forge independent national identities. The United States tended to approve of this movement, for colonialism, by its very nature, contradicted the American ideal of national self-determination and democracy. In addition, the decline of colonial control offered new opportunities for the expansion of American economic and diplomatic influence. This changing situation presented the United States with three challenges: how to promote independence and democracy in the new nations; how to expand American influence and markets without alienating these new countries; and how to fend off the spread of communism, which was attractive to the anticolonial independence movements. This effort to deal with the new nations remained entangled in the larger struggle to maintain a balance of power with the Soviet Union.

Both the United States and the Soviet Union, aware of the catastrophic dangers of a direct confrontation, saw the emerging nations as an arena in which they could engage each other without the risk of nuclear war. Kennedy's strategy was to attempt to insure stability in the Third World. If the United States and the other Western nations assisted the old colonies in a peaceful transition to independence, the argument went, then there would be little opportunity for communist insurgents to exploit discontent. The centerpiece of this strategy was financial aid.

FOREIGN-AID PROGRAMS

Guided by the same thinking that led to the Marshall Plan, Kennedy introduced an expanded program of foreign aid to assist in the economic development of the new nations. The United States made grants and loans directly to developing nations as well as contributing to United Nations projects and other international organizations. American businesses also invested in these countries by making loans and building factories. Among the innovations of the Kennedy administration were the Agency for International Development (created to oversee foreign-aid programs) and the Alliance for Progress, an American-led program for the economic development of Latin America based upon the cooperative efforts of all the nations in the region. Kennedy's favorite program was the Peace Corps, which was created in March 1961. The Peace Corps sent young American volunteers to developing nations to act as teachers, technicians, public health workers, and advisors. The Peace Corps proved to be immensely popular at home and abroad and was one of Kennedy's greatest foreign policy successes.

The United States also provided military aid to these countries. Assistance came in different forms, including cash, loans, equipment, arms, and training. The United States wanted these nations to be able to defend themselves and, if necessary, suppress communist insurgency on their own. Training, therefore, constituted an important aspect of this program. Some foreign military officers received training in the United States, but, for the most part, the United States sent army personnel and CIA operatives overseas to act as military advisors.

ANIMOSITY TOWARD THE UNITED STATES

The results of this policy were mixed. In many cases the United States won the good will of the people and governments of the emerging nations and helped them maintain stability in the early years of nationhood. In other cases the policy failed, for the potential for instability in the Third World was far greater than the planners in Washington anticipated. The vestiges of colonialism—poverty, underdevelopment, social inequality, inequitable land distribution, nondemocratic government—continued to plague the new nations. This less-than-distinguished legacy hampered American efforts, for the people of the Third World distrusted the Western nations. Their newly established national pride led them to resent American aid, for the patronage of a highly developed nation reminded them too much of colonial domination. Furthermore, their colonial heritage left them suspicious of the more powerful nations. They rightly suspected that the United States wanted something in return.

Another vestige of colonialism that greatly contributed to instability was the presence of hostile ethnic and religious groups in the same nations. The Europeans drew the boundaries of their colonies with little regard to ethnic, religious, or tribal relations. When independence came and colonial control was removed, civil war erupted as hostile factions fought over control of territory. Frequently, the only way to insure stability was through military dictatorship. This alternative conflicted with the stated American goal of establishing democratic governments, but often—in an attempt to create stability and fend off communist control—the United States backed these governments.

Together, all these factors bred suspicion of the West and internal instability. It is not surprising that warring factions, eager for support, accepted the aid offered by the Soviets. It is likewise not surprising that Third World revolutionaries, schooled in the exploitation and neglect of the Western nations, found communism attractive and gravitated toward the Soviet Union, particularly when the United States became the chief patron of dictatorships that were as corrupt, oppressive, and tyrannical as any colonial government. In both cases colonialism left a bitter heritage that drove a wedge of animosity between the United States and the emerging nations.

Soviet-American Relations

THE ARMS RACE

Shortly before Kennedy became president reports began to circulate in the United States that the Soviet Union had a larger and more effective nuclear arsenal than the United States did. This fear of a "missile gap," coupled with Eisenhower's policy of massive nuclear deterrence, resulted in a program to increase the nation's nuclear capability. When the reports proved to be false, Kennedy, who wanted to slow down the arms race, reduced the emphasis on nuclear weapons and urged an increased reliance on conventional land, sea, and air forces. Soviet leader Nikita Khrushchev also wanted an end to the arms race. Relations between the two leaders were stormy, but negotiations eventually led to the first of a series of nuclear arms limitation treaties. In August 1963 the United States, the Soviet Union, and ninety-seven other nations signed a treaty that prohibited testing of nuclear weapons in the air, under water, or in outer space.

BERLIN

In June 1961 the Soviet Union once again announced that it wanted the Western nations to withdraw from Berlin. After a bitter exchange of words between the United States and the Soviet Union, the United States, determined to show its commitment to the containment of communism in Europe, increased the shipment of arms to NATO, stationed more troops in Europe, and called up reserve forces and the National Guard. Tension increased when the Soviets built a wall separating East and West Berlin in an effort to stop the flow of refugees to the West. The crisis dissipated in October 1961 when the Soviets backed off from their demands and announced that they were satisfied with Western efforts to reach an agreement on the occupation of Berlin. Tension over the city remained, however, and the Berlin Wall became a symbol of repression as East Germans braved gunfire and tried to breach the wall in an effort to escape communist rule. In 1963 Kennedy visited Berlin and, in a speech delivered near the wall, reaffirmed America's commitment to the defense of Berlin.

CUBA

The United States refused to accept Fidel Castro's ascendance to power in Cuba, and in 1960 the CIA began training a force of Cuban exiles for an attack on their homeland. The CIA, which had declared war on Castro and waged a campaign of subversion against him—including poorly planned assassination attempts—believed that the Cuban people were ready to revolt. The initial plan was for the refugees to return home and instigate an insurgent movement. This plan was scrapped in favor of a military invasion. President Eisenhower and other top-level officials in Washington approved the invasion, but Kennedy, who inherited the scheme, was less than enthusiastic about it. It was poorly planned and hardly a secret. Despite his doubts, Kennedy gave permission for the attack, which ended as a monstrous failure. A force of 1,500 Cubans landed at the Bay of Pigs in April 1961. Castro, anticipating the attack, crushed the invasion in three days and took 1,200 prisoners. The expected revolt of the Cuban people never occurred. On the contrary, this obvious act of aggression abetted an already strong anti-American feeling in Cuba and increased Castro's popularity. The invasion also sullied America's reputation in the international community.

Castro, now firmly in the Soviet camp, began to receive increased arms shipments from Russia. The United States raised no objection to this but warned the Soviets against placing offensive weapons—that is, missiles capable of hitting targets in the United States—in Cuba. In October 1962 the United States announced that the Soviets were building missile bases in Cuba and demanded that the missiles be removed. Kennedy placed all military forces on emergency alert, declared a naval quarantine of Cuba, and ordered American warships to search all vessels headed for the island. Several days later Khrushchev agreed to withdraw the missiles provided the United States end the quarantine and promise not to invade Cuba. He also asked the United States to withdraw its missiles from Turkey, a NATO nation that bordered Russia on the south. Kennedy publicly accepted the first two conditions and privately assented to the third. Shortly thereafter, the Soviets dismantled the bases and removed the missiles.

THE SPACE RACE

The Russians initiated a new era of history in October 1957 when they successfully launched the *Sputnik*, a small earth-orbiting satellite. Four months later the United States orbited its first satellite, and the space race was on. These first satellites were, of and by themselves, of limited significance. Their implications for the future, however, were great, for earth orbiters have since come to have great value as scientific, military, and communication devices. Furthermore, the development of space flight technology contributed to advancements in computers, communications, and other forms of electronic technology. Equally at stake in the space race was national prestige. At first the Russians were ahead. They launched the first satellite and in April 1961 orbited a man around the earth. President Kennedy, alarmed at any sign of Soviet superiority, called for an all-out effort to surpass the Russians and land a man on the moon by the end of the decade.

During the 1960s the United States and the Soviet Union launched a large number of unmanned earth orbiters; they also sent unmanned explorers to neighboring planets. The primary goal, however, was a manned flight to the moon. The first step came in 1961 when the Russians orbited a man around the earth. The United States followed suit in 1962 when John Glenn became the first American to orbit the globe. Over the next several years both countries engaged in a variety of space maneuvers: endurance flights, space walks, the rendezvous of space craft, docking of two vehicles, and lunar orbits. The American effort soon outstripped that of the Soviets. By early 1969 the United States had logged 4,000 man-hours in space to the Russians' 868; had launched nineteen manned flights compared to twelve for the Soviets; and had executed more space walks, docking maneuvers, and lunar orbits. In July 1969 the United States won the race when Neil Armstrong and Edwin Aldrin landed on the moon. Over the next four years the United States sent six more crews to the moon.

THE WAR IN VIETNAM

Laos

The civil war in Vietnam received only limited attention from American policymakers in 1961. They assumed that the large American-backed South Vietnamese army was equal to the task of defeating the reportedly small force of Viet Cong guerrillas. Of much greater interest was the question of what position the United States should take on the conflict in Laos. Like Vietnam, Laos was a former part of French Indochina and, also like Vietnam, was in the midst of a civil war between pro-Western and communist forces. President Kennedy, ruling that Laos was not that important to American interests, reversed Eisenhower's policy of aiding the pro-Western government and assented to the establishment of a neutral coalition government in 1962.

Kennedy's Position on Vietnam

President Kennedy was unsure on how to proceed in Vietnam. He felt bound to honor earlier American commitments, and he wanted to stop the spread of communism. At the same time, he was hesitant to get heavily involved in the Vietnamese war and rejected calls for direct military intervention. Kennedy's chief concern was with the corruption of the government in Saigon and its seeming inability to defeat a greatly outnumbered enemy. The United States sent advisors, supplies—including helicopters and crews to transport Vietnamese soldiers—and money, but the South Vietnamese made little headway in the war. Despite a massive infusion of American aid the South Vietnamese army—comprised primarily of conscripts and led by corrupt and inefficient officers—was no match for the smaller but better disciplined and highly dedicated forces of the Viet Cong.

During 1962 and 1963 conditions in Vietnam worsened as corruption and repression became more widespread. Support for President Diem declined, and antigovernment demonstrations—highlighted by the self-immolation of protesting Buddhist monks—spread across the country. In early November 1963 a group of army officers, encouraged by American officials in Vietnam, overthrew the government and assassinated Diem. What effect this would have had on Kennedy's thinking is not clear, since he himself was assassinated shortly thereafter. Up to the very end he gave mixed signals on Vietnam. He continued to oppose an American combat role in Vietnam and even ordered the Pentagon to draw up a plan for American withdrawal in 1965. But he also continued to increase the American military presence. When he took office there were 900 American advisors in Vietnam; when he died there were over 16,000.

Escalation of the War

JOHNSON'S POSITION

When Lyndon Johnson became president in 1963 he devoted most of his energy to the passage of civil rights and Great Society legislation. During the summer of 1964, however, the president's attention began to shift to Vietnam. The change of government in Saigon and the increase in American aid seemed to have no affect on the war. Indeed, the Viet Cong seemed to be growing stronger. Unlike Kennedy, Johnson believed that a greater American involvement was the solution to the problem. He and his advisors formulated a new plan that called for the use of American troops in combat and an air war against the Viet Cong and their North Vietnamese allies. This aggressive new role would, the argument ran, rally the South Vietnamese and discourage the Viet Cong. It would also demonstrate America's continued opposition to the spread of communism. Another factor in the decision to involve American troops in combat was Johnson's attitude toward the war. The war in Vietnam was, for the most part, a minor conflict in a distant country that most Americans had never heard of. Johnson, a man of direct action, believed that a country like North Vietnam would be unable to withstand the might of the United States: American troops would quickly destroy the Viet Cong and bring the war to an end.

THE GULF OF TONKIN RESOLUTIONS

For all Johnson's bravura, he was not sure he could win congressional or public support for American involvement in combat in Vietnam. An opening to gain support came in July 1964. By that time American involvement had shifted from an advisory role to one of limited but direct combat support. In July North Vietnamese patrol boats attacked two American warships that were participating in South Vietnamese raids on North Vietnam. Johnson exploited this event and reported to Congress that the North Vietnamese had made an unprovoked attack on American warships in international waters in the Gulf of Tonkin off North Vietnam. The president ordered air strikes against North Vietnam and asked Congress for authority to commit American troops to combat, which was granted in the Gulf of Tonkin Resolutions. It was not until 1968 that Congress learned the true nature of the situation.

THE 1964 ELECTION

Since 1964 was an election year, Johnson was careful to deny any intention of increased American involvement in Vietnam. Indeed, he was very successful in portraying his opponent, Republican candidate Barry Goldwater, as a warmonger. Goldwater, a senator from Arizona, favored an escalation of the war, but he also considered the war to be a minor issue. Goldwater's main concern was domestic policy. He was an arch conservative who opposed the increased government activism of the New Deal and the Great Society. Johnson, running as a great reformer and the heir of John Kennedy, won a resounding victory (see Appendix B).

AMERICANS ENTER COMBAT

Escalation of the war came in February 1965 when a Viet Cong raid killed seven Americans and wounded 109 others. When retaliatory air strikes failed to deter the Viet Cong, Johnson ordered American troops into combat. American troop strength jumped from 25,000 to 184,000 by the end of the year. This move changed the conflict from a civil war to a war between the United States and North Vietnam. South Vietnam became a secondary player. Its government remained corrupt and ineffective, its army was unwilling to fight, and its people lost what little faith they had in the government.

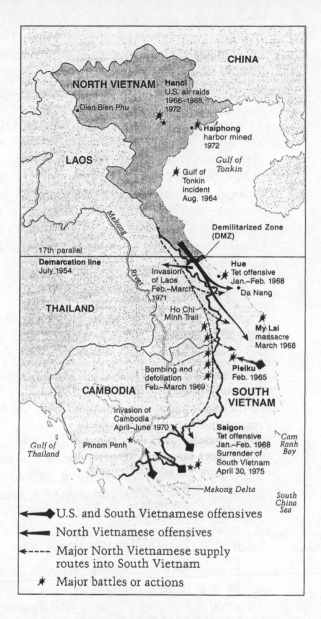

Fig. 10.1 The Vietnam War

Over the next three years American ground troops battled the Viet Cong and the North Vietnamese, while American bombers pounded Viet Cong positions, supply depots in North Vietnam, and supply lines to the south. But the war effort seemed to make little headway. General William Westmoreland, the American commander in Vietnam, reported on the gradual destruction of the Viet Cong and repeatedly announced that the end of the war was in sight. Meanwhile, more and more soldiers went to

Vietnam—American forces in Vietnam numbered 184,000 in 1965, 385,000 in 1966, 485,000 in 1967, and 536,000 in 1968.

Vietnam was a new kind of war for the United States. The American military was schooled in the massive head-on fighting of World War II where troop strength and superior equipment made a difference. Postwar training and equipment were designed to fight a war against a similarly trained and equipped Soviet army in Europe. The American army was ill-prepared to fight a guerrilla war in the jungles of southeast Asia. Tanks, helicopters, jet fighters, and B-52 bombers gave Americans mobility and firepower, but they were of limited use against an enemy that could dissipate into the jungle and disappear. Nor were they any help against an enemy that could melt into a sympathetic civilian population. This ability to intermingle with the population added a new dimension of terror to the war for American soldiers. Unable to tell an enemy soldier from a civilian, every civilian became a potential enemy.

THE TET OFFENSIVE

The heaviest fighting of the war came in early 1968 when the Viet Cong launched a massive offensive against 116 cities and towns in South Vietnam. Intelligence sources had warned of an impending attack during Tet (the Vietnamese new year holiday), but the Americans and South Vietnamese were unprepared for the magnitude of the offensive. Communist forces swept into Saigon and even penetrated the walls of the American embassy before they were driven out; they captured the city of Hue and held it for a month; and they battled American forces at Khe Sahn for seventy-six days before they were forced to withdraw. The offensive failed militarily, but it was a great political success, for it showed that the Viet Cong could attack where and when they pleased and that reports of their imminent destruction were false.

Opposition to the War

DISSENT WITHIN THE GOVERNMENT

In 1964 an overwhelming majority of Americans supported American action in Vietnam. But as the war continued, American involvement deepened, and the number of casualties grew—1,369 dead in 1965, 5,008 in 1966, 9,378 in 1967, and 14,592 in 1968—many people began to doubt the wisdom of the war. In Congress, a number of senators and representatives challenged the administration on the issue of the war. Senator William Fulbright of Arkansas spearheaded the opposition and used his position as chairman of the Senate Foreign Relations Committee to make the committee a forum on Vietnam policy. Discord also infected Johnson's cabinet. Secretary of Defense Robert McNamara, the principal architect of American policy in Vietnam, declared the war a failure in 1967. His successor, Clark Clifford, shared McNamara's belief that a military solution to the problem in Vietnam was unattainable and urged Johnson to seek a negotiated settlement.

STUDENT PROTEST

The center of opposition to the war was the college campus, where students from Berkeley to Boston protested the war by the thousands. Student leaders, schooled in the civil rights movement, used the same tactics to protest the war. By 1967 they were able to rally hundreds of thousands of protesters to march in massive demonstrations against the war. Antiwar marches in Washington, New York, and San Francisco were among the largest political demonstrations ever mounted in the United States. As the war dragged on, casualties mounted, the draft continued, and taxes increased, middle-class adults added their voices to the protest: Vietnam was simply not worth the cost in life and money.

REASONS FOR OPPOSITION

Opponents attacked the war on several grounds. They claimed that it was unnecessary, that Vietnam was not a threat to the United States. They argued that it was immoral and unjust, that the United States had no right to intervene in another country's civil war. And they said that it was racist and imperialist: The United States, like the European colonial powers, was trying to force its will on a poor non-white country. Supporters of the war responded that American intervention was indeed necessary and just. Communist leaders in Moscow and Peking, intent on world domination, were the aggressors, not the United States. If we did not stop fight them in Vietnam, the argument went, we would have to fight them in California.

TELEVISION AND THE WAR

Television played an important role in the growing opposition to the war. Supporters of the war later argued that the news media undermined the war effort by presenting a biased and inaccurate account of the conflict. Subsequent studies—including one by the Pentagon—refuted this claim. But television had a negative impact, nevertheless. Night after night, Americans could see the brutality of the war: the fighting, the wounded and dead, the destroyed villages, the defoliated countryside. They could also see that, despite the claims of the government, the war was not winding down. Television did not hurt the war effort as much as it hurt the credibility of the administration and the military command.

The 1968 Election

THE DEMOCRATS

The 1968 presidential campaign was the most turbulent in American history. The campaign began when Senator Eugene McCarthy of Minnesota, a leading opponent of the war, announced that he would seek the Democratic nomination for president. In early March 1968 he scored an astounding upset when he polled 42 percent of the vote to President Johnson's 48 percent in the presidential primary in conservative New Hampshire. Several days later Robert Kennedy—brother of the slain president, former attorney general, U.S. senator from New York, critic of the war—announced his candidacy. At the end of the month President Johnson dropped two bombshells. First, he announced that he had ordered a halt to the bombing of North Vietnam and that he would seek negotiations with the North Vietnamese. More astounding was his announcement that he would not run for reelection. Battered and exhausted by the controversy over the war and facing the very real possibility that he would lose the election, Johnson decided to retire. This decision opened the way for Vice-President Hubert Humphrey to enter the race.

Kennedy quickly became the leading candidate for the nomination. His family name, his civil rights record, his opposition to the war, and his personal charisma won him support from a broad spectrum of the public. McCarthy, inexperienced and little known except for his stand on the war, garnered little support. Humphrey, like Johnson, had been a champion of civil rights and reform in the Senate; also like Johnson, he had long harbored presidential aspirations. He too promised to end the war, but his association with the Johnson administration limited his appeal. The picture changed in June when Kennedy was assassinated after winning the California primary (which had all but assured his nomination). Humphrey, a party regular, won the nomination at the convention in Chicago. What happened on the convention floor seemed secondary to the events outside where Chicago police went on a rampage against protesters gathered to demonstrate against the war. People across the nation watching their televisions saw policemen attack and beat demonstrators and bystanders alike.

THE REPUBLICANS

The Republicans, for their part, added to the unusual atmosphere by nominating former vice-president Richard Nixon who, following his defeats for the presidency in 1960 and for governor of California in 1962, was considered a political has-been. For many people the country seemed to be out of control. The United States was fighting a half-hearted and unpopular war without direction or commitment. Riots had become a regular feature of ghetto life. Students across the country participated in civil disobedience and massive antiwar demonstrations. Assassination had become all too common: Martin Luther King was shot in April and Robert Kennedy in June. Nixon appealed to these people by promising to restore law and order. He also announced that he had a secret plan to end the war.

GEORGE WALLACE

The third candidate in the race was Governor George Wallace of Alabama, who had gained national attention by his personal efforts to prevent the desegregation of the University of Alabama in 1962. Wallace took a hard-line conservative stand against civil rights, antiwar demonstrators—his suggested response to people demonstrating in the streets was to run over them—the Washington bureaucracy, and the Supreme Court. His running mate, General Curtis LeMay, advocated dropping nuclear bombs on North Vietnam.

THE ELECTION

The outcome of the election had remained uncertain right up to election day, as Humphrey and Nixon ran neck and neck. Several unusual circumstances contributed to the closeness of the race. One was Johnson's resentment of Humphrey's antiwar position. The president gave only lukewarm support to his party's candidate and on several occasions went so far as to express his desire for a Nixon victory. Another unusual factor was the interference of Nixon campaign managers in the negotiations with North Vietnam. Fearful that progress in the peace talks would benefit Humphrey, several of Nixon's top aides persuaded the South Vietnamese government to delay the negotiations until after the election.

In 1960 Nixon lost the presidential election by 100,000 votes; in 1968 he won by 500,000. Nixon polled 31,783,000 vote (43 percent), Humphrey 31,271,000 (42 percent), and Wallace 9,899,000 (13.5 percent). A smattering of other candidates divided the rest of the vote (see Appendix B).

The War Under Nixon

PEACE NEGOTIATIONS

The centerpiece of Nixon's secret plan to end American involvement in Vietnam was "Vietnamization." According to this plan, the Vietnamese would assume responsibility for fighting the war as American troops gradually withdrew. At the same time, Nixon's chief advisor on foreign affairs, Henry Kissinger, began negotiations with the North Vietnamese. The peace talks continued on an intermittent basis for several years without resolution. The main point of contention was Kissinger's demand that American and North Vietnamese troops withdraw simultaneously, a proposal that the North Vietnamese refused to accept.

CAMBODIA

Nixon ordered the first troop withdrawal during the summer of 1969. Troop strength fell from 536,000 in 1968 to 475,000 by the end of 1969. But he also escalated the war. American warplanes intensified the bombing of North Vietnam and, for the first time, struck at Viet Cong supply lines in Laos (where the CIA had been conducting secret operations since 1962) and in Cambodia. In March 1970 a coup overthrew the neutral monarchy in Cambodia and established a pro-American government. A month later American and South Vietnamese troops attacked Viet Cong bases in Cambodia. These raids had little effect on the war effort in Vietnam, but they did have several immediate results. Insurgent forces in Cambodia, which had been dormant under the monarchy, rose up and began a brutal civil war. In the United States, the antiwar movement swelled as thousands of people joined the protest against the invasion of Cambodia. Riots broke out on campuses across the nation when National Guardsmen in Ohio killed four students at Kent State University during a demonstration against the invasion and police in Mississippi killed two students at Jackson State College. Congress expressed its disapproval of Nixon's expansion of the war by repealing the Gulf of Tonkin Resolutions, which had given President Johnson authority to commit troops to combat in 1964.

AMERICAN WITHDRAWAL

The last American combat troops left Vietnam during the summer of 1972, but American warplanes continued to bomb North Vietnam and fly missions in support of the South Vietnamese army. In January 1973 the United States, dropping its demand for the withdrawal of North Vietnamese forces, signed an agreement with North Vietnam that provided for the total withdrawal of American troops and a cease-fire. The last American troops pulled out in April, but the cease-fire never went into effect. The United States continued to supply military aid to South Vietnam and Cambodia until 1975, when their armies disintegrated and both governments collapsed.

CASUALTIES

The war took a heavy toll in southeast Asia and at home. War-torn Vietnam and Cambodia were devastated by the fighting that began in 1941 and continued into the 1990s. Millions of soldiers and civilians were killed, and millions more fled to other countries. Forests and farmland were defoliated, and cities, towns, and villages damaged or destroyed. Between 1955 and 1973, 57,000 Americans were killed and over 300,000 wounded. Many of the 2.8 million Americans who served in Vietnam suffered severe emotional distress caused by the terrors of guerrilla war and a sense of failure. At home the war created a terrible division within the American people. Several people were killed protesting the war, and thousands more injured or jailed. Over 30,000 young men went to jail or fled the country rather than serve in the war.

PROTEST MOVEMENTS

The civil rights movement and the antiwar movement spawned a number of other movements that challenged the status quo in the United States. Many Americans, particularly young people, saw racism, poverty, and the war as the natural results of the iniquities of American society. For them, simple reform was not enough.

The
Counterculture

BEATNIKS

During the 1950s most middle-class adults and their children embraced the prosperity, materialism, and conformity of the 1950s. But a small group of Americans, known as beatniks, chose to live their lives outside the mainstream of American society. They refused to hold regular steady jobs; lived in near poverty; and became acolytes and practitioners of avant garde jazz, abstract art, and free-form poetry. The poetry of Alan Ginsberg and the novels of Jack Kerouac, particularly *On the Road*, described and celebrated the beatnik life.

HIPPIES

In the 1960s the beatniks gave way to hippies. Hippies were, for the most part, young middle-class whites fleeing from what they viewed as the materialism and rigidity of their parents' society. Their goal was to develop a system of values based upon interpersonal relationships rather than the acquisition of material wealth. They lived in self-enforced poverty; practiced communal living; advocated a relaxation of sexual inhibitions; and experimented with meditation, eastern religions, and hallucinogenic drugs to promote introspection, increase self-awareness, and achieve a new way of perceiving the world. The hippie movement began as an urban phenomenon, with enclaves in San Francisco, New York, Los Angeles, and other large cities. In the mid-1960s, however, a "back to the land" movement began, as many hippies moved to the country and sought a simpler mode of living by engaging in self-sufficient farming.

The hippie movement at first espoused a repudiation of the ills of American society by severing itself from the political, economic, and social structure of the nation. The escalation of the war in Vietnam put an end to that isolation. By the late 1960s thousands of young middle-class whites had found the counterculture of the hippie movement to be an attractive alternative to what they considered to be the increasingly obvious racism, imperialism, and materialism of mainstream American society. At the same time, they felt a moral imperative to support the civil rights movement and oppose the war. By 1968 the hippie movement and the antiwar movement had combined and evolved into what is best described as a youth movement.

Sociologists and journalists coined the phrase "the generation gap" to describe the division that was emerging in American society. Not all young Americans embraced this movement, but enough did to make it the identifying factor of their generation.

MUSIC

Folk music and rock and roll played an important part in the youth movement. The folk song revival began in coffee houses frequented by beatniks and then found wider popularity with the general public. Many folk singers sang traditional American songs, but others followed the lead of Woody Guthrie and composed songs in the folk style but with lyrics dealing with contemporary social and political issues. During the early 1960s Bob Dylan emerged as the preeminent folk singer-songwriter. His music, which dealt with war, poverty, civil rights, and contemporary American society, became emblematic of the "protest song."

Rock and roll began in the 1950s as a cross between black rhythm and blues and white country music. Rock's lower-class origins and its oblique references to sex made it distasteful to mainstream America; from its inception in the 1950s and on into the 1990s, conservatives condemned rock and roll as an evil, corruptive influence on the youth of America. Young people, for their part, loved it, and the phenomenal success of Elvis Presley and the Beatles gave the music a new legitimacy. At first, most rock and roll songs were simple love songs. In the mid-1960s, however, rock became more political, as lyrics began to reflect the social and political concerns of the young.

Both rock and roll and folk music helped popularize the reform movements of the 1960s. The appeal of the music and the performers attracted thousands of new adherents to the civil rights, antiwar, and hippie movements. The burgeoning market for phonograph recordings created a new forum in which young people across the nation could hear the music and its message. Public performances—particularly folk and rock festivals—also promoted both the music and the cause. The Woodstock Music Festival, which attracted an estimated 350,000 to 500,000 people in 1969, was as much a political rally as it was an entertainment event.

Campus Unrest   During the 1960s college enrollments skyrocketed, and the hundreds of thousands of young men and women gathered on campuses across the country formed the core of the protest movements. The youth movement that combined the hippie movement with the civil rights and antiwar campaigns was largely a student one. As students gathered together to assert their independence and protest the war, they also began to challenge college administrators and teachers.

The student movement had its beginnings in 1964 at the University of California at Berkeley when university officials ordered students to stop distributing pamphlets on the civil rights movement. The students, outraged at this violation of their right to free speech, resisted the order and touched off a pattern of college protest that spread across the nation. By the end of the decade students were combining their demands for campus reform with their calls for an end to racism and the war. Students asked for curriculum reform, a relaxation of college control of student behavior, increased admission of minority students, and a voice in the formulation of campus policy.

The accumulation of complaints led to an increasing militancy among students. When administrators ignored student requests and tried to suppress campus demonstrations, students occupied campus buildings and battled with police. When National Guard troops killed four students at Kent State University, riots erupted at dozens of colleges.

The Women's Movement

The most important offshoot of the civil rights and antiwar movements was the women's movement. Women played an important role in these movements—in terms of both leadership and numbers of supporters—just as they had in earlier reform movements. And like those earlier movements, the campaign for civil rights and peace reminded women of their own status as second-class citizens. Beginning in the mid-1960s women began to organize in an effort to achieve a wide program of goals.

EQUAL OPPORTUNITY

As more and more women began to join the work force, they began to demand an end to economic discrimination. They sought access to a better education and to professional schools; access to jobs in all occupations and professions; access to management and administrative positions; access to public office; access to loans and credit independent of their husbands; membership in male-only clubs and associations; and equal pay. These goals were identical to those sought by blacks. And like blacks, women encountered strong resistance to this program. But the passage of civil rights legislation—with its prohibition of sexual discrimination—benefited women as well as blacks.

FAMILY ROLES

Women also sought more control over sexual reproduction and their role in the family. Women's rights advocates argued that married women should have the opportunity to decide how many children they were going to have, when they were going to have them, and who would care for them. They argued that women should have easy access to all forms of birth control—including abortion—and that child-care facilities should be available for working mothers. Family-planning organizations such as Planned Parenthood supported this position with a variety of arguments: Family planning offered more freedom and personal satisfaction to mothers and fathers both; it was better for the children; it was necessary in light of the impending overpopulation of the planet.

The desire of women to find employment and control reproduction affected the way they viewed the family. Many women were no longer willing to accept the "traditional" arrangement in which the husband was the dominant income earner and head of the family. These women sought a voice in matters affecting their families, repudiated the notion that housework was "women's work," made arrangements for care of their children outside the home while they were working, and demanded the right to decide whether they would stay at home or find a job. A sign of this new independence was an increase in the divorce rate. As women became better able to support themselves and their children, a great many of them terminated unsatisfactory marriages.

THE CAMPAIGN FOR WOMEN'S RIGHTS

The women's rights movement faced a difficult task, for its goal was not a tangible one such as abolishing legally mandated segregation or ending an unpopular war. Its primary task was to change attitudes about the proper role of women in American society. Women's rights advocates had to persuade employers, public officials, husbands, men in general, and women themselves of the benefits and justice of sexual equality. They also had to combat the image of women as sexual objects. Much of the early campaign was directed against sexual exploitation such as beauty pageants, skin magazines, the use of women in advertising, and more serious problems such as rape, wife abuse, and sexual harassment in the workplace. Rights activists wrote books, published magazines, and staged public demonstrations to convey their message. The foremost organization in the battle for equal rights was the National Organization of Women (NOW), founded in 1966.

Like the civil rights movement, the women's rights movement made frequent use of lawsuits in its fight for equality. The Civil Rights Act of 1964 contained a clause outlawing job discrimination based on gender, but federal officials, more interested in civil rights for blacks, gave little attention to discrimination against women. Women were, however, able to use this law against employers. On the issue of control of reproduction, the Supreme Court gave women's rights advocates two important victories. In 1964 the Court struck down a Connecticut law outlawing the sale and use of contraceptives, and in 1973 the controversial *Roe* v. *Wade* decision legalized abortion. The struggle for equality and the resistance they encountered convinced many women that they needed a constitutional guarantee of equality. This led to a campaign for a women's rights amendment to the

Constitution. In 1972 Congress submitted a proposed amendment to the states which read: "Equality of rights under the law shall not be denied or abridged by the United States or by any State on account of sex."

The New Left

During the middle and late 1960s a small number of protesters abandoned the moderate tactics of the civil rights and antiwar movements and began to advocate more radical solutions to the problems facing the United States. They had become disillusioned by what they saw as widespread and deep-seated opposition to change: the assassination of Martin Luther King and Robert Kennedy; the popularity of conservatives such as Richard Nixon and reactionaries such as George Wallace; the continuing escalation of the war; continuing racism; continuing poverty. They accepted the teachings of Karl Marx and condemned capitalism as the cause of the social, economic, and political problems in the United States. Eschewing reform as superficial and ineffective, the radical wing of the movement called for revolution. The New Left, as it was called, was never a serious threat; its members were few in number and divided by philosophy and goals. For several years, however, they waged a campaign of violence: rioting, bombing buildings, robbing banks, and killing policemen.

Opposition to the Protest Movements

The war in Vietnam created a great polarization of the American people. Conservative-minded Americans looked upon the reform movements as a challenge to what they considered to be traditional American society. These people believed that the United States was the greatest nation on earth: It was the victor in World War II, was an industrial giant, and enjoyed immense prosperity. They were bewildered when protesters began to criticize the country. The world they had struggled to build seemed to be falling apart. Blacks were marching in the streets and rioting in the ghettos. Young people were leaving clean, comfortable homes to live in self-imposed poverty. Thousands of people were demonstrating against the war and accusing the United States of being aggressive and imperialist. Women were rejecting their traditional place in the home.

CONSERVATIVE REACTION

The war, especially, generated harsh feelings. During the first several years of American involvement, supporters of the war argued that it was necessary to stop the spread of communism, for the Viet Cong were the pawns of communist leaders in Peking and Moscow who were out to destroy the United States and conquer the world. But as opposition to the war mounted, supporters of the war shifted their rhetoric to the protesters. Conservatives advertised themselves as great patriots and accused the protesters of being anti-American. The United States was at war, and the true patriot, they claimed, supported the government whether he liked the war or not; protesters were nothing but dirty, lazy, long-haired cowards afraid to defend their country. Public opposition to the war while soldiers were fighting and dying was treason, it was aiding the enemy. They refused to accept the notion that it was patriotic to urge the government to terminate a war if one considered the war to be unjust or improper. The conservatives became the arbiters of patriotism; "America: love it or leave it" was their slogan. When Richard Nixon became president he exploited this polarization by dubbing the conservative faction "the silent majority"—as opposed to the noisy minority—of protesters. Nixon was a master of the politics of division. He won support in the South by curtailing federal support for civil rights, and he curried favor with conservatives by playing upon their notions of patriotism.

GOVERNMENT REACTION

Nixon's attitude toward protesters was indicative of the government's position on the antiwar movement. Government at all levels had little tolerance for the protest movements and conducted one of the most flagrant campaigns of political repression that the country has ever witnessed. The FBI and the army both engaged in domestic surveillance, spying on reform leaders (including Martin Luther King) and using infiltrators to provoke violence and disorder that would justify a show of force by the police. Reform leaders were arrested on minor charges and given stiff jail sentences; several were killed in confrontations with the police. Demonstrators were killed, beaten, and arrested. A special animosity developed between the police and demonstrators. Many police officers shared the conservatives' view that the country was on the border of chaos and looked upon themselves as the preservers of order. They looked upon hippies and demonstrators as common criminals: They used illegal drugs, engaged in civil disobedience, participated in disorderly demonstrations, evaded the draft, and rioted. Any young person who looked like a hippie was considered suspicious and was subject to harassment and abuse.

REACTION TO THE WOMEN'S MOVEMENT

Opposition to women's rights was particularly fierce, for it threatened many diverse groups. Opposition came from expected sources such as conservatives who saw it as a threat to the established order and from political and business leaders who feared a diminishment of their power. But it also came from leaders of the reform movements. Many advocates of civil rights for blacks and an end to the war scoffed at the women's movement. Resistance also came from women. Some echoed the conservative argument that a woman's place was at home, taking care of her children and her husband. More important was the gulf between the advocates of careers for women and those who chose to remain at home. The women's movement placed great emphasis on expanding roles for women in the workplace and fighting the notion that women should remain home. Women who chose to remain at home felt that the movement belittled their lives and therefore had little sympathy for it.

DETENTE WITH THE SOVIET UNION

Throughout the 1960s and early 1970s the United States and the Soviet Union engaged in a deadly game of world diplomacy. They fought each other in proxy wars throughout the Third World and waged a continual battle of propaganda and rhetoric. Their armies faced each other in Eastern Europe; their submarines and aircraft probed each other's borders. Most dangerous of all, both continued to stockpile newer and more lethal nuclear weapons. This existence on the brink of disaster scared both countries into a series of negotiations intended to relieve the ongoing tension and avert any chance of nuclear war.

The Kennedy Years

Both the United States and the Soviet Union subscribed to the belief that superior might was necessary to guarantee peace. Neither, therefore, could show any sign of weakness. At the same time, both desired an easing of tension and favored top-level negotiations. American President John Kennedy and Soviet Premier Nikita Khrushchev exemplified this attitude. Kennedy traveled to the Berlin Wall—to the very gates of the Soviet empire—and declared his intention to defend Europe against Soviet aggression. Khrushchev pounded his shoe on his desk at a meeting of the United Nations, denounced the West as imperialists, and threatened to annihilate the United States. On the other hand, Kennedy acknowledged that the United States existed in a "world of diversity" in which there was a place for both the United States and communist Russia. Khrushchev, for his part, called for "peaceful coexistence" between the two nations. A meeting in Vienna between Kennedy and Khrushchev in 1961 bore little fruit, but in 1963 the United States and the Soviet Union opened the "hot line," a telecommunications link between the White House and Soviet headquarters at the Kremlin designed to provide immediate communications between leaders of the two nations at a time of crisis. Also in 1963, the two countries were parties to a multinational nuclear test ban treaty.

The Johnson Years

Lyndon Johnson, saddled with an expanding war in Vietnam, sought to maintain stable relations with Russia. In 1967 the two countries ratified a treaty pertaining to the maintenance of consulates in each other's country. This was the first bilateral treaty between the United States and the Soviet

Union since 1917. That same year they were signatories to multinational treaties banning nuclear weapons in outer space and in South America. It was also in 1967 that the hot line received its first use. When war broke out in the Middle East in June, Soviet Premier Aleksei Kosygin and President Johnson used the hot line to assure each other of their mutual noninvolvement in the conflict. Later that month the two held an informal conference when Kosygin visited the United Nations headquarters in New York.

The Nixon Years

THE SOVIET UNION

Soviet-American relations cooled during the summer of 1968 when the Red Army crushed an incipient pro-democracy movement in Czechoslovakia. The tension soon eased, however, and shortly after Richard Nixon became president both countries ratified a multinational nuclear non-proliferation treaty in which the signatories agreed not to provide nuclear weapons technology to countries that did not already possess nuclear weapons.

In May 1972 Nixon visited Moscow and attended the first of several meetings with Soviet leaders. This meeting culminated several years of negotiations between the two countries. The high point of the conference was the signing of two treaties limiting the deployment of nuclear weapons. Other agreements called for improved commercial relations and cooperation in technological, scientific, space, and health research. Soviet Party Secretary Leonid Brezhnev returned Nixon's visit in June 1973. No major agreements resulted from this meeting, but it did symbolize the new spirit of cooperation between the two nations. A third meeting between the two in Moscow in June 1974 failed to produce any new agreement. These meetings and treaties did little to end or even slow the nuclear arms race, for both nations continued to develop more sophisticated and more deadly weapons. They did, however, confirm the willingness of both nations to find a peaceful settlement to their differences.

CHINA

Nixon, like his predecessors, became mired down in southeast Asia. In his dealings with the Soviet Union and China, however, he proved himself to be an adept and daring hand at foreign policy. His greatest diplomatic coup came in February 1972 when he made a week-long visit to Red China. Nixon, the conservative red basher, did what no liberal president could have done: He normalized relations with Communist China. Beginning in 1969 his administration introduced a number of measures that eased restrictions on travel to and trade with China. In 1971 the United States jettisoned its support of the Nationalist government on Taiwan by voting in favor of a resolution that admitted Communist China to the United Nations and expelled Taiwan. Nixon's visit to Peking and his meetings with Premier Chou

En-Lai and Mao Tse-tung cemented the change in policy. The countries did not exchange ambassadors, but they did establish diplomatic missions in 1973.

THE THIRD WORLD

Detente with the Soviets and the Chinese had little effect on American policy in the Third World. Despite improved relations with the Soviets, Nixon and his foreign policy advisor (and later secretary of state) Henry Kissinger continued to subscribe to the Cold War belief that the United States needed to block Soviet influence in the Third World. Accordingly, the United States extended support to any government that was anticommunist. As a result, right-wing dictatorships around the globe found a patron in Washington. Brutal and repressive governments in Greece, Pakistan, Rhodesia, and South Africa found favor with the Nixon administration. And, of course, left-wing governments remained targets. In 1970 Kissinger authorized the CIA to "destabilize" the elected marxist government of Salvador Allende in Chile. In 1973 the United States gave at least tacit approval to a coup that overthrew and killed Allende and replaced him with a right-wing military government.

THE MIDDLE EAST

A desire to check Soviet expansion also influenced American policy in the Middle East. In 1972 Nixon visited Iran and forged a new alliance with the shah, a brutal despot whose father had risen to power in a CIA-engineered coup in 1953. Under the new arrangement, the United States supplied Iran with billions of dollars worth of modern weapons and made it a bulwark against Soviet expansion in the region.

The Middle East was a highly complex and volatile region where hostile nations were constantly on the brink of war. Dealing with this region taxed Nixon's and Kissinger's diplomatic skills to the utmost. The United States had conflicting interests in the region. It was the primary supporter of Israel; it relied heavily on Arab oil; and it wanted to limit Soviet influence with the Arab nations. In October 1973 the United States found itself facing a double crisis: War erupted between Israel and its Arab neighbors, and the Arab-controlled Organization of Petroleum Exporting Nations (OPEC) stopped the export of oil to the United States in retaliation for American aid to Israel. Secretary of State Kissinger assumed the role of mediator and in November arranged a cease-fire. During the winter and spring of 1973–1974 Kissinger made numerous trips to the capitals of the Middle Eastern countries in his attempt to mediate a peace settlement. He persuaded the Israelis to withdraw from their advanced position in Egypt, and in return, the Arabs ended the oil embargo. In June 1974 Nixon made a tour of the region in an effort to affirm American friendliness for all Middle Eastern nations.

WATERGATE

If Richard Nixon's great strong point was foreign diplomacy, his fatal weaknesses were his paranoia and his penchant for secrecy. He distrusted Congress, the federal bureaucracy, and even many of his own appointees, believing that they were set on sabotaging his administration.

Trouble with Congress

Nixon was at war with the Democratic majority in Congress from the beginning of his presidency. Aware that he would get little support from Congress for his programs, Nixon decided to bypass the legislature and use his extensive powers as chief executive to attain his goals. A major point of contention between the two was Vietnam. By 1969 the Democrats were committed to an early withdrawal from Vietnam. The president, knowing that Congress would oppose an escalation of the war, ordered secret attacks on Cambodia and informed Congress of them after the fact. Congress disapproved of this action, but with American troops in the field, there was little it could do. It revoked the Gulf of Tonkin Resolutions, but this was, for the most part, a symbolic gesture. In domestic matters, Congress passed many measures that Nixon opposed. Unable to stop the enactment of these laws, Nixon impounded the funds—that is, as chief executive he refused to allocate money for programs he opposed. Other presidents had believed in strong executive power, but Nixon's actions raised the theory of executive dominance in government to new levels. His desire for White House guards to wear military-style uniforms more suitable to a nineteenth-century European imperial court than to a twentieth-century democracy underscored Nixon's attempt to establish what critics called an "imperial presidency."

Presidential Staff

Nixon's fear of interference with his own plans shaped the conduct of his administration. Nixon surrounded himself with a cadre of advisors loyal to him alone, and these men formulated policy and ran the government. The cabinet was almost superfluous, and senior officials in the various departments were mostly ignored. At the center of this group was Nixon's longtime friend and advisor Attorney General John Mitchell. Mitchell, assisted by Chief of Staff H. R. Haldeman and domestic advisor John Ehrlichman, controlled access to the president and determined who and what received his attention. Henry Kissinger (special advisor, 1969–1973; secretary of state, 1973–1974) advised the president on foreign affairs, and the two of them conducted foreign diplomacy without the assistance or knowledge of the State Department or the Pentagon. These four, assisted by a host of other advisors, insulated the president from the rest of the government and the public. The wall of secrecy became so great, in fact, that the Pentagon spied on the White House in an effort to gain information on national security matters.

Intolerance of Dissent

One important duty of the White House staff was to shelter the president from divergent points of view, for Nixon had little tolerance for dissent. Indeed, Nixon's hatred of opposition was so great that he ordered his advisors to compile an "enemies list": a roster of Democrats, public officials, news correspondents, civil rights and antiwar activists, and anyone else who challenged Nixon's policies. He then launched a campaign of surveillance and harassment to embarrass and, if possible, incriminate the opposition, all to be done in the name of national security. The goal was, in the words of one advisor, to "use the available federal machinery to screw our political enemies."

Hatred of the Antiwar Movement

Nixon bestowed his greatest hatred on the opponents of the war in Vietnam. Indeed, the enemies list, the domestic surveillance, and the harassment of dissenters were directed primarily at the antiwar movement. At one point Nixon and his aides discussed hiring thugs from organized crime syndicates to beat up protesters. Nixon was particularly outraged by the publication of the Pentagon Papers, in 1971. This history of the early years of the Vietnam war documented the poor planning of policy and the falsification of information presented to Congress and the public. Unable to stop publication of the papers, Nixon ordered his staff to use every means available—legal and illegal—to discredit Daniel Ellsberg, the Defense Department aide who had "leaked" the papers, and the newspapers that published them. Ellsberg was indicted for theft and espionage (the case was dismissed) and became the victim of harassment by White House agents.

The Watergate Burglary

By early 1972 Nixon was obsessed with the upcoming presidential election. Mitchell resigned as attorney general to become director of Nixon's reelection campaign. (Mitchell had been campaign director in 1968.) The main task of the White House staff became the reelection of Richard Nixon. In typical fashion they organized the Committee to Reelect the President (CRP) and operated independently of the Republican party. Within the CRP was—also in typical fashion—a "security wing." Originally organized to investigate the leaking of sensitive information, such as the Pentagon Papers, these "plumbers" soon turned their attention to sabotaging the Democratic party.

THE BREAK-IN

During May and June 1972 a team of burglars, armed with cameras and wire-tapping equipment and acting on Mitchell's orders but apparently without Nixon's knowledge, staged several break-ins at Democratic party headquarters in the Watergate Hotel in Washington. What these burglaries were supposed to accomplish was never made clear; they were, for the most part, just another example of the lawlessness and paranoia of the Nixon administration. On the evening of June 17 the burglars were caught and their ties to CRP quickly discovered.

THE COVER-UP

The White House immediately began a cover-up of the operation. Officials denied any involvement by the CRP or the White House, claiming that the burglars were renegades acting on their own. Meanwhile, the White House staff destroyed documents, pressured the FBI to halt its investigation of the burglary, paid for the defense of the burglars, and paid them hush money. Nixon publicly announced that an internal investigation had failed to find any evidence of involvement by White House staff. In reality, there had been no investigation. Mitchell, claiming personal reasons, resigned as chief of CPR.

The 1972 Election

The election itself is almost a footnote to the Watergate scandal. The Democrats nominated Senator George McGovern of South Dakota, who ran on what was primarily an antiwar platform. Governor George Wallace of Alabama, once again the candidate for the American Independent party, withdrew from the race after he was critically wounded in an assassination attempt. McGovern, running with a badly organized campaign and a worn-out issue, did poorly. Even the growing Watergate scandal failed to help him. Nixon won easily, polling 47 million votes to McGovern's 27 million (see Appendix B). His victory did little to help the Republican party, however, for the Democrats retained control of Congress.

The Investigation

The White House continued to deny any involvement in the Watergate burglary, but suspicion in the case would not go away. Bob Woodward and Carl Bernstein, two reporters for the *Washington Post*, continued to unearth evidence linking John Mitchell to the break-in. At the trial of the burglars (all of whom were convicted) in January 1973 Judge John Sirica stated his belief that others were involved in the case and urged a continuation of the criminal investigation. In February 1973 the Senate appointed a committee headed by Sam Ervin of North Carolina to begin its own investigation.

SENATE HEARINGS

These investigations increased pressure on the White House staff, and in bits and pieces different members admitted participation in the efforts to cover up White House involvement. As the trail drew closer to the president, staff members began to resign in order to protect Nixon. Haldeman, Ehrlich-man, and Attorney General Richard Kleindienst—who had directed the prosecution of the burglars—quit in late April. Lower-level advisors, fearful that they would be offered as scapegoats, testified before the Senate committee. The American public watched the hearings on television and saw the accumulating evidence of the president's involvement in the cover-up. The most important revelation was that Nixon had tape-recorded all his conversations and meetings.

SPECIAL PROSECUTOR

In May 1973 Nixon appointed Archibald Cox as special prosecutor to investigate the cover-up. Both Cox and the Senate committee subpoenaed the tapes, but Nixon, claiming executive privilege, refused to release them. When Cox continued to press for their release, Nixon ordered Attorney General Elliot Richardson and his assistant William Ruckelshaus to fire Cox. When they refused, Nixon fired them; Solicitor General Robert Bork, who agreed to dismiss Cox, became acting attorney general. The public outrage at this was so great that Nixon agreed to appoint a new special prosecutor and to release the tapes. Meanwhile, the House of Representatives began to consider impeachment.

Evidence of Corruption

Nixon surrendered seven tapes in November 1973, stating that they were the only ones relevant to the investigation. The tapes contained no direct evidence of the president's involvement in the cover-up, but they were damaging nonetheless, for they revealed Nixon to be a vindictive, foul-mouthed, and amoral man. In addition, the investigations uncovered a history of corruption in the administration: burglaries, illegal campaign contributions, lucrative gifts to Nixon—including cash and real estate—in exchange for political favors, and the enemies lists. They also revealed that Nixon had not paid his taxes between 1969 and 1972.

The Resignation of Spiro Agnew

Also contributing to Nixon's downfall was the conviction of Vice-President Spiro Agnew for income-tax evasion. Agnew had proved to be a great asset in Nixon's attack on his political enemies, for he was a master at coining catchy phrases in his public assaults on antiwar protesters, the news media, and liberals in general. In August 1973 Agnew was indicted for accepting bribes while governor of Maryland and while vice-president. In October he agreed to a plea bargain, resigned from the vice-presidency, and was convicted of a single count of income-tax evasion.

Nixon's Resignation

Pressure on Nixon continued to mount during the early months of 1974. In March Mitchell, Haldeman, Ehrlichman, and three others were indicted by a grand jury. Unsure about the constitutionality of indicting the president, the grand jury named Nixon as an unindicted co-conspirator. Ordered by the courts to release more tapes, Nixon provided edited transcripts that, while implicating him in the cover-up, never proved it. In May the Supreme Court ordered Nixon to surrender even more tapes.

In late July 1974 the House Judiciary Committee voted three articles of impeachment, accusing Nixon of obstructing justice, abusing presidential power, and refusing to answer congressional subpoenas. On August 5 Nixon released transcripts of three tapes that proved his knowledge of the break-in immediately after it happened and revealed that he had ordered the FBI to halt its investigation. This proof of guilt destroyed any remaining support that Nixon had. His advisors at the White House and leading Republicans in Congress urged him to resign. Reluctant to do so, Nixon gave up and resigned on August 8, 1974.

Aftermath

Gerald Ford, a Congressman from Michigan whom Nixon had appointed vice-president in October 1973 when Agnew resigned, assumed the duties of the presidency. A month later Ford granted Nixon a complete and unconditional pardon for any crimes he may have committed. Nixon's aides did not fair so well. Over forty of them, including Haldeman, Ehrlichman, and three former cabinet members—Attorney General John Mitchell, Attorney General Richard Kleindienst, and Commerce Secretary Maurice Stans—were convicted of crimes relating to the break-in and cover-up.

What began in 1961 as an era of optimism and high moral purpose ended in 1975 in disillusionment and moral corruption. Millions of Americans saw their faith in the country shaken by the assassination of the two Kennedys and Martin Luther King; by the failure of an ill-conceived policy and poorly conducted war in Vietnam; and by the abuse of power that led to the resignation of the president of the United States. The energy and resources that should have gone into the civil rights movement and the war on poverty had been diverted to fighting and protesting the war in Vietnam. By the mid-1970s Americans found themselves morally exhausted. They were worn out by the fear, anger, and bitterness created by the turmoil of the era, particularly Vietnam and Watergate.

Selected Readings

Bernstein, Carl, and Bob Woodward. *All the President's Men* (1974)
_____. *The Final Days* (1976)
Evans, Sara. *Personal Politics: The Roots of Women's Liberation in the Civil Rights Movements and the New Left* (1979)
Friedan, Betty. *The Feminine Mystique* (1963)
Garthoff, Raymond L. *Detente and Confrontation: American-Soviet Relations from Nixon to Reagan* (1985)
Gitlin, Todd. *The Sixties: Years of Hope, Days of Rage* (1987)
Halberstam, David. *The Best and the Brightest* (1972)
Heath, Jim. *Decade of Disillusionment: The Kennedy-Johnson Years* (1975)
Herring, George. *America's Longest War: The United States and Vietnam, 1950– 1975,* 2nd ed. (1986)
Kerouac, Jack. *On the Road* (1955)

Kutler, Stanley, *The Wars of Watergate: The Last Crisis of Richard Nixon* (1991)
Parmet, Herbert. *Richard Nixon and His America* (1990)
Sheehan, Neil. *A Bright Shining Lie: John Paul Vann and America in Vietnam* (1988)
Wolfe, Tom. *The Electric Kool-Aid Acid Test* (1968)

11

The Shift to Conservatism: 1976–1988

1977 Jimmy Carter becomes president

Carter grants pardon to Vietnam-era draft evaders

Panama Canal Treaty

1978 Carter mediates treaty between Israel and Egypt

1979 United States establishes diplomatic relations with China

Iranians capture American embassy in Teheran

Three Mile Island accident

1981 Ronald Reagan begins first term as president

Iran releases American hostages

CIA begins aiding Contras in Nicaragua

First AIDS case reported

1982 Equal Rights Amendment fails to win ratification

American troops land in Lebanon

1983 American troops sent to Grenada

American troops withdraw from Lebanon

1985 Reagan begins second term as president

1986 American planes bomb Libya

U.S. warships sent to the Persian Gulf

1987   Iran-Contra scandal made public

1989   George Bush becomes president

*F*or the second time in the twentieth century (the first being the 1920s) the American people in the late 1970s and the 1980s retreated from the social activism of the preceding years. Conservatism had remained strong during the 1960s—Barry Goldwater had suffered a devastating defeat in the 1964 presidential election, but Richard Nixon and George Wallace had won a majority of the votes in 1968—but the mood of the country had been one of liberal reform. In the late 1970s that mood changed. Many people remained dedicated to the goals of the reform movement, but the country as a whole wanted a respite from the turmoil of Vietnam, civil rights, and Watergate.

This change in mood resulted from a dissatisfaction with the outcome of the reform movements. Certainly, there had been many successes. If racial segregation had not been eradicated completely, it had been greatly reduced. The political system was open to more people than it had been before. Millions of people who could not vote in 1960 could do so in 1976. Barriers to economic opportunity for both blacks and women had been breached. But there were many failures as well. The continued existence of poverty, crime, and racism accented the weakness of the Great Society programs. Indeed, the campaign to eradicate these problems brought them to new prominence and made them appear to be worse than before the reform programs started. The civil rights movement led to the worst riots ever witnessed in the United States. The war in Vietnam failed to stop the spread of communism abroad and created misery and turmoil at home.

The hostility encountered by the reform movement, the corruption of the Nixon administration, and the failure of American policy in Vietnam left the country with a sense of disillusionment. The inability of the United States to defeat North Vietnam had badly bruised the ego of the nation. The animosity directed toward the civil rights and antiwar movement created a feeling of cynicism, as many people began to doubt the country's commitment to justice and equality. Worst of all was the sense of betrayal engendered by the Watergate scandal. Richard Nixon had asked the American people to trust him, and many came to regret that they had. The great crusade to reform the nation and the world had, it seemed, failed.

This sense of failure led to a disenchantment with the federal government. John Kennedy and Lyndon Johnson saw the federal government as a tool for solving problems. By 1976 Americans at both ends of the spectrum saw it as a source of trouble. Liberals viewed Washington as a center of imperialism, repression, and corruption; conservatives saw it as the home of an inept and intrusive bureaucracy. Candidates from both sides adopted the tactic of running as outsiders committed to taming the federal government. "Government cannot solve our problems," President Jimmy Carter *announced in 1978. Ronald Reagan went even further. "Government is not the solution to our problem," he proclaimed in his first inaugural address in 1981; "it is the problem."*

THE 1976 ELECTION

Gerald Ford

Gerald Ford was the first American president to hold office without having been elected either to the presidency or vice-presidency. During the two years of his term he worked to be more than just a caretaker president. In 1976 he legitimized his claim to the office when he overcame a strong challenge from Ronald Reagan and won the Republican nomination for president. Despite this impressive effort, Ford's presidency and reelection campaign suffered from three insurmountable burdens. The first was the onus of Watergate and the Nixon pardon. The outrage caused by the Watergate scandal remained great enough to damage the chances of any Republican candidate. Ford's unconditional pardon of Richard Nixon sullied his reputation as an honest man and tied him directly to the scandal. The second problem was America's continued difficulties abroad, highlighted by the fall of Vietnam and Cambodia in 1975.

If these two were not enough, Ford faced a third and more immediate problem: a slumping economy at home. When Ford took office inflation was already on the rise. Government spending for the war and domestic programs contributed to the problem, but the primary reason for inflation was the increased cost of imported oil following the OPEC oil embargo of 1973. Ford, unwilling to institute price and wage controls (tactics used by Nixon), sought to control inflation by tightening the money supply and raising interest rates. This policy worked—inflation fell from 12 percent in 1974 to less than 5 percent in 1976—but at a price, for it resulted in the worst economic decline since the Great Depression. In 1975 unemployment stood at nearly 12 percent.

Jimmy Carter

The Democratic nomination went to Jimmy Carter, a former governor of Georgia. Carter was an enigmatic candidate. As a conservative southern Democrat, he was able to win support in the South. At the same time, he was a strong supporter of civil rights and social reform, positions that appealed to blacks and liberals. Carter's main campaign strategy was to run as an outsider against the Washington establishment—he had never held federal office, while Ford had been a Congressman for twenty-three years—and against the corruption of Watergate. "I'll never lie to you," Carter promised the American people.

The 1976 election pitted two honest and competent—but uninspiring—men against each other. The burden weighing upon Ford proved to be too heavy, however, and Carter won, garnering 40 million votes to Ford's 38 million (see Appendix B).

THE CARTER ADMINISTRATION

Domestic Policy

THE FEDERAL GOVERNMENT

Carter employed a strange combination of liberal and conservative ideas in his conduct of public business. He made great progress in opening the government to minorities. He appointed more women and blacks to office than did any of his predecessors and appointed three women to his cabinet—the first to hold such high-level offices since 1955. He strengthened federal protection of consumers, workers, and the environment and successfully urged the creation of three new government departments: Energy, Education, and Health and Human Services. At the same time, he believed that federal interference in economic matters had become too great. He particularly favored a reduction of federal regulation of business and advocated deregulation of the airlines, the trucking industry, banking, railroads, and the oil industry.

ECONOMIC DECLINE

Economic problems proved to be Carter's greatest domestic worry. Inflation, which had been on the decline when Carter took office, began to rise rapidly in 1977. Like Ford, Carter favored currency regulation rather than price and wage controls. His attempt to curb inflation by tightening the money supply and raising interest rates failed miserably. By 1980 the country suffered from continued inflation (13.5 percent), unprecedented interest rates (20 percent), and high unemployment (almost 8 percent). The federal deficit grew, industrial output declined, and worker productivity hit its lowest point since World War II. At the same time, incomes continued to rise and more people than ever participated in American prosperity. Economists, baffled by this strange combination of factors, were unable to offer a solution to the problem.

THE ENERGY CRISIS

A central contributing factor to the economic crisis was the rising price of fuel. The United States continued to produce a large amount of oil, natural gas, and coal, but these supplies were inadequate to the nation's needs. As a result, the country imported an ever-increasing amount of expensive foreign oil. The growing demand and the rising cost of fuel underscored the need for a national energy policy. The federal government created the Department of Energy, deregulated the oil industry, set fuel efficiency standards for automobiles, and urged consumer conservation. These measures did little to stem the use of oil or to create a coherent national policy. Nuclear-generated electricity offered an alternative to the use of imported oil, but the potential catastrophic danger of a nuclear power plant accident limited its appeal. Indeed, the poor safety record of existing plants and the near disaster at the Three Mile Island facility in Pennsylvania in 1979 turned many people against nuclear power.

Foreign Affairs   HUMAN RIGHTS

President Carter, influenced by detente with the communist powers and public reaction to the Vietnam war, initiated a new foreign policy. Carter hoped to restore America's prestige in the international arena (and in the eyes of its own citizens) by shifting from what appeared to be an imperialistic and militaristic policy to one based on morality and diplomacy. The centerpiece of his new policy was an insistence on the importance of human rights. It was no longer enough, Carter argued, for the United States to set a moral example for the rest of the world. The nation should, instead, take an active role in support of human rights in other nations. The United States would now deal with other nations based upon the extent to which they extended liberty and justice to their citizens.

CENTRAL AMERICA

One of Carter's goals in foreign affairs was to improve relations with Latin America. Overall, his human rights policy offered an avenue to better relations by urging Latin American leaders to improve economic and social conditions within their countries. More specifically, Carter sought to reverse the practice of American dominance of Latin America and end American support for despotic leaders. His first success in this field was the Panama Canal Treaty, which was ratified in 1978 and arranged for transfer of control of the canal to Panama in the year 2000. This treaty raised a firestorm of opposition among conservatives, who saw it as a further weakening of the United States. Latin Americans, however, hailed it as a positive step. In a way, the treaty was only symbolic, for everyone knew that the United States would continue to consider the canal as its special province and would take action to prevent any hostile measures that jeopardized national security.

Carter's efforts to reduce American ties to despotic governments were less conclusive. In 1979 a revolution erupted in Nicaragua against the dictatorial and exploitative Somoza family. Carter tried to persuade Somoza to institute reforms but failed. When the revolutionary Sandinista party came to power Carter made friendly but guarded overtures to the new leftist government. The success of this revolt encouraged a similar uprising in neighboring El Salvador. At first, Carter stopped aid to the right-wing government in an effort to induce reform. The revolution soon degenerated into a civil war between the government and communist insurgents, however, and the United States once again began to support the government.

MIDDLE EAST PEACE ACCORDS

The great diplomatic victory of the Carter administration was the peace treaty between Israel and Egypt. In 1977 Egypt initiated peace talks with Israel. When these negotiations broke down, Carter invited Egyptian President Anwar Sadat and Israeli Prime Minister Menachem Begin to the United States and personally assumed the role of mediator. The resulting treaty, signed in September 1978, did not resolve the great issues of the Arab-Israeli conflict, but it did end the thirty-year state of war that existed between Israel and Egypt and it improved American relations with Egypt.

SOVIET-AMERICAN RELATIONS

Despite Carter's efforts at a new style of diplomacy, relations with the Soviet Union remained as difficult as ever. Detente continued, but both sides remained suspicious of the other. The two countries engaged in arms-control negotiations, but a balance of power—not arms reduction—was their goal. While continuing to amass huge arsenals, they negotiated a treaty that did not reduce armaments but only provided a cap on the number of nuclear weapons each country could possess. The friendly faces shown by Carter and Soviet leader Brezhnev at the signing of the Strategic Arms Limitation Treaty in Vienna in 1979 masked the growing tension. The Soviets resented Carter's public support for Soviet dissidents and his call for human rights. They were also alarmed by American diplomatic recognition of their rival to the east, Communist China.

Relations between the United States and the Soviet Union degenerated in 1979 when the Soviet Union sent troops into Afghanistan to support a wavering marxist government. Carter condemned the invasion, withdrew the arms limitation treaty from consideration by the Senate, canceled a grain sale to the Soviet Union, boycotted the 1980 Olympics in Moscow, provided aid to Afghani rebels, and declared the invasion of Afghanistan to be a threat to American interests. By the end of his term, Carter was as much a Cold Warrior as any of his predecessors.

IRAN

If Carter's greatest diplomatic triumph occurred in the Middle East with the Israeli-Egyptian peace settlement, his greatest failure also occurred there with the Iran crisis. The shah of Iran had been America's chief ally in the Middle East since the 1950s, and the United States had helped him modernize his country and build up an extensive military force. The Soviet invasion of Afghanistan and the increasing dependence of the United States on Middle Eastern oil lent new importance to this alliance. It was, however, an alliance that put Carter's human rights policy to the test, for the shah was one of the most brutal, corrupt, and repressive rulers in the Middle East.

In the late 1970s a wave of religious fundamentalism swept through the Islamic nations. This movement was decidedly political as well as religious. It emphasized a return to traditional Islamic social practices and a repudiation of Western customs that had been introduced into the region. The United States, as leader of the Western nations and chief patron of Israel, became the central target of fundamentalist attack. The shah of Iran—with his repressive regime, his desire for modernization, and his close ties to the United States—was especially vulnerable to this new movement. In early 1979 revolutionary forces forced him to flee the country.

The Carter government was torn over what action to take. Carter's national security advisor Zbigniew Brezinski, a hard-line Cold Warrior, favored an American-backed military coup to restore the shah. Secretary of State Cyrus Vance urged the president to repudiate the shah and work with the Iranian revolutionaries to establish a moderate government. While Carter remained undecided, radical fundamentalists led by the Ayatollah Khomeini cemented their control of the country. Ignoring warnings that any gesture of friendship to the shah would bring severe retaliation, Carter allowed him to enter the United States to receive medical treatment. In October 1979 the Iranians seized the American embassy in Teheran and took fifty Americans hostage. Carter spent the rest of his term trying to resolve this crisis. The Iranian revolutionaries, rejoicing in their victory, remained defiant and rejected all diplomatic overtures. An attempt by American military forces to launch a rescue mission encountered problems in its early stages and was called off.

The 1980 Election

THE CANDIDATES

Like his predecessor Gerald Ford, Jimmy Carter ran for reelection while bearing the burden of several overwhelming problems. The crisis in Iran, uncontrolled inflation, and high interest rates had turned people against him. Many Americans admired Carter for his hard work, intelligence, and moral integrity, but after four years a significant number of voters had concluded that he simply did not have the ability to be a good president. Particularly lacking was a talent for instilling confidence in the American people.

After the trauma of Vietnam, Watergate, and the civil rights movement, and after the challenge of the Iranian revolution, the American people wanted a leader who would restore their pride and confidence in themselves and their country. They found that leader in Ronald Reagan, the Republican candidate. Reagan had one great asset: his easy-going, grandfatherly image.

A former actor, Reagan knew how to use television to convey a positive image of himself. He had the ability to smile at people, tell them everything was okay, and have them believe him. His ability to reassure people contrasted sharply with Carter's tendency to be a little too honest in assessing the gloomy side of national affairs.

A third candidate in the race was John Anderson, a liberal Republican, who ran as an independent. Anderson, a long-time congressman from Illinois, was never a threat to the main parties, but he ran a highly visible campaign and offered the voters a serious alternative to Carter and Reagan.

REAGAN'S PLATFORM

Much of Reagan's appeal came from his image as a strong, but at the same time, congenial man. But he also espoused a political program that was in tune with the country's conservative mood. He openly repudiated the government activism of the New Deal and the Great Society and, like Carter, portrayed himself as an outsider who would tame the Washington bureaucracy. He took a strong anticommunist, anti-Soviet stance and advocated a massive military buildup. Reagan showed little concern for the plight of the poor and the disadvantaged; civil rights was not an important item on his agenda. His economic program was based upon the assumption that existing federal policy interfered with economic growth. His proposals, which were decidedly pro-business, included a reduction of federal regulations of all sorts, corporate and individual tax cuts, reductions in government spending, and a balanced federal budget.

THE ELECTION

Reagan took an early lead in the campaign and held on until his victory in the election. Reagan received 44 million votes to Carter's 35 million and Anderson's 6 million. Reagan recaptured the South for the Republicans, but the black vote went almost entirely to Carter. In the congressional elections the Republicans won a majority in the Senate for the first time since 1952.

THE RELEASE OF THE IRANIAN HOSTAGES

A closing footnote to the election was the release of the hostages held in Iran. Carter announced on his last day in office that their release had been obtained. The timing of the announcement—just before Reagan's inauguration—made it seem to be more of a triumph for Reagan than for Carter. The role and influence of Reagan's campaign and election in the release of the hostages remains unclear.

THE REAGAN ADMINISTRATION

Economic Policy

THE TAX CUT AND DEREGULATION

The central tenet of Reagan's domestic policy was that a reduction of government spending and government activism would solve the nation's problems. Reagan and his supporters argued that a massive tax cut, a reduced federal bureaucracy, and an end to government regulation of the economy would spur economic growth and erase the federal deficit. A tax cut—particularly for business and the wealthy—would, the argument ran, stimulate the economy to such an extent that revenue on increased profits would offset the reduction from the tax cut. Congress accepted the administration's proposal and passed a new tax law with lower rates. Reagan also accelerated the deregulation of business that had begun under Carter and attempted to declaw many of the regulatory agencies in the executive branch. Neither the tax cut nor deregulation stimulated the economy to the level predicted. The recession continued until 1983 when continued high interest rates finally drove down inflation and unemployment.

Reagan's promise to scale down the size of the federal government proved to be unattainable. Everyone agreed in principle that the government should be reduced, but too many people depended upon or wanted the services of federal programs for there to be any significant reduction. Reagan's policy of shifting some social service programs to the states simply resulted in an increase in state and local taxes and bureaucracies.

TRADE DEFICIT

The United States remained prosperous, but the country was still beset by economic problems that could not be cured by the Reagan program. The increasing cost of labor, material, and production made American manufacturing vulnerable to foreign competition, particularly from Japan and other Asian nations. This resulted in an unfavorable balance of trade, with imports exceeding exports. Some people called for a protective tariff to shore up American manufacturing, but the Reagan administration opposed trade barriers and argued that its economic program would solve the problem.

FEDERAL DEFICIT

Reagan's inability to reduce federal programs, a high rate of military spending, and lost revenue due to the tax cut resulted in an astronomical increase in the federal deficit. The national debt grew from $935 billion in 1981 to $2.7 trillion in 1988. This huge debt created a need for foreign investment and changed the United States from a creditor nation to the world's largest debtor nation. In 1980 foreign countries owed the United States $150 billion; in 1988 the United States owed $400 billion. Reagan's economic policies did not, by themselves, cause these many problems. But by failing to recognize the complexity of these problems, the Reagan administration was ineffective in combating them.

Foreign Policy

President Reagan, like many other Americans, wanted to restore America's prestige as the world's greatest and strongest nation after the fiasco of Vietnam. To accomplish this end he engaged in a war of rhetoric and propaganda, authorized military and covert action, and advocated a massive buildup of nuclear and conventional weapons. At the same time, significant changes in the world situation provided an opportunity to strengthen the nation's position through negotiation.

THE WORLD'S POLICEMAN

Reagan, an inveterate Cold Warrior, believed that the United States was engaged in a life-and-death struggle with the Soviet Union. He condemned the Soviet Union as an "evil empire" and blamed it for all the trouble in the world. Once again American policymakers dismissed the notion that Third World nations had legitimate grievances that needed to be addressed. If it were not for Soviet-backed subversion, Reagan claimed, "there wouldn't be any hot spots in the world." The United States, in an effort to reassert itself as the leader of the free world, assumed the responsibility of counteracting these measures. This led to American involvement in such scattered places as Cambodia, Afghanistan, Angola, Libya, Lebanon, the Persian Gulf, Grenada, and Central America. Involvement included financial and military aid, military intervention, and covert operations.

ANGOLA

Reagan's simplification of the problem had mixed results. In Angola the situation would have been comical had it not been so bloody. The United States was supplying extensive aid to rebels fighting against the marxist government of the country. Cuba, with a large black population descended from slaves who had come from Angola, sent troops to assist the government. Several American oil companies had large refineries in Angola and had reached a working agreement with the government, which needed the revenue from oil exports. These refineries were a primary target of the rebels. This led to a strange situation in which Cuban troops protected American-owned oil refineries against attacks by rebels supported by the American government.

LEBANON

The situation in Lebanon was tragic. This small country was ripped apart by a civil war among an assortment of Christian and Islamic sects. Invasion by Syrian and Israeli forces added to the carnage. In 1983 Reagan dispatched a contingent of Marines to Lebanon in an effort to restore order. The mission, which was poorly conceived, ended in tragedy in October 1983 when a terrorist driving a truck laden with explosives crashed into a barracks and killed 241 Marines while they were sleeping. Terrorist attacks, including car bombings, were a common tactic in Lebanon; as recently as April 1983 a car bomb had destroyed the American embassy in Beirut and killed sixty-three people. The American command ignored this danger and failed to provide adequate security for the barracks: Gates to the compound had never been installed and the guards carried unloaded weapons. Shortly after this attack the Marines left the country. This was not a withdrawal, Secretary of Defense Caspar Weinberger insisted, but a "strategic redeployment" to warships off the coast.

GRENADA

Within days of this debacle, the United States invaded the tiny Caribbean island of Grenada. The pretext for the attack was that the marxist government served as a conduit for weapons for insurgents and that Americans resident on the island were in danger because of local political turmoil. American soldiers landed on the island in October 1983 and quickly subdued a force of Cuban militia (the Grenadans had no army). The easy conquest and the happiness of the Grenadans at the removal of an inept and unpopular government enabled Reagan to declare this a great victory and to deflect attention away from the Marine deaths in Lebanon.

CENTRAL AMERICA

Reagan's greatest concern in the Third World was with the civil wars in Central America. The United States gave aid to Honduras and to the brutally repressive right-wing government of El Salvador in the fight against leftist rebels. Most attention, however, was focused on the marxist Sandinista government of Nicaragua. President Carter had tried initially to work with the new government but had reduced aid in protest of the curtailment of individual rights by the Sandinistas. When Reagan became president he declared Nicaragua to be a threat to the United States and to hemispheric stability. The CIA began to provide major assistance to the antigovernment rebels, known as Contras. In 1982 Congress forbade the use of funds for covert operations in Nicaragua, but the CIA ignored this ban. CIA agents even went so far as to place mines in Nicaraguan harbors. This led Congress to outlaw all military assistance to the Contras. The Latin American nations urged a negotiated settlement to the conflict, but Reagan, intent on destroying the Sandinistas, gave little support to these measures.

TERRORISM

Revolutionary groups, aware that they could not directly challenge the might of the United States or the other Western nations, resorted to terrorism as a means of waging war. Terrorist tactics included assassination, kidnapping, hijacking and bombing airliners, and bombing or attacking crowded civilian facilities such as airports. President Reagan took a hard line on terrorism and vowed never to negotiate with terrorists. He also promised to attack any group or nation that could be identified as supporting terrorist activities. In most cases the identity of terrorists could not be discovered, but in 1986 American planes bombed Libya in retaliation for a terrorist attack on a cruise ship in which an American citizen was killed.

THE IRAN-CONTRA SCANDAL

One of Ronald Reagan's chief assets was his image as a friendly and charming man. Many of his advisors, however, displayed a sense of arrogance that led them to disregard the law and engage in practices that benefited themselves personally or promoted their political goals. Several were convicted for criminal activity and others forced to resign their offices. The most blatant and arrogant disregard of the law was exposed in the Iran-Contra scandal.

In 1947 Congress created the National Security Council, a body comprised of top government officials, to advise the president on international affairs. Different presidents treated the NSC differently. Truman and Eisenhower relied on it heavily; Johnson disregarded it. Nixon entrusted foreign affairs to his national security advisor (Henry Kissinger) and ignored the State Department. Reagan made little use of the council itself, but relied heavily upon his national security advisor. The NSC staff, operating out of the White House, assumed a new duty for itself and began to conduct covert operations. In 1985 National Security Advisor Robert McFarlane oversaw a highly convoluted scheme in which military equipment was sold to Iran in an effort to secure the release of Americans held prisoner by Islamic radicals in Lebanon. McFarlane arranged for Israel to sell arms to Iran and for the United States to replace the equipment that Israel sold. This was in direct violation of America's pledge to honor a ban on arms sales to Iran. It also contradicted repeated statements by Reagan that the United States would not negotiate for the release of hostages. The arms were sold at a highly inflated price, which enabled the arms dealers who brokered the deal to make a healthy profit. Colonel Oliver North, an NSC staff member in charge of another illegal activity—raising money for the Contras—arranged to transfer the remaining profits from the Iranian arms sales to the Contras.

When knowledge of this affair became public North and other NSC staff members scrambled to destroy evidence while Reagan and his advisors made a number of misleading statements in an effort to defuse the scandal.

Congressional investigations and criminal proceedings led to the conviction of McFarlane, Admiral John Poindexter (McFarlane's successor as national security advisor), former army general Richard Secord, and Colonel North. Another, and perhaps the key figure in the matter, CIA Director William Casey—a close friend and advisor of Reagan—died shortly after the scandal became known.

President Reagan's involvement in the affair remains unclear. When asked if he knew about a critical memo outlining NSC staff activities, Reagan admitted that he did. After meeting with his advisors, however, he changed his answer and said he did not. When asked again, he replied that he could not remember. During the 1990 trial of John Poindexter, Reagan once again claimed ignorance of the matter and even seemed to be surprised to learn that McFarlane had gone to jail for his role in the affair. In any case, the scandal reflected poorly on Reagan. Either he did approve of the illegal arms sales and diversion of funds or else he had no knowledge of what was going on in his administration.

SOVIET-AMERICAN RELATIONS

During his first term Reagan took a very hard line against the Soviets, accusing them of being the source of all the problems in the world. To offset a supposed military advantage enjoyed by the Soviets, the Reagan administration engaged in a massive increase in both nuclear and conventional weapons. Reagan and his advisors put special emphasis on nuclear weapons, including the proposed Strategic Defense Initiative, an elaborate and largely unworkable system of space-based surveillance equipment and weapons. They even suggested that the United States could win a nuclear war if it were properly armed. During his second term Reagan, under attack from a growing antinuclear movement both in the United States and abroad, began to moderate his language. He even claimed that he had always been a strong proponent of arms reduction.

Relations with the Russians improved dramatically in 1985 when Mikhail Gorbachev came to power as the Soviet head of state. The Soviet Union was beset by extensive internal problems, and Gorbachev decided that he needed peace with the Western nations in order to concentrate on solving his problems at home. Gorbachev and Reagan met in 1985 and again in 1986. These meetings, although congenial, had no concrete results. In 1987 the two met once more and signed a nuclear arms reduction treaty. The weapons in question constituted only a minute portion of the Soviet and American arsenals. The feeling of good will that accompanied these meetings suggested, however, that an end to the nuclear arms race and the long-standing hostility between the two countries was possible.

**Continued
Republican
Dominance**

Ronald Reagan coasted to an easy victory in the 1984 presidential election. His personal charm and his message of a strong America continued to appeal to voters. His reelection was also the result of a weak and badly divided Democratic party. During the 1960s and 1970s the Democratic party had become an alliance of liberals and minorities and, as such, lacked a leader or issue that could unite it and provide a program that would appeal to a wide spectrum of the American public. The Democratic candidate, Walter Mondale—a long-term senator and vice-president under Carter—suffered a devastating defeat. Reagan carried every state except Minnesota (Mondale's home) and the District of Columbia (see Appendix B). The most noteworthy aspect of Mondale's campaign was his vice-presidential candidate: Geraldine Ferraro, a member of Congress from New York and the first woman to run for such a high office for a major party.

The Republicans also won the presidency in 1988. Vice-President George Bush, aided by Reagan's popularity and the continuing conservative mood of the country, defeated Massachusetts Governor Michael Dukakis, who was plagued by the continued division within the Democratic ranks and by a poorly run campaign (see Appendix B). Republican dominance was not absolute, however, for the Democrats recaptured the majority in the Senate in 1986 and continued to control the House of Representatives.

SOCIAL MOVEMENTS AND GROUPS

**Conservative
Movements**

RELIGIOUS FUNDAMENTALISM

Christian fundamentalism was the most notable conservative social movement of the 1980s. A large number of people, distressed by the tension of the 1960s and bewildered by the rapid changes in modern society, found solace in the simple, direct message of fundamentalist teaching and by the sense of community offered by religious congregations. A distinguishing feature of this religious revival was that it was overtly political and right-wing. At the head of the movement was a cadre of television evangelists who urged their audiences to become politically active on behalf of candidates who espoused the values of conservative Christianity and issues such as prayer in public school, an end to abortion, and the teaching of creationism. The most prominent of these evangelists was Jerry Falwell, whose organization, the Moral Majority, became a major force in the candidacy of Ronald Reagan. These religious leaders remained powerful throughout most of the decade. Their influence began to wane in the late 1980s, however, a decline that was underscored by the downfall of popular evangelist Jim Bakker following revelations of his involvement in a sex scandal and his conviction for fraud.

CONSUMERISM

One of the defining characteristics of the youth movement of the 1960s was a rejection of the materialism of their parents' generation. Young people lived in a state of elective poverty, occupying substandard housing and wearing plain and sometimes shabby clothing. The 1980s, by way of contrast, celebrated wealth and consumerism. The Reagan administration, with its close ties to the upper class and its ostentatious show of wealth, set the tone. The desire for wealth and personal well-being, the conservatives argued, was the primary source of human motivation. Making money became the great goal, and a master of business administration became the most highly prized college degree. On the business level this spirit was epitomized by corporate raiding: the purchase of a large corporation for the purpose of making a profit not by marketing a product, but by reselling the company and its subsidiaries. The general public, for its part, went on a spending binge. This spending had a positive side, for it helped bring an end to the recession. The downside of this trend was that Americans borrowed heavily to finance their purchases, thereby adding to the country's indebtedness.

THE ABORTION DEBATE

The most divisive and emotional issue of the era was the debate over abortion. In 1973 the Supreme Court, in the landmark *Roe v. Wade* decision, struck down state laws that outlawed abortion. Many people saw this as a positive step, for it gave women another means of birth control in a country where the availability of family planning and contraceptives was uneven. Advocates of abortion saw it as a health measure as well. Women sought abortions whether they were legal or illegal. It was much better, supporters argued, for women to receive safe abortions at approved medical facilities than to risk injury and death from illegal methods.

Opponents, however, advanced a very simple argument: Human life begins at conception, and the abortion of a fetus is murder. While doctors and scientists argued over when human life begins, anti-abortion activists staged mass demonstrations, picketed abortion clinics, and engaged in civil disobedience to draw attention to what they considered a moral wrong. Anti-abortion forces agitated for local and state restrictions on abortion, but their primary goal was a reversal of *Roe* v. *Wade*. Their great hope was that Reagan and Bush would be able to appoint enough conservatives to the Supreme Court to win a new ruling.

The Environmental Movement

One liberal movement that began in the 1960s and continued to flourish was the campaign to protect the earth's environment. As technology improved, humankind's ability to do rapid and irreparable damage to the earth increased. During the 1970s and 1980s the potential for immediate and long-term disaster became more evident. Air pollution from industrial and automotive emissions created respiratory problems for humans, endangered vegetation, and, by damaging the earth's protective ozone layer, threatened the life-supporting environment of the planet. The mining and harvesting of raw materials scarred the earth, threatened the depletion of valuable natural resources and the extinction of entire species of animals, and, like air pollution, endangered the entire ecosystem of the planet. The widespread use of chemicals endangered animals and polluted the air and water; the production and transportation of oil resulted in spills that caused extensive damage; the storage and disposal of no-longer-usable toxic materials became a major health problem.

These problems became so great that government action to control them became essential. The first federal legislation on clean air and water occurred in the mid-1960s as part of the Great Society program. In 1970 President Nixon created the Environmental Protection Agency to coordinate government environmental policy. Over the next twenty years federal and state governments set emissions standards for industry and automobiles, regulated the use and disposal of chemicals, and set standards for water and air quality. President Reagan, in his drive for deregulation, attempted to neutralize the Environmental Protection Agency, the Department of the Interior, and other agencies dealing with conservation and environmental safety. Popular support for environmental issues remained strong, however, and regulation continued despite Reagan's efforts.

Organizations concerned with environmental issues targeted two problems in particular. One was the environmental damage caused by the vast consumption of natural resources in the United States. Environmentalists urged people to reduce consumption and to recycle reusable refuse. Americans were not much interested in curtailing their consumption, but recycling proved to be an increasingly popular alternative. The second and perhaps the greatest concern of environmentalists was the proliferation of nuclear-powered electrical generating plants. Those facilities posed two threats. They produced a large amount of long-lasting radioactive waste, and they posed a serious safety risk. If a major accident occurred at a nuclear power plant, critics noted, the damage would be catastrophic. Proponents of nuclear power argued that it was a safe source of energy and that it provided an alternative to dependence on foreign oil supplies. The evidence for either side was not overwhelming. Nuclear plants produced an increasing amount of electricity across the country without a serious accident, but their safety records were not good. At times half the plants in the country were closed for safety violations. A near disaster occurred at the Three Mile Island plant in eastern Pennsylvania when a mechanical failure produced a large quantity of radioactive water and steam. The operators of the facility prevented a release of any radioactive material into the atmosphere, thereby averting a major catastrophe. The crisis was great enough, however, to accredit fears about the danger of nuclear energy.

Blacks

ADVANCES

During the late 1970s and the 1980s blacks began to consolidate the gains made during the previous decade. The curtailment of discrimination in education and hiring enabled many blacks to establish themselves in business and the professions. It was government and the military, however, that offered the best avenues for advancement. The military proved to be particularly attractive to young black men, for it offered them chances for security, advancement, and self-respect that were not as readily available in the civilian world. The opportunity for black advancement in the military was emphasized when General Colin Powell became head of the joint chiefs of staff.

INVOLVEMENT IN GOVERNMENT

Many blacks found employment in local, state, and federal government and moved into upper management positions. More important was the increasing number of elected black officials. In 1982 over 6,000 blacks held elected office across the country, including mayors in such major cities as Washington, Los Angeles, Chicago, Detroit, and New York. In both 1984 and 1988 Jesse Jackson, a noted civil rights activist, made an impressive showing in his campaign for the Democratic nomination for president. No black was a candidate for a major party for president or vice-president, but blacks did serve as members of the president's cabinet. Robert Weaver, the first black to hold a cabinet post, served as secretary of housing and urban development under Lyndon Johnson from 1966 to 1969. Nixon did not appoint any black department heads, but Ford did. Since 1975 there has been a black in every cabinet. Blacks held other high-level appointments as well. Thurgood Marshall, an attorney for the NAACP (he argued the *Brown* v. *Board of Education* case before the Supreme Court), became a justice of the Supreme Court in 1967. Civil rights leader Andrew Young served as ambassador to the United Nations under Carter, and General Powell was national security advisor to President Reagan before joining the joint chiefs of staff.

POVERTY

Unfortunately, the decline of black fortunes was as remarkable as the gains. The economic reverses of the 1970s and 1980s and the decline of American manufacturing were particularly hard on blacks. Black unemployment remained high—usually double the rate for whites—and in 1986 42 percent of black families were living in poverty, an increase of 8 percent over 1981. Severe social problems also remained. Infant disease and mortality, unemployment, substandard housing, crime, school dropouts, drug abuse, and alcoholism plagued the black community. During the late 1980s homicides resulting from gang warfare and drug dealing reached epidemic proportions among young black men.

AFFIRMATIVE ACTION

The leading political issue relating to blacks during the 1980s was affirmative action, a program began in the 1960s to assure that blacks and other minorities had access to education, hiring, and promotion. During the 1980s conservatives argued that affirmative action was unjust and counterproductive. They claimed that affirmative action, by its very nature, established a system of quotas that favored minorities. This created injustice by establishing reverse discrimination, which disqualified whites because of their race. It also hurt the country, they argued, by giving less talented people precedence over the more qualified. Supporters of the program insisted that continued economic and educational inequality made affirmative action necessary to insure that minorities had access to educational institutions, jobs, and advancement.

Women

EMPLOYMENT OPPORTUNITIES

Women, like blacks, found many new employment opportunities in the 1970s and 1980s. The number of women in management, business, law, medicine, and other professions increased dramatically. Even such male-dominated areas as the clergy and the military opened up; some churches allowed women to be ordained, and women were given a greater role in the military, including admission to the service academies. The most prominent advances came in government. Sandra O'Connor's appointment to the Supreme Court in 1981, Geraldine Ferraro's candidacy for vice-president on the Democratic ticket in 1984, and the regular appointment of women to cabinet positions revealed a new willingness to accept women in positions of high leadership. Women had served in the cabinet in previous administrations—Frances Perkins (the first woman to head a federal department) served as secretary of labor throughout Franklin Roosevelt's presidency, and Oveta Hobby served as Eisenhower's secretary of health, education and welfare from 1953 to 1955—but regular appointments did not begin until 1975 when Gerald Ford appointed Carla Hills secretary of housing and urban development. Carter and Reagan both had three women in their cabinets, and Bush appointed two. Other high appointments included Jeanne Kirkpatrick's assignment as American ambassador to the United Nations.

Several states elected women governors, and a number of cities had women mayors and council members.

These high-level positions indicated a change in attitude toward women in leadership positions. Equally important was the increasing number of jobs available to women. This resulted from the integration of women into almost all avenues of employment and from changes in the economy. The shift from an industrial to a service economy created many new jobs that were considered suitable for women. The increasing importance of office and retail work offered women new chances for employment and advancement. Women also benefited from affirmative-action programs.

JOB-RELATED PROBLEMS

All was not as rosy as it seems at first, however. Many of these new jobs were considered menial or semi-skilled and were low paying. Discrimination also remained a problem. On average, women were paid considerably less than men for comparable work. And despite the increased visibility of women in high-level positions, the upper echelons of management remained the almost exclusive domain of men. Another major problem of the workplace was sexual harassment. Many women discovered, to their dismay, that their new-found professionalism did not protect them from the unwanted sexual advances of their male colleagues or, worse, from their bosses.

FAMILY

By 1988 over 50 percent of the women in the United States worked outside the home. Among mothers, almost half of those who had preschool-age children had jobs. The entry of so many women into the work force affected the way they thought about families. Control of reproduction became critical. Women demanded better access to all forms of contraception, they limited the number of children they bore, and many of them delayed child-bearing until later in life. Child care also became an issue. Child-care centers proliferated, with many of them being sponsored by employers. Interestingly, as more jobs became available to women, and as women became more comfortable in the workplace, the old tension between women holding jobs and those who stayed at home diminished. Staying home and raising children became a career choice like any other job; indeed, many working women took time off from their jobs to be with their small children. In many businesses extended maternity leave became a normal fringe benefit.

One aspect of the new independence of women that had both good and bad features was the increase in divorce. As women became more economically independent they showed less willingness to remain in unhappy marriages. In 1980 there were 1.2 million divorces—one divorce for every two marriages that year. Divorce proved to be a viable solution for adults to a discordant marriage, but the impact of the high divorce rate on children—the tension of divorce, living with a single working parent, living with a stepparent in case of remarriage—is not yet known.

THE EQUAL RIGHTS AMENDMENT

The great disparity between the rights of men and the rights of women convinced many people that a constitutional amendment was necessary to end this inequality. In 1972 Congress passed a proposed amendment to the Constitution that stated "Equality of rights under the law shall not be denied or abridged by the United States or any state on account of sex." Thirty-five states quickly ratified the amendment; thirty-eight were needed for passage. During the late 1970s and early 1980s ratification of the Equal Rights Amendment (ERA) became the primary goal of the women's movement. As the country turned toward conservatism, however, opposition increased. The opposing sides fought a bitter battle for several years, but by 1982 it was clear that the amendment would not win ratification.

Asians and Hispanics

ASIANS

The 1970s and 1980s saw a huge flow of Asian immigrants into the United States. Millions of Filipinos, Chinese, Koreans, Vietnamese, Cambodians, Indians, and other Asians fled the turmoil and poverty of their homelands. Abetted by a new immigration law (passed in 1965) that allowed an increased number of Asian immigrants, these people resettled in the United States. Most Asian immigrants adapted easily to their new country. They were, for the most part, educated, and many of them had some money. The Asian immigrants possessed a strong entrepreneurial spirit, and many of them were successful at starting small businesses.

MEXICAN FARM WORKERS

Hispanic immigrants, on the other hand, had a much harder time. For years Mexicans had been entering the United States to work as farm laborers in the southwest. Most of these workers entered the country illegally, but their labor was needed, and officials did little to stop them. Unfortunately, their illegal status and the poverty of their homeland made them vulnerable to exploitation by their American employers. Mexican farm workers received horribly low wages and lived in shacks in what frequently amounted to prison camps. In the 1960s these migrant farm workers began to unionize and after a long struggle won recognition.

CENTRAL AMERICAN IMMIGRANTS

The political turmoil in Central America in the 1980s added to the flow of immigrants from the south. Millions of Hispanics fled the war, poverty, and oppression of their native countries and used the illegal networks established by Mexican migrant workers to enter the United States. Conditions in the United States were not always better, however. Like millions of immigrants before them, the Hispanics settled in large cities in hope of finding jobs. Once there they encountered the problems faced by all immigrants before them, including the many Puerto Ricans and Cubans who had been migrating to the United States since the 1950s and 1960s: menial labor, overcrowded and overpriced housing, a foreign language, and an already racially tense atmosphere. Hispanic immigrants in New York, Washington, Miami, Los Angeles, and a host of other cities found themselves at odds with whites and blacks alike.

Table 11.1. Immigration to the United States, 1971–1988			
1971	370,000	1980	531,000
1972	385,000	1981	597,000
1973	400,000	1982	594,000
1974	395,000	1983	560,000
1975	386,000	1984	544,000
1976	399,000	1985	570,000
1977	462,000	1986	602,000
1978	601,000	1987	602,000
1979	460,000	1988	643,000

Table 11.2. Immigration from selected Asian nations, 1971–1988			
	1971–1980	1981–1988	Total
Philippines	360,200	374,500	734,700
Korea	272,000	272,300	544,300
China	202,500	295,500	498,000
Vietnam	179,000	314,900	493,900
India	176,800	200,000	376,800
Iran	46,200	108,600	154,800
Cambodia	8,400	105,300	113,700
All Asia	**1,633,800**	**2,166,700**	**3,800,500**

IMMIGRATION POLICY

The government, for its part, did not know what to do with an influx of millions of illegal aliens. Immigration policy was confused and unevenly enforced. Immigrants from Nicaragua could gain entry as political refugees, but Salvadorans and Hondurans fleeing the death squads and civil wars of their countries could not. Immigration officers played hide and seek with people crossing the Mexican border but lacked the ability stop the flow of illegal entrants. A 1986 law granted amnesty to illegal aliens who had been in the country since 1982 and imposed penalties on employers who hired illegal aliens.

The Gay Rights Movement

The most controversial movement of the 1980s was the gay rights movement. Homosexuals, following the lead of other minority groups, began to organize in the late 1960s and demand rights long denied to them. Gay men and women wanted to be able to express their sexuality openly and end the many legal restrictions against them. They also sought equal access to employment and promotion. Gays came from all walks of life and all levels of society. The age-old taboos against homosexuality remained strong—particularly among religious fundamentalists—and opposition to gay rights persisted.

Gays found themselves confronted with a new problem with the outbreak in 1981 of AIDS (acquired immune deficiency syndrome). AIDS attacked men and women, heterosexual and homosexual alike. A high incidence of the disease among gay men, however, made it an issue of special concern for them. During the 1980s much gay activism centered on demands for better medical care and more money for research to find a cure. The disease also spread among intravenous drug users and their children. By 1988 over 50,000 people had died from the disease and a reported 100,000 were infected with it.

*T*he shift to conservatism manifested itself in many ways: twelve years of conservative presidents; the defeat of the Equal Rights Amendment; verbal assaults on big government and the liberal policies of the past; a renewed commitment to an aggressive American role in world affairs. For all that, the conservatism of the 1980s was relative. Despite their rhetoric and despite the ardent wishes of many of their supporters, Carter and Reagan were not able to reduce the size of the federal government nor undo the social and economic legislation of the previous two decades. Indeed, the federal bureaucracy grew during their administrations, and demands on the government necessitated the creation of three new departments during Carter's presidency.

Nor were the conservatives successful in their efforts to roll back the social changes experienced by the country. They were able to defeat the ERA, but there was little they could do about the new roles that blacks, *women, and other minorities assumed in American society. They could condemn the antipoverty programs of the Great Society as failures, but by 1988 it was clear that conservative remedies for poverty did not work very well either.*

Foreign policy followed this same pattern. Strong anticommunist rhetoric, massive arms buildup, and foreign intervention were hallmarks of conservative policy. At the same time, a post-Vietnam cautiousness permeated American foreign policy. Even in his most aggressive actions, Reagan was careful to avoid committing the United States to a confrontation that could not be easily won or quickly terminated. The American people generally supported Reagan's foreign policy, but there was enough opposition—especially to American involvement in Central America—to remind the government that the country's citizens would not tolerate another ill-advised foreign war.

Selected Readings

Arnson, Cynthia. *Crossroads: Congress, the Reagan Administration and Central America* (1989)

Bill, James. *The Eagle and the Lion: The Tragedy of American-Iranian Relations* (1988)

Cannon, Lou. *President Reagan: The Role of a Lifetime* (1991)

Hargrove, Erwin. *Jimmy Carter as President: Leadership and the Politics of the Public Good* (1989)

Epilogue: The Challenge of the 1990s

It is trite to say that the twentieth century was a time of great, rapid, and unforeseen change, for this was true of most centuries. The year 1890 was as different from 1800 as 1990 was from 1900, and the steamboat and railroad were as revolutionary to the nineteenth century as the automobile and airplane were to more recent times. Nevertheless, the United States underwent tremendous change during the twentieth century. Not even the most visionary proponent of the United States as a world power could have imagined in 1900 the power of the United States in 1990. Nor could the most ardent reformer have envisioned the social changes that occurred. Multiple-warhead intercontinental ballistic missiles and black female police officers would have been inconceivable to them. From the viewpoint of 1991 these things are everyday facts of life.

In reviewing the past ninety years there is much to be proud of and much that could have been done better. The United States maintained an exceptionally high standard of living and continued to be a bastion of liberty and freedom. At the same time, Americans did not always live up to their high ideals in their treatment of other nations or in their treatment of each other. The present task is to study the past so that the nation can continue its successes and avoid the repetition of failures.

This is no easy task, for old challenges persist and new ones arise daily. At home, the perennial problems of poverty, racism, and discrimination continue to plague the United States. Great and good things were accomplished during the century, but liberty, equality, and economic security for all remains an unfulfilled goal.

On the international scene, opportunity seems to beckon. The revolutionary changes in the Soviet Union, the collapse of communist power in Eastern Europe, the reunification of Germany, and the removal of the Berlin Wall—the symbol of the division between East and West—indicate an improvement in worldwide foreign relations. The changes are not completely positive, however, for the decline of communist power unleashed a host of economic, ethnic, and territorial problems in the Soviet Union and Eastern Europe that need to be resolved. These changes in eastern Europe and the possibility of a quasi-union of the Western European nations pose a challenge to the economic and diplomatic future of the United States.

Changes in other parts of the globe present new challenges as well. The easing of political tension in Africa, southeast Asia, and Latin America is a positive sign, but grave social and economic problems—particularly extreme poverty—provide a continual threat to peace and stability. A more direct challenge is the rising economic power of Japan, Korea, and other Asian nations, especially in light of America's declining industrial base and other economic problems. The Middle East remains volatile and continues to pose a potential threat. The United States scored an impressive victory over Iraq in the Persian Gulf war, but the animosity that exists among the various ethnic, religious, and political groups is a severe problem in a region that is of great strategic importance to the United States.

Equally challenging is the growing possibility of worldwide environmental catastrophe. Ozone depletion, deforestation, global warming, overpopulation, famine, and the spreading AIDS epidemic are issues as serious as any geopolitical problem.

In 1989 the United States began its third century as a nation. During the first two hundred years it wrestled with a host of problems: establishing a new government, preserving national unity during a bitter civil war, fighting a number of popular and unpopular wars, resolving a variety of economic and social problems. Throughout its history the United States has been able to rise to the many challenges confronting it, although there have been many false steps and failures along the way. The world of the 1990s is not the world of the 1790s or the 1890s, and we cannot hope to duplicate the world of the past. The lessons of history are there to learn, however. Let us hope we learn them.

Appendix A

Presidential Profiles: 1901–1991

WILLIAM MCKINLEY (REPUBLICAN)

1843	Born in Niles, Ohio
1861–1865	Serves in Union Army
1867	Begins to practice law in Canton, Ohio
1877–1882; 1885–1890	Member, U. S. House of Representatives from Ohio
1892–1895	Serves two terms as governor of Ohio
1897–1901	First term as president of the United States
1901	Second term as president
1901	Assassinated in Buffalo, New York

THEODORE ROOSEVELT (REPUBLICAN)

1858	Born in New York City
1880	Graduates from Harvard University
1882–1884	Member, New York State Assembly
1886	Unsuccessful candidate for mayor of New York
1889–1895	U.S. civil service commissioner
1895–1897	Police commissioner of New York City
1897–1898	Under–secretary of the navy

1898   Colonel, 1st U.S. Volunteer Cavalry; sees action against Spanish in Cuba

1899–1900   Governor of New York

1901   Vice-president of the United States

1901–1905   First term as president of the United States

1905–1909   Second term as president

1906   Wins the Nobel Peace Prize

1912   Unsuccessful candidate for president of the Progressive party

1912   Wounded in assassination attempt

1919   Dies

WILLIAM HOWARD TAFT (REPUBLICAN)

1857   Born in Cincinnati, Ohio

1878   Graduates from Yale University

1880   Begins to practice law in Cincinnati

1887–1889   Judge of state court of appeals

1892–1900   Federal judge

1900   President of Philippine Government Commission

1901–1904   Governor of the Philippine Islands

1904–1908   Secretary of war

1909–1913   President of the United States

1912   Unsuccessful candidate for reelection to the presidency

1913–1921   Professor of law at Yale University

1921–1930   Chief justice of the United States

1930   Dies

WOODROW WILSON (DEMOCRAT)

1856   Born in Staunton, Virginia

1879   Graduates from Princeton University

1886   Receives Ph.D. from Johns Hopkins University

1885–1902   University professor: Bryn Mawr College, 1885–1888; Wesleyan College, 1888–1890; Princeton University, 1890–1902

1902–1910   President of Princeton University

1911–1912   Governor of New Jersey

1913–1917   First term as president of the United States

1917–1921   Second term as president of the United States

1919   Suffers a stroke

1920   Receives Nobel Peace Prize

1924   Dies

WARREN G. HARDING (REPUBLICAN)

1865   Born in Corsica, Ohio

1884   Becomes owner and editor of Marion (Ohio) *Star*

1900–1904   Member, Ohio State Senate

1904–1906   Lieutenant governor of Ohio

1910   Loses election for governor of Ohio

1915–1921   U.S. senator from Ohio

1921–1923   President of the United States

1923   Dies in San Francisco

CALVIN COOLIDGE (REPUBLICAN)

1872   Born in Plymouth, Vermont

1895   Graduates from Amherst College

1897   Admitted to bar in Northampton, Massachusetts

1907–1908   Member, Massachusetts General Court

1910–1911   Mayor of Northampton

1912–1915   Member, Massachusetts State Senate

1916–1918   Lieutenant governor of Massachusetts

1919–1920   Governor of Massachusetts

1921–1923   Vice-president of the United States

1923–1925   First term as president of the United States

1925–1929   Second term as president

1933   Dies

HERBERT HOOVER (REPUBLICAN)

1874   Born in West Branch, Iowa

1895   Graduates from Stanford University; embarks on career as mining engineer

1914–1918   Chairman, American Relief Committee

Chairman, Commission for Relief in Belgium

Chairman, U.S. Food Administration

1921–1928   Secretary of commerce

1929–1933	President of the United States
1947–1949:	Chairman, Commission on Organization of the Executive Branch
1953–1955	
1964	Dies

FRANKLIN D. ROOSEVELT (DEMOCRAT)

1882	Born in Hyde Park, New York
1904	Graduates from Harvard
1907	Graduates from Columbia Law School; begins to practice law in New York City
1911–1913	Member, New York State Senate
1913–1920	Assistant secretary of the navy
1920	Unsuccessful candidate for vice-president
1921	Stricken with polio
1929–1932	Serves two terms as governor of New York
1933	Escapes an assassination attempt without injury
1933–1937	First term as president of the United States
1937–1941	Second term as president
1941–1945	Third term as president
1945	Begins fourth term as president
1945	Dies at Warm Springs, Georgia

HARRY S TRUMAN (DEMOCRAT)

1884	Born in Lamar, Missouri
1906–1917	Farmer
1917–1919	Officer in U.S. Army
1922–1934	County judge
1935–1945	U.S. senator from Missouri
1945	Vice-president of the United States
1945–1949	First term as president of the United States
1949–1953	Second term as president
1950	Uninjured in an assassination attempt
1972	Dies

DWIGHT D. EISENHOWER (REPUBLICAN)

1890	Born in Denison, Texas

1915	Graduates from the U.S. Military Academy
1942–1945	Commander of U.S. forces in Europe
1944–1945	Commander of Allied forces in Europe
1945–1948	Chief of staff of the army
1948–1951	President of Columbia University
1952	Commander of Allied forces in Europe
1953–1957	First term as president of the United States
1957–1961	Second term as president
1969	Dies

JOHN F. KENNEDY (DEMOCRAT)

1917	Born in Brookline, Massachusetts
1940	Graduates from Harvard
1941–1945	Officer in U.S. Navy
1947–1953	Member, U.S. House of Representatives from Massachusetts
1953–1961	U.S. senator from Massachusetts
1957	Pulitzer Prize for *Profiles in Courage*
1961–1963	President of the United States
1963	Assassinated in Dallas, Texas

LYNDON B. JOHNSON (DEMOCRAT)

1908	Born near Stonewall, Texas
1930	Graduates from Southwest State Teachers College
1930–1932	Schoolteacher in Houston, Texas
1935–1937	State director, National Youth Administration
1937–1949	Member, U.S. House of Representatives from Texas
1949–1961	U.S. senator from Texas
1953–1955	Senate minority leader
1955–1961	Senate majority leader
1961–1963	Vice-president of the United States
1963–1965	First term as president of the United States
1965–1969	Second term as president
1973	Dies

RICHARD NIXON (REPUBLICAN)

1913	Born in Yorba Linda, California
1934	Graduates from Whittier College
1937	Graduates from Duke Law School
1937–1942	Attorney in Whittier, California
1942–1946	Officer in U.S. Navy
1947–1951	Member, U.S. House of Representatives from California
1951–1953	U.S. senator from California
1953–1957	First term as vice-president of the United States
1957–1961	Second term as vice-president
1960	Defeated in election for president
1962	Defeated in election for governor of California
1963–1968	Attorney in New York City
1969–1973	First term as president of the United States
1973–1974	Second term as president
1974	Resigned from the presidency
1974	Receives complete presidential pardon for any offenses he may have committed while president

GERALD FORD (REPUBLICAN)

1913	Born in Omaha, Nebraska
1935	Graduates from University of Michigan
1941	Graduates from Yale Law School
1941–1945	Officer in U.S. Navy
1949–1972	Member, U.S. House of Representatives from Michigan
1973	Appointed vice-president of the United States
1974–1977	President of the United States
1975	Uninjured in two assassination attempts
1976	Defeated for reelection to the presidency

JIMMY CARTER (DEMOCRAT)

1924	Born in Plains, Georgia
1946	Graduates from the United States Naval Academy
1946–1953	Officer in U.S. Navy
1953–1971	Farmer in Plains, Georgia

1962–1966	Member, Georgia State Senate
1966	Unsuccessful candidate for governor of Georgia
1971–1974	Governor of Georgia
1977–1981	President of the United States
1980	Defeated for reelection to presidency

RONALD REAGAN (REPUBLICAN)

1911	Born in Tampico, Illinois
1932	Graduates from Eureka College
1932–1937	Radio sports broadcaster
1937–1967	Actor
1964	Unsuccessful candidate for governor of California
1967–1974	Serves two terms as governor of California
1981–1985	First term as president of the United States
1981	Wounded in assassination attempt
1985–1989	Second term as president

GEORGE BUSH (REPUBLICAN)

1924	Born in Milton, Massachusetts
1948	Graduates from Yale University
1942–1945	Officer in U.S. Navy
1948–1966	Oil company executive
1964	Unsuccessful candidate for U. S. Senate
1967–1971	Member, House of Representatives from Texas
1970	Unsuccessful candidate for U. S. Senate
1971–1973	Ambassador to the United Nations
1973–1974	Chairman of the Republican National Committee
1974–1975	Liaison officer to China
1976–1977	Director of the CIA
1981–1985	First term as vice-president of the United States
1985–1989	Second term as vice-president
1989–	President of the United States

Appendix B

Presidential Elections: 1900–1988

MINOR PARTIES

Throughout the history of the United States, presidential elections have been dominated by the two-party system. Occasionally third parties have been important—in the twentieth century the Socialist party fielded a major candidate in the elections of the first two decades, as did the Progressive party in 1912 and 1924, the States Rights party in 1948, and the American Independent party in 1968—but with the exception of the 1912 election, the two major parties have far and away outpolled any other candidates. In every election, however, a number of smaller parties have run candidates for the presidency. These were, for the most part, small regional and special interest parties. Their continual presence reminds us that the political spectrum in the United States extends beyond the Democrats and the Republicans, and that no matter how overwhelmingly dominant the two leading parties are, there is a considerable number of people outside the mainstream of American politics willing to support these dissident groups.

The presence of these candidates can also indicate trends within the electorate. During the late nineteenth and early twentieth centuries voters in the southern states gave their allegiance to the Democratic party. In 1944 the first signs of a revolt against the Democrats appeared when voters in several states refused to support Franklin Roosevelt. This revolt continued through the 1950s and 1960s as the Democrats became identified as the patrons of civil rights and other liberal causes. It culminated in 1964 when Barry Goldwater carried six southern states and in 1968 with the candidacy of George Wallace on the American Independent ticket. The defection of conservative southerners to the Republican Party after 1972 confirmed this trend.

ROLE OF THE STATES

The states play a key role in the election of the president. State officials manage the elections and count the votes. State delegations meet at national conventions and select the candidates for the major parties. State officials set the qualifications that determine which minor-party candidates will appear on the ballot. Most important, the states elect the president. The winner of the most votes in a state receives—with an occasional exception— all the electoral votes of that state. The number of votes a state receives is determined by its population. It is possible, although it has not happened in the twentieth century, for the candidate with the highest popular vote nationwide not to receive a majority of the electoral vote and not to become president. It is also possible, because of the apportionment of electoral votes, that a candidate can carry a majority of the states but not receive a majority of the electoral vote. This happened in 1960 (Nixon carried twenty-four states and Kennedy twenty-two) and in 1976 (Ford won twenty-seven, Carter twenty-four).

POPULAR ELECTORAL STATES

		Popular Vote	Electoral Vote	States Carried
1900	William McKinley, Republican	7,218,039	292	28
	William Jennings Bryan, Democrat	6,358,345	155	17
	John Wooley, Prohibition	209,004		
	Eugene Debs, Socialist	86,935		
	Wharton Barker, People's	50,340		
	Joseph Malloney, Socialist Labor	40,900		
	Seth Ellis, Union Reform	5,693		
	Other	1,214		

		Popular Vote	Electoral Vote	States Carried
1904	Theodore Roosevelt, Republican	7,626,593	336	32
	Alton Parker, Democrat	5,082,898	140	13
	Eugene Debs, Socialist	402,489		
	Silas Swallow, Prohibition	258,596		
	Thomas Watson, People's	114,051		
	Charles Corregan, Socialist Labor	33,156		
	Other	1,181		
1908	William Howard Taft, Republican	7,676,258	321	29
	William Jennings Bryan, Democrat	6,406,801	162	17
	Eugene Debs, Socialist	420,380		
	Eugene Chafin, Prohibition	252,821		
	Thomas Hisgen, Independence	82,537		
	Thomas Watson, People's	28,376		
	August Gilhaus, Socialist Labor	14,018		
	Other	1,482		
1912	Woodrow Wilson, Democrat	6,293,152	435	40
	Theodore Roosevelt, Progressive	4,119,207	88	6
	William Howard Taft, Republican	3,486,333	8	2
	Eugene Debs, Socialist	900,369		
	Eugene Chafin, Prohibition	207,972		
	Arthur Reimer, Socialist Labor	29,374		
	Other	4,556		
1916	Woodrow Wilson, Democrat	9,126,300	277	30
	Charles Evans Hughes, Republican	8,546,789	254	18
	Allen Benson, Socialist	589,924		
	J. Frank Hanly, Prohibition	221,030		
	Progressive—Unspecified	35,234		
	Arthur Reimer, Socialist Labor	15,284		
	Other	461		

		Popular Vote	Electoral Vote	States Carried
1920	Warren Harding, Republican	16,133,314	404	37
	James Cox, Democrat	9,140,884	127	11
	Eugene Debs, Socialist	913,664		
	Parley Christensen, Farmer Labor	264,540		
	Aaron Watkins, Prohibition	188,391		
	James Ferguson, American	47,812		
	William Cox, Socialist Labor	30,418		
	Black and Tan Republican—Unspecified	27,198		
	Robert Macauley, Single Tax	5,690		
	Other	1,875		
1924	Calvin Coolidge, Republican	15,717,553	382	35
	John Davis, Democrat	8,386,169	136	12
	Robert LaFollette, Progressive	4,814,050	13	1
	Herman Faris, Prohibition	54,833		
	William Foster, Workers	38,080		
	Frank Johns, Socialist Labor	28,368		
	Gilbert Nations, American	24,215		
	Socialist—Unspecified	5,134		
	William Wallace, Single Tax	2,919		
	Other	4,638		
1928	Herbert Hoover, Republican	21,411,991	444	40
	Alfred Smith, Democrat	15,000,185	87	8
	Norman Thomas, Socialist	266,453		
	William Foster, Workers	48,170		
	William Varney, Prohibition	34,489		
	Verne Reynolds, Socialist Labor	21,608		
	Frank Webb, Farmer Labor	6,390		
	Other	1,078		
1932	Franklin Roosevelt, Democrat	22,825,016	472	42
	Herbert Hoover, Republican	15,758,397	59	6
	Norman Thomas, Socialist	883,990		
	William Foster, Workers	102,221		

	Popular Vote	Electoral Vote	States Carried
William Upshaw, Prohibition	81,916		
William Harvey, Liberty	53,199		
Verne Reynolds, Socialist Labor	34,028		
Jacob Coxey, Farmer Labor	7,431		
Other	3,184		
1936 Franklin Roosevelt, Democrat	27,747,636	523	46
Alfred Landon, Republican	16,679,543	8	2
William Lemke, Union	892,492		
Norman Thomas, Socialist	187,785		
Earl Browder, Communist	79,211		
D. Leigh Colvin, Prohibition	37,668		
John Aiken, Socialist Labor	12,790		
Other	5,178		
1940 Franklin Roosevelt, Democrat	27,263,448	449	38
Wendell Willkie, Republican	22,336,260	82	10
Norman Thomas, Socialist	116,827		
Roger Babson, Prohibition	58,625		
Earl Browder, Communist	48,548		
John Aiken, Socialist Labor	14,883		
Other	1,792		
1944 Franklin Roosevelt, Democrat	25,611,936	432	36
Thomas Dewey, Republican	22,013,372	99	12
Texas Regulars—Unspecified	135,411		
Norman Thomas, Socialist	79,000		
Claude Watson, Prohibition	74,733		
Edward Teichert, Socialist Labor	45,179		
Southern Democrat—Unspecified	7,799		
Independent Democrat	4,016		
1948 Harry Truman, Democrat	24,105,587	303	28
Thomas Dewey, Republican	21,970,017	189	16
Strom Thurmond, States Rights	1,169,134	39	4
Henry A. Wallace, Progressive	1,157,057		

		Popular Vote	Electoral Vote	States Carried
	Norman Thomas, Socialist	138,973		
	Claude Watson, Prohibition	103,489		
	Edward Teichert, Socialist Labor	29,038		
	Farrell Dobbs, Socialist Worker	13,614		
	Other	5,533		
1952	Dwight Eisenhower, Republican	33,936,137	442	39
	Adlai Stevenson, Democrat	27,314,649	89	9
	Vincent Hallinan, Progressive	140,416		
	Stuart Hamblen, Prohibition	73,413		
	Eric Hass, Socialist Labor	30,250		
	Darlington Hoopes, Socialist	20,065		
	Douglas MacArthur, Constitution	17,205		
	Farrell Dobbs, Socialist Worker	10,312		
	Henry Krajewski, Poor Man's	4,203		
	Other	4,473		
1956	Dwight Eisenhower, Republican	35,585,245	457	41
	Adlai Stevenson, Democrat	26,030,172	73	7
	Walter Jones, Democrat		1	
	Unpledged to candidate	153,352		
	T. Coleman Andrews, Constitution	108,055		
	Eric Hass, Socialist Labor	44,300		
	Independent—Unspecified	42,961		
	Enoch Holtwick, Prohibition	41,937		
	Farrell Dobbs, Socialist Worker	7,797		
	Harry Byrd, States Rights	2,657		
	Darlington Hoopes, Socialist	2,044		
	Henry Krajewski, American Third Party	1,829		
	Other	5,023		
1960	John Kennedy, Democrat	34,221,344	303	22
	Richard Nixon, Republican	34,106,671	219	26
	Orval Faubus, States Rights	214,541		
	Harry Byrd, Democrat	116,248	15	2
	Eric Hass, Socialist Labor	47,522		

		Popular Vote	Electoral Vote	States Carried
	Rutherford Decker, Prohibition	44,087		
	Farrell Dobbs, Socialist Worker	40,166		
	Charles Sullivan, Constitutional	18,170		
	J. Bracken Lee, Conservative	8,708		
	C. Benton Coiner, Conservative	4,204		
	Other	7,299		
1964	Lyndon Johnson, Democrat	43,126,584	486	45
	Barry Goldwater, Republican	27,177,838	52	6
	Unpledged Democrats	210,732		
	Eric Hass, Socialist Labor	45,187		
	Clifton DeBerry, Socialist Worker	32,701		
	E. Harold Munn, Prohibition	23,266		
	John Kasper, States Rights	6,953		
	Joseph Lightburn, Constitution	5,060		
	Other	12,783		
1968	Richard Nixon, Republican	31,785,148	301	32
	Hubert Humphrey, Democrat	31,274,503	191	14
	George Wallace, American Independent	9,901,151	46	5
	Hennings Blomen, Socialist Labor	52,591		
	Dick Gregory, Peace and Freedom	47,097		
	Fred Halstead, Socialist Worker	41,390		
	Peace and Freedom—Unspecified	27,887		
	Eugene McCarthy—Unspecified	25,552		
	E. Harold Munn, Prohibition	14,915		
	American Independent Democrat	10,518		
	Eldridge Cleaver, Peace and Freedom	8,736		
	Other	13,882		
1972	Richard Nixon, Republican	47,170,179	520	49
	George McGovern, Democrat	29,171,791	17	2
	John Schmitz, American Independent	1,090,673		
	Benjamin Spock, People's	78,751		
	Louis Fisher, Socialist Labor	53,811		
	Socialist Worker—Unspecified	43,114		

		Popular Vote	Electoral Vote	States Carried
	Linda Jenness, Socialist Worker	37,423		
	Gus Hall, Communist	25,343		
	Evelyn Reed, Socialist Worker	13,878		
	E. Harold Munn, Prohibition	13,505		
	John Hospers, Libertarian	3,671	1	
	Other	25,451		
1976	Jimmy Carter, Democrat	40,830,763	297	24
	Gerald Ford, Republican	39,147,793	240	27
	Ronald Reagan, Republican	1		
	Eugene McCarthy, Independent	756,691		
	Roger MacBride, Libertarian	173,011		
	Lester Maddox, American Independent	170,531		
	Thomas Anderson, American	160,773		
	Peter Camejo, Socialist Worker	91,314		
	Gus Hall, Communist	58,992		
	Margaret Wright, People's	49,024		
	Lyndon Larouche, U.S. Labor	40,043		
	Benjamin Bubar, Prohibition	15,934		
	Jules Levin, Socialist Labor	9,616		
	Frank Zeidler, Socialist	6,038		
	Other	45,366		
1980	Ronald Reagan, Republican	43,904,153	489	44
	Jimmy Carter, Democrat	35,483,883	49	7
	John Anderson, Independent	5,720,060		
	Ed Clark, Libertarian	921,299		
	Barry Commoner, Citizen's	234,294		
	Gus Hall, Communist	45,023		
	John Rarick, American Independent	41,268		
	Clifton DeBerry, Socialist Worker	38,737		
	Ellen McCormack, Right to Life	32,327		
	Maureen Smith, Peace and Freedom	18,116		
	Deidre Griswold, Worker's World	13,300		
	Benjamin Bubar, Statesman	7,212		
	David McReynolds, Socialist	6,898		

	Popular Vote	Electoral Vote	States Carried
Percy Greaves, American	6,647		
Andrew Pulley, Socialist Worker	6,272		
Richard Congress, Socialist Labor	4,029		
Kurt Lynen, Middle Class	3,694		
Other	27,086		
1984 Ronald Reagan, Republican	54,455,074	525	49
Walter Mondale, Democrat	37,577,137	13	2
David Bergland, Libertarian	228,314		
Lyndon LaRouche, Independent Democrat	78,807		
Sonia Johnson, Citizen's	72,200		
Bob Richards, Populist	66,336		
Dennis Serrette, Independent	46,852		
Gus Hall, Communist	36,386		
Mel Mason, Socialist Worker	24,706		
Larry Holmes, Workers World	15,329		
Delmar Dennis, American	13,161		
Ed Winn, Workers League	10,801		
Earl Dodge, Prohibition 4,242			
Other	23,448		
1988 George Bush, Republican	47,946,422	426	40
Michael Dukakis, Democrat	41,016,429	112	11
Lloyd Bentsen, Democrat	1		
Ron Paul, Libertarian	432,179		
Lenora Fulani, New Alliance	217,219		
David Duke, Populist	47,047		
Eugene McCarthy, Consumer	30,905		
Warren Griffin, American Independent	27,818		
Lyndon LaRouche, Independent	25,562		
William Marra, Right to Life	20,504		
Ed Winn, Workers League	18,693		
James Warren, Socialist Worker	15,604		
Herbert Lewin, Peace and Freedom	10,370		
Earl Dodge, Prohibition	8,002		
Larry Holmes, Workers World	7,846		

	Popular Vote	Electoral Vote	States Carried
Willa Kenoyer, Socialist	3,882		
Delmar Dennis, American	3,475		
Other	30,532		

Note: The category "Other" comprises candidates and parties that received fewer than 1,000 votes and votes that could not be awarded positively to any candidate or party.

Source: Congressional Quarterly's Guide to U.S. Elections, 2nd ed. (1985); Richard Scammon and Alice McGillivray, eds., American Votes 18: A Handbook of Contemporary American Election Statistics: 1988 (1989)

Appendix C

Presidential Cabinets: 1901–1991

*O*ver the two hundred years of its existence, the president's cabinet has changed in size and in the duties of its members. These changes reflect the changing role of the federal government in American society, the priorities of the country and of the presidents, and the changing demands of an evolving federal bureaucracy.

GROWTH OF THE CABINET

The first cabinet, organized in 1789, had five members. One hundred years later it had expanded to eight members. It remained that size until 1903 when the number of members increased to nine. In 1989—the two hundredth anniversary of its founding—the cabinet consisted of the vice-president and fourteen department heads. The change was greater than the net increase suggests, for four offices that existed in 1903 were gone in 1989.

New Departments

The first change of the twentieth century was the establishment of the Department of Commerce and Labor in 1903; in 1913 Congress divided Commerce and Labor into two separate departments. The creation of a vast military establishment during World War II led to the next modification. The Department of War (one of the original departments established in 1789) and the Department of the Navy (organized in 1798) were combined in the Department of Defense. The creation of the Department of Health, Education, and Welfare in 1953 reflected the federal government's increasing role in social matters. The pressing problems of the nation's cities necessitated the organization of the Department of Housing and Urban Development in 1966. The Department of Transportation followed in 1967. The establishment of the U. S. Postal Service as a quasigovernmental operation in 1971 led to the removal of the postmaster general from the cabinet. The organization of the Department of Energy occurred in 1977. The federal government's increased role in social welfare matters led to the division of the Department of Health, Education, and Welfare into the Department of Health and Human Services and the Department of Education in 1979. The newest office, the Department of Veteran Affairs, was founded in 1989.

Duties of Department Heads

Advisors to Congress

The duties of the cabinet officers changed as well, reflecting the growth of the government, party politics, and the administrative practices of the various presidents. During the early years of the United States department heads were as much advisors to Congress as they were to the president, for they regularly provided Congress with information necessary to the enactment of laws. This practice still continues, but it has become more political. In the eighteenth and early nineteenth century department heads provided information at Congress's behest. In the twentieth century department heads and their aides presented information to Congress in order to promote the legislative program of the administration.

Administrative Duties

During the twentieth century the federal bureaucracy grew tremendously and with it the department heads' administrative duties. As the federal government increased its involvement in the economic and social affairs of the nation, cabinet officers found themselves responsible for the direction of thousands of employees charged with rendering services to the public. As department heads they were responsible for the formation of policy for and the general management of a specific segment of government operations. Correspondingly, their roles as general advisors to the president decreased.

Advisors to the President

The reliance of the chief executive on his cabinet varied from president to president. During the administrations of Harding and Coolidge, the cabinet dominated the government, setting policy as well as running the business of the nation. This contrasts sharply with Richard Nixon, who, for the most part, excluded his cabinet from any role in formulating central policy, and with Jimmy Carter, who was reluctant to delegate authority on even the most trivial matters. As the century progressed and the business of the government grew, presidents tended to rely on special advisors for the formulation of overall policy and leave the cabinet members to manage their departments.

THE VICE-PRESIDENT

The role of the vice-president has always been, and remains, nebulous. Constitutionally, the vice-president is charged with presiding over the Senate and assuming the duties of the chief executive should the president die or otherwise become unable to continue in office. Harry Truman's ascendancy to the presidency in 1945 and Richard Nixon's nomination as the Republican candidate in 1960 brought a new importance to the vice-presidency. After 1960—and particularly after Lyndon Johnson became president—the vice-president was considered a leading contender for the presidency. Indeed, between 1945 and 1988 every vice-president except Alban Barkley, Spiro Agnew, and Nelson Rockefeller has been either president or a candidate for president. As a result, the vice-president has assumed a new role as cabinet member and presidential advisor. The extent of the vice-president's influence remains unclear and varies from president to president, but it seems to be increasing with each succeeding administration.

CABINET MEMBERS

(Officers are listed according to the creation of their departments)

William McKinley, 1901

Vice-President	Theodore Roosevelt	1901
State	John Hay	1901
Treasury	Lyman Gage	1901
War	Elihu Root	1901
Justice	Philander Knox	1901
Post Office	Charles Smith	1901
Navy	John Long	1901
Interior	Ethan Hitchcock	1901
Agriculture	James Wilson	1901

Theodore Roosevelt, 1901–1909

Vice-President	Vacant	1901–1905
	Charles Fairbanks	1905–1909
State	John Hay	1901–1905
	Elihu Root	1905–1909
	Robert Bacon	1909
Treasury	Lyman Gage	1901–1902
	Leslie Shaw	1902–1907
	George Cortelyou	1907–1909
War	Elihu Root	1901–1904
	William Howard Taft	1904–1908
	Luke Wright	1908–1909
Justice	Philander Knox	1901–1904
	William Moody	1904–1906
	Charles Bonaparte	1906–1909
Post Office	Charles Smith	1901–1902
	Henry Payne	1902–1904
	Robert Wynne	1904–1905
	George Cortelyou	1905–1907
	George Meyer	1907–1909
Navy	John Long	1901–1902
	William Moody	1902–1904
	Paul Morton	1904–1905
	Charles Bonaparte	1905–1906
	Victor Metcalf	1906–1908
	Truman Newberry	1908–1909
Interior	Ethan Hitchcock	1901–1907
	James Garfield	1907–1909
Agriculture	James Wilson	1901–1909
Commerce and Labor	George Cortelytou	1903–1904
	Victor Metcalf	1904–1906
	Oscar Straus	1906–1909
	Charles Nagel	1909

William Howard Taft, 1909–1913

Vice-President	James Sherman	1909–1913
State	Philander Knox	1909–1913
Treasury	Franklin MacVeagh	1909–1913
War	Jacob Dickinson	1909–1911
	Henry Stimson	1911–1913
Justice	George Wickersham	1909–1913
Post Office	Frank Hitchcock	1909–1913
Navy	George Meyer	1909–1913

Interior	Richard Ballinger	1909–1911
	Walter Fisher	1911–1913
Agriculture	James Wilson	1909–1913
Commerce and Labor	Charles Nagel	1909–1913

Woodrow Wilson, 1913–1921

Vice-President	Thomas Marshall	1913–1921
State	William Jennings Bryan	1913–1915
	Robert Lansing	1915–1920
	Bainbridge Colby	1920–1921
Treasury	William McAdoo	1913–1918
	Carter Glass	1918–1920
	David Houston	1920–1921
War	Lindley Garrison	1913–1916
	Newton Baker	1916–1921
Justice	James McReynolds	1913–1914
	Thomas Gregory	1914–1919
	A. Mitchell Palmer	1919–1921
Post Office	Albert Burleson	1913–1921
Navy	Josephus Daniels	1913–1921
Interior	Franklin Lane	1913–1920
	John Payne	1920–1921
Agriculture	David Houston	1913–1920
	Edwin Meredith	1920–1921
Commerce	William Redfield	1913–1919
	Joshua Alexander	1919–1921
Labor	William Wilson	1913–1921

Warren Harding, 1921–1923

Vice-President	Calvin Coolidge	1921–1923
State	Charles Evans Hughes	1921–1923
Treasury	Andrew Mellon	1921–1923
War	John Weeks	1921–1923
Justice	Harry Daugherty	1921–1923
Post Office	Will Hays	1921–1922
	Hubert Work	1922–1923
	Harry New	1923
Navy	Edwin Denby	1921–1923
Interior	Albert Fall	1921–1923
	Hubert Work	1923
Agriculture	Henry C. Wallace	1921–1923
Commerce	Herbert Hoover	1921–1923
Labor	James Davis	1921–1923

Calvin Coolidge, 1923–1929

Vice-President	Vacant	1923–1925
	Charles Dawes	1925–1929
State	Charles Evans Hughes	1923–1925
	Frank Kellogg	1925–1929
Treasury	Andrew Mellon	1923–1929
War	John Weeks	1923–1925
	Dwight Davis	1925–1929
Justice	Harry Daugherty	1923–1924
	Harlan Stone	1924–1925
	John Sargent	1925–1929
Post Office	Harry New	1923–1929
Navy	Edwin Denby	1923–1924
	Curtis Wilbur	1924–1929
Interior	Hubert Work	1923–1928
	Roy West	1928–1929
Agriculture	Henry C. Wallace	1923–1924
	Howard Gore	1924–1925
	William Jardine	1925–1929
Commerce	Herbert Hoover	1923–1928
	William Whiting	1928–1929
Labor	James Davis	1923–1929

Herbert Hoover, 1929–1933

Vice-President	Charles Curtis	1929–1933
State	Henry Stimson	1929–1933
Treasury	Andrew Mellon	1929–1932
	Ogden Mills	1932–1933
War	James Good	1929
	Patrick Hurley	1929–1933
Justice	William Mitchell	1929–1933
Post Office	Walter Brown	1929–1933
Navy	Charles Adams	1929–1933
Interior	Ray Wilbur	1929–1933
Agriculture	Arthur Hyde	1929–1933
Commerce	Robert Lamont	1929–1932
	Roy Chapin	1932–1933
Labor	James Davis	1929–1930
	William Doak	1930–1933

Franklin Roosevelt, 1933–1945

Vice-President	John Garner	1933–1941
	Henry W. Wallace	1941–1945
	Harry Truman	1945

State	Cordell Hull	1933–1944
	Edward Stettinius	1944–1945
Treasury	William Woodin	1933–1934
	Henry Morgenthau	1934–1945
War	George Dern	1933–1936
	Henry Woodring	1936–1940
	Henry Stimson	1941–1945
Justice	Homer Cummings	1933–1939
	Frank Murphy	1939–1940
	Robert Jackson	1940–1941
	Francis Biddle	1941–1945
Post Office	James Farley	1933–1940
	Frank Walker	1940–1945
Navy	Claude Swanson	1933–1940
	Charles Edison	1940
	Frank Knox	1940–1944
	James Forrestal	1944–1945
Interior	Harold Ickes	1933–1945
Agriculture	Henry A. Wallace	1933–1940
	Claude Wickard	1940–1945
Commerce	Daniel Roper	1933–1939
	Harry Hopkins	1939–1940
	Jesse Jones	1940–1945
	Henry A. Wallace	1945
Labor	Frances Perkins	1933–1945

Harry Truman, 1945–1953

Vice-President	Vacant	1945–1949
	Alban Barkley	1949–1953
State	James Byrnes	1945–1947
	George Marshall	1947–1949
	Dean Acheson	1949–1953
Treasury	Fred Vinson	1945–1946
	John Snyder	1946–1953
War	Robert Patterson	1945–1947
	Kenneth Royall	1947
Justice	Tom Clark	1945–1949
	J. Howard McGrath	1949–1952
	James McGranery	1952–1953
Post Office	Frank Walker	1945
	Robert Hannegan	1945–1947
	Jesse Donaldson	1947–1953
Navy	James Forrestal	1945–1947

Interior	Harold Ickes	1945–1946
	Julius Krug	1946–1949
	Oscar Chapman	1949–1953
Agriculture	Clinton Anderson	1945–1948
	Charles Brannan	1948–1953
Commerce	Henry A. Wallace	1945–1946
	W. Averell Harriman	1946–1948
	Charles Sawyer	1948–1953
Labor	Lewis Schwellenbach	1945–1948
	Maurice Tobin	1948–1953
Defense	James Forrestal	1947–1949
	Louis Johnson	1949–1950
	George Marshall	1950–1951
	Robert Lovett	1951–1953

Dwight Eisenhower, 1953–1961

Vice-President	Richard Nixon	1953–1961
State	John Foster Dulles	1953–1959
	Christian Herter	1959–1961
Treasury	George Humphrey	1953–1957
	Robert Anderson	1957–1961
Justice	Herbert Brownell	1953–1958
	William Rogers	1958–1961
Post Office	Arthur Summerfield	1953–1961
Interior	Douglas McKay	1953–1956
	Fred Seaton	1956–1961
Agriculture	Ezra Benson	1953–1961
Commerce	Sinclair Weeks	1953–1958
	Lewis Strauss	1958–1959
	Frederick Mueller	1959–1961
Labor	Martin Durkin	1953
	James Mitchell	1953–1961
Defense	Charles Wilson	1953–1957
	Neil McElroy	1957–1959
	Thomas Gates	1959–1961
Health, Education, & Welfare	Oveta Hobby	1953–1955
	Marion Folsom	1955–1958
	Arthur Flemming	1958–1961

John Kennedy, 1961–1963

Vice-President	Lyndon Johnson	1961–1963
State	Dean Rusk	1961–1963
Treasury	C. Douglas Dillon	1961–1963

Justice	Robert Kennedy	1961–1963
Post Office	J. Edward Day	1961–1963
	John Gronouski	1963
Interior	Stewart Udall	1961–1963
Agriculture	Orville Freeman	1961–1963
Commerce	Luther Hodges	1961–1963
Labor	Arthur Goldberg	1961–1962
	W. Willard Wirtz	1962–1963
Defense	Robert McNamara	1961–1963
Health, Education, & Welfare	Abraham Ribicoff	1961–1962
	Anthony Celebrezze	1962–1963

Lyndon-Johnson, 1963–1969

Vice President	Vacant	1963–1965
	Hubert Humphrey	1965–1969
State	Dean Rusk	1963–1969
Treasury	C. Douglas Dillon	1963–1965
	Henry Fowler	1965–1969
Justice	Robert Kennedy	1963–1964
	Nicholas Katzenbach	1965–1967
	Ramsey Clark	1967–1969
Post Office	John Gronouski	1963–1965
	Lawrence O'Brien	1965–1968
	Marvin Watson	1968–1969
Interior	Stewart Udall	1963–1969
Agriculture	Orville Freeman	1963–1969
Commerce	Luther Hodges	1963–1964
	John Conner	1964–1967
	Alexander Trowbridge	1967–1968
	Cyrus Smith	1968–1969
Labor	W. Willard Wirtz	1963–1969
Defense	Robert McNamara	1963–1968
	Clark Clifford	1968–1969
Health, Education, & Welfare	Anthony Celebrezze	1963–1965
	John Gardner	1965–1968
	Wilbur Cohen	1968–1969
Housing &Urban Development	Robert Weaver	1966–1969
	Robert Wood	1969
Transportation	Alan Boyd	1967–1969

Richard Nixon, 1969–1974

Vice-President	Spiro Agnew	1969–1973
	Gerald Ford	1973–1974

State	William Rogers	1969–1973
	Henry Kissinger	1973–1974
Treasury	David Kennedy	1969–1970
	John Connelly	1970–1972
	George Schultz	1972–1974
	William Simon	1974
Justice	John Mitchell	1969–1972
	Richard Kleindeinst	1972–1973
	Elliot Richardson	1973
	William Saxbe	1973–1974
Post Office	Winton Blount	1969–1971
Interior	Walter Hickel	1969–1971
	Rogers Morton	1971–1974
Agriculture	Clifford Hardin	1969–1971
	Earl Butz	1971–1974
Commerce	Maurice Stans	1969–1972
	Peter Peterson	1972–1973
	Frederick Dent	1973–1974
Labor	George Schultz	1969–1970
	James Hodgson	1970–1973
	Peter Brennan	1973–1974
Defense	Melvin Laird	1969–1973
	Elliot Richardson	1973
	James Schlesinger	1973–1974
Health, Education, & Welfare	Robert Finch	1969–1970
	Elliot Richardson	1970–1973
	Caspar Weinberger	1973–1974
Housing & Urban Development	George Romney	1969–1973
	James Lynn	1973–1974
Transportation	John Volpe	1969–1973
	Claude Brinegar	1973–1974

Gerald Ford, 1974–1977

Vice-President	Nelson Rockefeller	1974–1977
State	Henry Kissinger	1974–1977
Treasury	William Simon	1974–1977
Justice	William Saxbe	1974–1975
	Edward Levi	1975–1977
Interior	Rogers Morton	1974–1975
	Stanley Hathaway	1975
	Thomas Kleppe	1975–1977
Agriculture	Earl Butz	1974–1976
	John Knebel	1976–1977

Commerce	Frederick Dent	1974–1975
	Rogers Morton	1975–1976
	Elliot Richardson	1976–1977
Labor	Peter Brennan	1974–1975
	John Dunlop	1975–1976
	William Usery	1976–1977
Defense	James Schlesinger	1974–1975
	Donald Rumsfeld	1975–1977
Health, Education, & Welfare	Caspar Weinberger	1974–1975
	Forrest Mathews	1975–1977
Housing & Urban Development	James Lynn	1974–1975
	Carla Hills	1975–1977
Transportation	Claude Brinegar	1974–1975
	William Coleman	1975–1977

Jimmy Carter, 1977–1981

Vice-President	Walter Mondale	1977–1981
State	Cyrus Vance	1977–1980
	Edmund Muskie	1980–1981
Treasury	W. Michael Blumenthal	1977–1979
	G. William Miller	1979–1981
Justice	Griffin Bell	1977–1979
	Benjamin Civiletti	1979–1981
Interior	Cecil Andrus	1977–1981
Agriculture	Bob Bergland	1977–1981
Commerce	Juanita Kreps	1977–1979
	Philip Klutznick	1979–1981
Labor	F. Ray Marshall	1977–1981
Defense	Harold Brown	1977–1981
Health, Education, & Welfare	Joseph Califano	1977–1979
	Patricia Harris	1979
Housing & Urban Development	Patricia Harris	1977–1979
	Moon Landrieu	1979–1981
Transportation	Brock Adams	1977–1979
	Neil Goldschmidt	1979–1981
Energy	James Schlesinger	1977–1979
	Charles Duncan	1979–1981
Health and Human Services	Patricia Harris	1979–1981
Education	Shirley Hufstedler	1979–1981

Ronald Reagan, 1981–1989

Vice-President	George Bush	1981–1989
State	Alexander Haig	1981–1982

	George Schultz	1982–1989
Treasury	Donald Regan	1981–1985
	James Baker	1985–1988
	Nicholas Brady	1988–1989
Justice	William Smith	1981–1985
	Edwin Meese	1985–1988
	Richard Thornburgh	1988–1989
Interior	James Watt	1981–1983
	William Clark	1983–1985
	Donald Hodel	1985–1989
Agriculture	John Block	1981–1985
	Richard Lyng	1985–1989
Commerce	Malcolm Baldrige	1981–1987
	C. William Verity	1987–1989
Labor	Raymond Donovan	1981–1985
	William Brock	1985–1987
	Ann McLaughlin	1987–1989
Defense	Caspar Weinberger	1981–1987
	Frank Carlucci	1987–1989
Housing & Urban Development	Samuel Pierce	1981–1989
Transportation	Andrew Lewis	1981–1983
	Elizabeth Dole	1983–1987
	James Burnley	1987–1989
Energy	James Edwards	1981–1982
	Donald Hodel	1982–1985
	John Herrington	1985–1989
Health and Human Services	Richard Schweiker	1981–1983
	Margaret Heckler	1983–1985
	Otis Bowen	1985–1989
Education	Terrel Bell	1981–1985
	William Bennett	1985–1988
	Lauro Cavazos	1988–1989

George Bush, 1989–

Vice-President	Dan Quayle	1989–
State	James Baker	1989–
Treasury	Nicholas Brady	1989–
Justice	Richard Thornburgh	1989–
Interior	Manuel Lujan	1989–
Agriculture	Clayton Yeutter	1989–
Commerce	Robert Mosbacher	1989–
Labor	Elizabeth Dole	1989–1991
	Lynn Martin	1991–

Defense	Dick Cheney	1989–
Housing & Urban Development	Jack Kemp	1989–
Transportation	Samuel Skinner	1989–
Energy	James Watkins	1989–
Health and Human Services	Louis Sullivan	1989–
Education	Lauro Cavazos	1989–1991
	Lamar Alexander	1991–
Veterans Affairs	Edward Derwinski	1989–

INDEX

A

Abortion, 180, 206
Affirmative action, 209
Afghanistan, Soviet invasion of, 197, 198
AFL (American Federation of Labor), 15, 143
AFL-CIO, 143
Africa, World War II in, 119
Agency for International Development, 165
Agnew, Spiro, resignation of, 189
Agricultural Adjustment Act (1933), 97
Agricultural Adjustment Act (1938), 103
Agricultural Adjustment Administration, 100
Agriculture
   and Great Depression, 90–91, 92
   Mexican farm workers in, 211
   and New Deal programs, 97, 103
   in 1920s, 84
   shift from, 4–5
   use of machine technology in, 5
AIDS, 213, 216
Airplane, invention of, 6
Alliance for Progress, 165
American Federation of Labor (AFL), 15, 143
American foreign policy
   early overseas interests, 22–23
   free trade as basic tenet of, 21
   isolation as basic tenet of, 22
   overseas expansion of, 23–25
American Railway Union, 15
Anderson, John, in election of 1980, 199
Angola, U.S. policy in, 201

Anticommunism, 137
Anti-Saloon League, 39
Antitrust suits, 47
Arab nationalist movement, 135
Arms race, 166
Art, public, 42
Atlantic Charter, 114, 123
Atomic bomb, 123
   attempts to control, 131–132
Atomic Energy Commission, 132
Austria, in World War I, 56
Austrian Empire, in Treaty of Versailles, 67
Automobile
   consolidation of, 13–14
   early development of, 13
   impact of, 84–85
Automobile industry, consolidation of, 13–14

B

Baby boom, 144
Bakker, Jim, 205–206
Balkans, in Treaty of Versailles, 67
Ballinger, Richard, 51
Baltimore and Ohio Railroad, 12
Bank holiday, 96
Banking Act (1933), 96
Banking, New Deal reforms in, 96
Barnett, Ross, 153
Batista, Fulgencio, 136
Beatniks, 177
Begin, Menachem, 197

Belgian Relief Program, 75
Belgium
  in Treaty of Versailles, 67
  in World War I, 56
  in World War II, 112
Berlin blockade, 129, 130, 134
Berlin Wall, 166–167, 183
Bernstein, Carl, 188
Birth control, 40
Black, Hugo, 103
Black Muslims, 157
Black Panthers, 157
Blacks. *See also* Civil rights
  advances, 208
  affirmative action, 209
  involvement in government, 208
  migration to north, 80
  in military, 149
  and New Deal, 104
  poverty of, 208–209
  in World War II, 116
Bonus army, 94–95
Bork, Robert, 189
Boston, police strike in, 74
Boxers, 32
Brezhnev, Leonid, 184
Brezinski, Zbigniew, 198
Brown v. *Board of Education of Topeka*,
      149–150, 208
Bryan, William Jennings, 66, 80
Bulgaria, in World War I, 56
Bulge, Battle of, 120
Bush, George
  cabinet of, 245–246
  in election of 1988, 205
  presidential profile of, 223
Business
  advertising, 82
  and decline of unions, 82–83
  federal reforms in, 46–47
  government support for, 81
  in Great Depression, 92
  growth of, 142
  and labor relations, 82
  mergers in, 81–82
  in New Deal, 101
  state regulation of, 44

Busing controversy, 159

C

Cabinet
  duties of department heads, 235–236
  growth of, 234–235
  of specific presidents, 236–246
Cambodia, 175–176
Camp David, Maryland, Eisenhower-Khrushchev
      meeting at, 134
Camp David Talks, 197
Campus unrest, 178–179
Capone, Al, 86
Caribbean, U.S. expansion into, 30–32
Carnegie, Andrew, 7, 11, 12, 16, 41
Carnegie Steel, 11
Carranza, Venustiano, 59
Carter, Jimmy
  cabinet of, 236, 244
  domestic policy under, 195–196
  in election of 1976, 194–195
  in election of 1980, 198–199
  foreign affairs under, 196–198
  human rights under, 196
  presidential profile of, 222–223
Casey, William, 204
Castro, Fidel, 136–137, 167
Central America. *See also* Latin America
  under Carter administration, 196–197
  immigrants from, 211–212
  U.S. policy in, 30–32, 202
Chambers, Whittaker, 137
Chiang Kai-shek, 111, 119, 130
Chicago
  gang warfare in, 86
  growth of, and transportation improvements,
      10
Child labor laws, 47
China
  civil war in, 130
  Nixon's visit to, 184–185
  U.S. interests in, 32
Chou En-Lai, 184–185
Christian fundamentalism, 205–206
Churchill, Winston, 113–114, 118–119, 120, 128
CIO (Congress of Industrial Organizations), 143

City government, reform measures in, 42–43
City planning, reform in, 44
Civil Rights Act (1964), 180
Civil rights bills, 150–151
Civil rights movement
  beginnings of, 148–151
  busing controversy, 159
  disenchantment with reform, 155–157
  national retreat on, 158–159
  in 1960s, 152–153
  and progressive movement, 40
  and school desegregation, 149–150
  urban riots, 158
Civilian Conservation Corps, 97
Clayton Antitrust Act, 52
Cleaver, Eldridge, 157
Cleveland, Grover, 26, 29
Cold war
  arms race in, 132
  beginning of, 127–32
  colonial revolutions, 132–133
  containment, 128
  detente, 183–185
  in Germany, 134
  and John F. Kennedy, 164–168
  Soviet-American relations in, 127–128, 204
  tension in Asia, 130–131
  tension in Europe, 128–130
  in Vietnam, 133–134
Colonialism, end of, 164
Commerce and Labor, Department of, 47, 234
Commerce, U.S. Department of, 47, 234
Committee on Public Information, 62
Committee to Reelect the President (CRP), 187
Communism
  in Soviet Union, 127
  in U.S., 78
Congress of Industrial Organizations (CIO), 101, 143
Congress of Racial Equality (CORE), 155
Congressional hearings, 137–138
Conservation, reforms in, 47–48
Conservative movements, 205–206
Consumer spending, in 1950s, 141–142
Consumerism, 206
Containment, 128
Coolidge, Calvin, 86, 235

Coolidge, Calvin (*cont'd*)
  cabinet of, 239
  in election of 1924, 74–75
  and Good Neighbor Policy, 77
  political philosophy of, 74, 81
  presidential profile of, 219
Coral Sea, Battle of, 122
CORE (Congress of Racial Equality), 155
Counterculture, 177–178
Cox, Archibald, 189
Cox, James, 69, 73
Crane, Stephen, 38
Crime, and prohibition, 86
Cuba
  and Bay of Pigs invasion, 167
  Castro takeover of, 136–137
  conquest of, 28
  establishment of American protectorate in, 31
  and missile crisis, 167
  revolution in, 25–26, 117
  U.S. interests in, 25

D

Darrow, Clarence, 80
Darwin, Charles, 24
Daugherty, Henry, 74
Davis, John W., 75
D-Day, 120
Debs, Eugene, 15, 16
  in election of 1912, 51–52
Deforestation, 216
DeLome, Dupuy, 27
DeLome letter, 27
Denby, Edwin, 74
Denmark, in World War II, 112
Dewey, George, 28
Dewey, Thomas
  in election of 1944, 117
  in election of 1948, 139
Dien Bien Phu, 133
Divorce, 210–211
Domestic markets, 8
Dominican Republic, revolution in, 59
Domino theory, 133
Douglas, William, 103
Draft, in World War I, 63

Dubois, W. E. B., 40
Dukakis, Michael, in election of 1988, 205
Duryea, Charles, 13
Duryea, Frank, 13
Dylan, Bob, 178

E

Economic decline, under Carter administration,
    195
Economic Opportunity Act, 154
Economic readjustment, in 1950s, 141
Edison, Thomas, 6
Education
    advances in, 83–84
    and busing, 159
    and campus unrest, 173, 178–179
    school desegregation, 149–150
    state reforms in, 45–46
Education, U.S. Department of, 195
Egypt, and Suez crisis, 135–136
Ehrlichman, John, 188, 190
Eighteenth Amendment, 39, 48
Einstein, Albert, 123
Eisenhower, Dwight D., 134, 140
    cabinet of, 241
    and civil rights, 150
    and Cold War, 134
    in election of 1952, 140
    in election of 1956, 140
    presidential profile of, 220–221
    on Vietnam, 169
    as World War II general, 119, 120
Elections
    of 1900, 225
    of 1904, 50, 226
    of 1908, 50, 226
    of 1912, 51–52, 226
    of 1916, 61, 226
    of 1920, 73, 227
    of 1924, 74–75, 227
    of 1928, 75, 227
    of 1932, 94–95, 227–228
    of 1936, 102, 228
    of 1940, 113, 228
    of 1944, 117, 228
    of 1948, 139, 228–229

Elections (cont'd)
    of 1952, 140, 229
    of 1956, 140, 229
    of 1960, 151, 229–230
    of 1964, 170, 230
    of 1968, 173–175, 230
    of 1972, 188, 230–231
    of 1976, 194–195, 231
    of 1980, 198–199, 231–232
    of 1984, 205, 232
    of 1988, 205, 232–233
Electricity, 6
Elk Hills, California, 74
Elkins Act (1903), 47
El Salvador, U.S. policy in, 197
Emergency Banking Relief Act, 96
Emergency Relief Appropriations Act (1935),
    100
Employment opportunities, for women, 209–210
Energy crisis, under Carter administration,
    195–196
Energy, U.S. Department of, 195
Environmental movement, 207–208
Environmental problems, and industrialization,
    17
Environmental Protection Agency, 207
Equal opportunity, 179
Equal Rights Amendment (ERA), 211
Ethiopia, Italy invasion of, 111
Europe, U.S. interests in, 33–34
Evers, Medgar, 153

F

Fair Labor Standards Act, 104
Fall, Albert, 74
Falwell, Jerry, 205
Family, 179–180, 210–211
Famine, 216
Farm Security Administration, 103
Fascism, rise of, 109–110
Faubus, Orval, 150
Federal deficit, under Reagan, 200–201
Federal Deposit Insurance Corporation, 96
Federal Emergency Relief Act, relief programs
    in, 97
Federal Home Loan Bank Act (1932), 94

Federal Housing Administration, 142
Federal reform, 46–49
Federal Reserve Board, 101
Federal Reserve System, 52, 96
Federal Trade Commission, 47, 52
Federated Republic of Germany (West Germany), 129
Ferdinand, Archduke, 56
Ferraro, Geraldine, 205, 209
   in election of 1984, 205
Financial institutions, 7
Financiers, 7
Financing, availability of, and growth of industrialism, 3
Fireside chats, 96
Fitzgerald, F. Scott, 87
Folk music, 178
Forbes, Charles, 74
Ford, Gerald, 194
   cabinet of, 243–244
   in election of 1976, 194, 195
   as president, 190
   presidential profile of, 222
Ford, Henry, 13
Foreign markets, 8
Forest, Argonne, 64
Fourteen Points, 65–66
   fate of, 67
France
   in Treaty of Versailles, 67
   and Vietnam, 133
   in World War I, 56
   in World War II, 112, 120
Frankfurter, Felix, 103
French, Daniel Chester, 42
Fulbright, William, 172

G

Gay rights movement, 213
General Electric, 81
General Motors, 81
Geneva Armanent Conference (1927), 77
German U-boat attacks, in World War I, 58
Germany
   Cold War in, 134
   division of, 134

Germany (*cont'd*)
   expansion of, 110–111
   invasion of, in World War II, 120
   postwar division of, 109–110, 129
   rearmament in, 110
   and Treaty of Versailles terms, 67
   in World War I, 56
Ginsberg, Alan, 177
Global warming, 216
Goldwater, Barry, in election of 1964, 170
Gompers, Samuel, 15, 16
Good neighbor policy, 77
Gorbachev, Mikhail, 204
Government Contracts Act (1936), 101
Government, responsibility for reform, 38
Great Britain
   relations with U.S., 113–114
   in World War I, 56
   in World War II, 112
Great Depression
   agriculture in, 90–91
   and election of 1932, 94–95
   end of, 116
   extent of, 91–93
   Hoover's recovery programs, 93–94
   international finance, 91
   and New Deal, 95–106
   and overproduction, 90
   and price and wage structure, 90
   and protective tariff, 91
   and real estate speculation, 89
   and stock market crash, 91–92
   and stock market speculation, 90
Great Society, 154–155, 207
Greece
   U.S. and Soviet confrontation in postwar, 128–129
   in World War I, 56
Grenada, U.S. policy in, 202
Guadalcanal, 122
Guatemala, revolution in, 136
Gulf of Tonkin resolutions, 170, 176, 186
Guthrie, Woody, 178

H

Haiti, 1915 revolution in, 59

Haldeman, H. R., 186, 188, 190
Harding, Warren, 235
    cabinet of, 73, 238
    death of, 74
    in election of 1920, 73
    and Good Neighbor Policy, 77
    and League of Nations, 69
    presidential profile of, 219
    scandals of administration, 73–74
Hawaii, U.S. interests in, 29
Hay, John, 32
Health and Human Services, U.S. Department of,
        195
Health care, advances in, 83–84
Hearst, William Randolph, 26
Highway Act (1956), 142
Hills, Carla, 209
Hippies, 177–178
Hiroshima, 123
Hispanics, and New Deal, 104
Hiss, Alger, 137–138
Hitler, Adolf
    rise of, 110
    suicide of, 120
    in World War II, 112
Ho Chi Minh, 133
Hobby, Oveta, 209
Holding company, 16
Home Owners Loan Corporation, 96
Homestead Steel Mill, 16
Hoover, Herbert
    background of, 75
    cabinet of, 239
    in election of 1928, 75
    in election of 1932, 95
    political philosophy of, 75–76
    presidential profile of, 219–220
    recovery programs of, 93–94
    as secretary of commerce, 73
Hooverilles, 94
Housatonic, sinking of, 61
House, Edward, 60
House Judiciary Committee, 190
Household conveniences, 83
Housing
    improvements in, 83
    reform in, 44

Housing and Urban Development, U.S. Depart-
        ment of, 154
Housing assistance programs, in New Deal, 100
Huerta, Victoriano, 59
Hughes, Charles Evans, 73, 76–77
    in election of 1916, 61
Hull House, 41
Human rights, under Carter administration, 196
Humphrey, Hubert, in election of 1968, 174, 175
Hunter, Robert, 38

I

Idealism, 24–25
Immigration
    Asians and Hispanics, 211–213
    nations for origin, 9
    restrictions on, 79–80
Income tax, 48
Industrialization
    automobile, 13–14
    emergence of, 3–10
    expanding markets, 8
    immigration, 8–9
    impact of machinery on, 7
    investment and financing, 7
    oil, 13
    problems resulting from, 14–17
    railroads, 12–13
    steel, 10–12
Internal combustion engine, 6–7
International finance, 91
Interstate Commerce Commission (ICC), 46–47,
        101
Iran
    coup in, 135
    hostage crisis in, 198, 199
    overthrow of Shah, 197–198
Iran-Contra scandal, 203–204
Isolation, as basic tenet of American foreign
        policy, 22
Israel, creation of, 135
Italy
    invasion of Ethiopia, 111
    and rise of Mussolini, 110
    in World War I, 56
    in World War II, 119

Iwo Jima, 122

J

Jackson, Jesse, 208
Japan
  and atomic bomb, 122
  bombing of Pearl Harbor, 114–115
  pre-World War I aggression of, 111
  relations with U.S. pre-World War II, 114
  U.S. interests in, 33
  U.S. occupation of, 130
  in World War I, 56
  in World War II, 122
Japanese-Americans, in World War II, 116–117
Jazz Age, 86–87
Job Corps, 154
Johnson, Hiram, 45
Johnson, Lyndon, 150
  cabinet of, 242
  and civil rights, 153–154, 158
  and Great Society, 154–155
  in election of 1964, 170
  presidential profile of, 221
  relations with Soviet Union, 183–184
  on Vietnam War, 169–170
Joint-stock companies, 7
Jungle, The (Sinclair), 47

K

Kellogg-Briand Pact, 77
Kennedy, John F.
  assassination of, 153
  and Bay of Pigs invasion, 167
  cabinet of, 241–242
  and civil rights, 152–153
  and Cold War, 164–168
  and Cuban missile crisis, 167
  domestic programs of, 151–152
  in election of 1960, 151
  presidential profile of, 221
  relations with Soviet Union, 183
Kennedy, Robert
  assassination of, 174, 181
  as attorney general, 152
  in election of 1968, 174
Kent State University, 176

Kerouac, Jack, 177
Khe Sahn, 172
Khomeini, Ayatollah, 198
King, Martin Luther, 150, 152, 155, 156–157, 182
  assassination of, 158, 174, 181
  "I have a dream" speech of, 153
Kirkpatrick, Jeanne, 209
Kissinger, Henry, 175, 185, 186, 203
Kleindienst, Richard, 188, 190
Korean War, 130–131
Kosygin, Aleksei, 184
Krushchev, Nikita, 134, 183
Ku Klux Klan, revival of, 81

L

Labor, U.S. Department of, 47, 234
Labor force
  availability of, and growth of industrialism, 3
  and industrialization, 14–16
  for manufacturing, 8
  post World War I, 79
  post World War II, 143
  women in, 179–180
Labor laws, state reforms in, 45
Labor relations
  and government support for business, 82
  in New Deal, 101, 104
LaFollette, Robert, 45, 75, 86
Landon, Alf, in election of 1936, 102
Laos, Vietnam War in, 168–169
Latin America
  Cuba, 136–137
  good neighbor policy in, 77
  Guatemala, 136
  resentment toward United States, 136
  U.S. involvement in, pre World War I, 59–60
  and World War II, 117–118
League of Nations, 66, 68
  fate of, 69
  ineffectiveness of, 111
  Republican policy on, 76
Lebanon, U.S. policy in, 201–202
Leisure time, in 1950s, 145
LeMay, Curtis, 175
Levittown, 144

Lewis, Sinclair, 87
Liberty Bonds, 62
Lindbergh, Charles, 87
Literacy test, 79
Little Rock, Arkansas, 150
London Armament Conference (1930), 77
Long, Huey, 99
Lusitania, sinking of, 58
Luxembourg, in World War II, 112

M

MacArthur, Douglas, 122
   and Korean War, 131
   and occupation of Japan, 130
Machinery
   impact of, on industrialization, 7
   proliferation of, 5–7
Maggie, A Girl of the Streets (Crane), 38
Maine, sinking of, 27
Malcolm X, 157
Manhattan Project, 123
Manifest destiny, 24, 25
Manufacturing, 3
   influence of, on urban growth, 9–10
   influence of railroads on, 12
   labor for, 8
   shift from agriculture to, 4
Mao Tse-tung, 111, 130, 185
Marne, second Battle of, 63
Marshall, George, 129
Marshall Plan, 129, 140, 165
Marx, Karl, 181
McCarran Act, 137
McCarthy, Eugene, in election of 1968, 173
McCarthy hearings, 138
McCarthy, Joseph, 138
McFarlane, Robert, 203, 204
McGovern, George, in election of 1972, 188
McKinley, William, 29
   assassination of, 50
   cabinet of, 236
   presidential profile of, 217
McNamara, Robert, 172–173
Medicaid, 154
Medicare, 154
Mellon, Andrew, 73, 81

Meredith, James, 153
Mexico
   Pancho Villa in, 60
   revolution in, 59
   and Vera Cruz, 59–60
Middle class, support for progressiveness, 36
Middle East
   Soviet incursions in, 134
   U.S. policy in, 185–186
Middle East Peace Accords, 197
Midway, Battle of, 122
Miller, Thomas, 74
Minorities
   under Carter administration, 195
   and New Deal, 104
   in World War II, 116–117
Mitchell, John, 186, 187, 188, 190
Mondale, Walter, in election of 1984, 205
Monopoly, 16–17
Monroe Doctrine, Roosevelt Corollary to, 30–31
Montgomery bus boycott, 150
Moral Majority, 205
Morgan, John Pierpont, 7, 11–12
Music
   folk, 178
   jazz, 86–87
   rock and roll, 178
Mussolini, Benito, 119
   execution of, 120
   rise of, 110
   in World War II, 112
Mutual defense pacts, 118

N

Nagasaki, 123
Nasser, Gamal Abdel, 135–136
Nation, Carrie, 39
National Association for Advancement of
   Colored People (NAACP), 40, 155
National Bituminous Coal Commission, 101
National Child Labor Committee, 45
National Commission for Conservation of
   Natural Resources, 48
National Endowment for Humanities, 154
National Guard, 113
National Housing Act, 104

National Labor Relations Act, 101
National Organization of Women (NOW), 180
National pride, 24
National Recovery Administration, 97–98, 100
National Security Council, 203
National Urban League, 40
National War Labor Board, 115
National Youth Administration, 100
NATO (North Atlantic Treaty Organization), 129–130
Naval Disarmament, 76–77
Naval Warfare, and World War II, 114
Navy, Department of, 234–235
Navy, U.S., in World War I, 63
Netherlands, in World War II, 112
Neutrality
    U.S. policy of, and World War I, 56–57
    U.S. policy of, and World War II, 112
    U.S. policy of toward Europe, 33–34
New Deal, 95–96
    agriculture in, 97, 103
    banking reform in, 96
    business regulation, 101
    close of, 104–105
    housing assistance programs, 100
    influence of World War II, 106
    labor relations in, 101
    and minorities, 104
    opening steps, 96
    principal legislation and programs, 105–106
    reaction to, 99–100
    recovery programs in, 97–98
    regulatory agencies in, 99
    relief programs in, 97, 98
    second, 100–103
    Social Security, 102
    subsequent legislation, 98–99
    and Supreme Court, 100, 102–103
    tax reform, 101–102
    third, 103–106
    unions, 101
    work relief programs, 100
    and World War II, 148–149
New left, 181
Newlands Reclamation Act (1902), 48
Newspaper coverage, of Spanish-American War, 26–27

Newton, Huey, 157
New York, growth of, and transportation improvements, 10
New York Birth Control League, 40
New York Central Railroad, 12
Ngo Dinh Diem, 133, 169
Nicaragua, 31
    immigrants from, 213
    revolution in, 77
    U.S. policy in, 196–197, 202
Nineteenth Amendment, 48
Nixon, Richard, 137
    cabinet of, 235–236, 242–243
    and civil rights, 158–159
    in election of 1960, 151
    in election of 1968, 174–175
    in election of 1972, 188
    hatred of antiwar movement, 187
    intolerance of dissent, 187
    presidential profile of, 222
    presidential staff of, 186
    relations with China, 184–185
    relations with Soviet Union, 184
    resignation of, 189–190
    and silent majority, 182
    troubles with Congress, 186
    as vice-president, 136
    Vietnam War under, 175–176
    and Watergate, 186–190
Norris, Frank, 38
Norris, George, 98
North Atlantic Treaty Organization (NATO), 129–130, 134, 140
North, Oliver, 203, 204
Northern de facto segregation, 156–157
Northern Pacific Railroad, 12
Northern Securities Company, 47
Norway, in World War II, 112
NOW (National Organization of Women), 180
Nye, Gerald, 112

O

O'Connor, Sandra Day, 209
Octopus (Norris), 38
Office of Price Administration (OPA), 115, 141

Office of Scientific Research and Development, 115
Oil, 13
Okinawa, 122
On the Road (Kerouac), 177
O'Neill, Eugene, 87
Open Door Policy, 32
Open Housing Law, 154
Oppenheimer, Robert, 137
Organization of Petroleum Exporting Nations (OPEC), 185
Overpopulation, 216
Ozone depletion, 216

P

Pacific, U.S. expansion into, 29–30
Pacific islands, U.S. interests in, 22
Palmer, A. Mitchell, 78
Panama Canal Treaty, 196
Panama Canal, U.S. interests in, 31–32
Parker, Alton, 50
Parks, Rosa, 150
Parties, minor, 224–225
Peace Corps, 165
Peace movement, in World War I, 57
Pearl Harbor, bombing of, 114–115
Pennsylvania Railroad, 12
Pentagon Papers, 187
Perkins, Frances, 101, 209
Pershing, John, 60, 63–64
Philadelphia, growth of, and transportation improvements, 10
Philanthropy, 41
Philippines
  acquisition of, 29–30
  guerrilla war in, 30
  Spanish-American War in, 27–28
Phillips, David, 38
Pinchot, Gifford, 51
Planned Parenthood, 40, 179–180
Platt Amendment, 117
Poindexter, John, 204
Poland, in World War II, 112
Political reform, states in, 45
Pool, 16
Population, growth of, in 1950s, 143–144

Potsdam, Germany, 119, 122, 129
Poverty
  and industrialization, 17
  in 1920s, 84
Poverty (Hunter), 38
Powell, Colin, 208
Progressive party, in election of 1924, 75
Progressivism
  diversity of movement, 36
  federal reform, 46–49
  influences on the Reform Movement, 37–38
  middle-class support for, 36
  private efforts at reform, 38–42
  state reform, 44–46
  types of reform, 37
  urban reform, 42–44
  vestiges of, 86
Prohibition, 39, 48, 85–86
Propaganda
  in World War I, 62
  in World War II, 115
Protective legislation, 47
Protest movements
  beatniks, 177
  hippies, 177–178
  music in, 178
  new left, 181
  opposition to, 181–183
  women's movement, 179–181
Public utilities, reform in, 43
Public vice, reform in, 43
Public Works Administration, 97–98
Pulitzer, Joseph, 26–27
Pullman Company, 16

R

Racism, as issue in overseas expansion, 23
Railroads, 7
  expansion and consolidation, 12–13
  influence of, on manufacturing, 12
Randolph, A. Philip, 116
Raw materials, availability of, and growth of industrialism, 3
Reagan, Ronald
  cabinet of, 244–245
  economic policy under, 200–201

Reagan, Ronald (*cont'd*)
  in election of 1980, 198–199
  in election of 1984, 205
  foreign policy, 201–204
  presidential profile of, 223
Real estate speculation, 89–90
Reconstruction Finance Corporation (RFC), 93
Regulatory agencies, 99
Regulatory commissions, 46–47
Religious fundamentalism, 80–81
Republican party, domination of, post World
        War I, 72–77
Rescue mission, 41
Resettlement Administration, 100
Revenue Act (1935), 101–102
Richardson, Eliot, 189
Riis, Jacob, 38
Rock and roll music, 178
Rockefeller, John D., 7, 13
Roe v. *Wade*, 180, 206
Rogers, Will, 86
Romania, in World War I, 56
Roosevelt, Eleanor, 102
Roosevelt, Franklin D.
  cabinet of, 239–240
  death of, 117
  in election of 1932, 95
  in election of 1936, 102
  in election of 1940, 113
  in election of 1944, 117
  image of, 94
  New Deal policies of, 95–106
  presidential profile of, 220
  and Soviet relations, 128
  and World War II, 118–119
Roosevelt, Theodore, 28
  as activist president, 50
  cabinet of, 237
  and conservation, 47–48
  and construction of Panama Canal, 31–32
  in election of 1904, 50
  in election of 1912, 51–52
  and mediation of Russo-Japanese War, 33
  presidential profile of, 217–218
  reforms under, 46
  and Roosevelt corollary, 30–31
Roosevelt Corollary, 30–31

Rosenberg, Ethel, 138
Rosenberg, Julius, 138
Rough Riders, 28
Ruckelshaus, William, 189
Rural Electrification Administration, 100
Russia. *See also* Soviet Union
  in Treaty of Versailles, 67
  in World War I, 56

S

Sacco, Nicola, 78
Sadat, Anwar, 197
St. Gauden, Augustus, 42
St. Mihiel, 64
Salvation Army, 41
San Francisco Conference (1945), 123
Sanger, Margaret, 40
School desegregation, 149–150
Scopes monkey trial, 80
Secord, Richard, 204
Segregation, Northern de facto, 156–157
Senate hearings, on Watergate, 188–189
Serbia, in World War I, 56
Service sector, 143
Settlement houses, 41
Seventeenth Amendment, 48
Share Our Wealth Society, 99
Sherman Memorial (St. Gauden), 42
Shopping center, development of, 144
Sinclair, Upton, 47
Sirica, John, 188
Sixteenth Amendment, 48
Smith, Alfred, 75
Smith, Jesse, 74
Social Darwinism, 24
Social justice movement, 37
Social Security, 102
Social theory, 37
Socialism, 78
  decline of, 82
Socialist party, 15
  in election of 1912, 51–52
Society of Fists, 32
Southern Christian Leadership Conference
        (SCLC), 155–156, 157
Soviet Union. *See also* Cold War; Russia

Soviet Union (*cont'd*)
  under Brezhnev, 184
  detente with, 183–185
  and division of Germany, 129
  expansion of, 127–128
  under Gorbachev, 204
  ideology in, 127
  under Khrushchev, 183
  under Kosygin, 184
  in Middle East, 134
  territorial security in, 127
  and World War II, 119, 120
Space race, 168
Spain, dwindling empire of, 25
Spanish-American War
  aftermath, 28–29
  background to, 25–27
  declaration of war, 27
  newspaper coverage, 26–27
  peace treaty, 28
  in Philippines, 27–28
  war with Spain, 27–29
Spanish Civil War, 111
Stalin, Josef, 119, 120
Standard of living, improvement in, 83
Standard Oil Company, 13
Standard Oil Trust, 13
Stans, Maurice, 190
State leadership, reforms in, 45
State reform, 44–46
States, role of, in presidential elections, 225
States Rights Democratic party (Dixiecrats), in
      election of 1948, 139
Steam engine, 6
Steam technology, 6
Steel, 10–12
Stevenson, Adlai, 140
Stock market crash, 91–92
  business losses in, 92
  farm losses in, 92
  unemployment in, 92–93
Stock market speculation, 90
Strategic Arms Limitation Treaty (1979), 197
Strategic Defense Initiative, 204
Student Nonviolent Coordinating Committee
      (SNCC), 157
Student protest, against Vietnam War, 173

Suburbs, growth of, 85, 144
Suez crisis, 135–136
Suffrage, 40
Sunday, Billy, 80
Supreme Court, U.S., and New Deal legislation,
      100, 102–103

T

Taft, William Howard
  administration of, 50–51
  cabinet of, 237–238
  in election of 1908, 50
  in election of 1912, 51–52
  presidential profile of, 218
  reforms under, 46
Taft-Hartley Act (1947), 143
Tariff, protective, 91
Tax reform
  in New Deal, 101–102
  under Reagan, 200
  states in, 45
Teapot Dome, Wyoming, 74
Technology, steam, 6
Television, 145
  and Vietnam War, 173
Tennessee Valley Authority, 98
Terrorism, 203
Third World, U.S. policy in, 164–166, 185
Three Mile Island, 208
Thurmond, Storm, 139
Trade deficit, under Reagan, 200
Trade, U.S. policy of free, 21, 57–58
Transcontinental line, 12
Transportation, improvements in, and urban
      growth, 10
Treason of Senate (Phillips), 38
Truman, Harry S
  and atomic bomb, 122
  cabinet of, 240–241
  and Cold War, 128–129
  domestic policies of, 139, 140
  in election of 1948, 139
  presidential profile of, 220
  and Korean War, 131
  and World War II, 119
Truman Doctrine, 128–129

Trust, 16–17
Turkey
  U.S. and Soviet confrontation in postwar,
      128–129
  in Treaty of Versailles, 67
  in World War I, 56

U

U-2 incident, 134
U-boat campaign, 64
Un-American Activities Committee of House of
      Representatives, 137–138
Unemployment, in Great Depression, 92–93
Unions
  decline of, 82–83
  early, 15
  and labor unrest, 16
  in New Deal, 101
United Nations, 123
  and atomic bomb, 131–132
U.S. imperialism
  in Caribbean and Central America, 30–32
  in Pacific, 29–30
U.S. Steel, 11–12
Urban growth
  and anti-black riots, 80
  and industrialization, 17
  influence of automobile on, 85
  influence of manufacturing on, 9–10
Urban reform, 42–44

V

Vance, Cyrus, 198
Vanzetti, Bartolomeo, 78
Vera Cruz, U.S. attack on, 59–60
Versailles, Treaty of, 67–68, 109
  opposition to, 68–69
Vertical integration, 11
Veterans Administration, 142
Vice-president, 236
  of specific presidents, 236–246
Vietnam
  American involvement in, 133
  civil war in, 133–134
  revolt against French, 133

Vietnam War
  American withdrawal from, 176
  casualties in, 176
  escalation of, 169–172
  Gulf of Tonkin resolutions, 170
  Kennedy's position on, 169
  in Laos, 168–169
  Lyndon B. Johnson on, 169–170
  under Nixon, 175–176
  opposition to, 172–173, 181–182
  and television, 173
  Tet offensive in, 172
  U.S. entrance into, 170–172
Villa, Pancho, 60
Virgin Islands, U.S. purchase of, 59
VISTA, 154
Volstead Act (1919), 48, 85–86

W

Wagner, Robert, 101
Wallace, George, 181
  in election of 1968, 175
  in election of 1972, 188
Wallace, Henry, 73, 139
War, Department of, 234
War Manpower Commission, 115
War Production Board, 115
Warsaw Pact, 130
Washington Armanent Conference (1921), 76–77
Washington, Booker T., 40
Watergate burglary, 187
  aftermath, 190
  break-in, 187–188
  cover-up, 188
  evidence of corruption, 189
  investigation, 188–189
  Nixon's resignation, 189–190
  resignation of Spiro Agnew, 189
  special prosecutor, 189
Watts, riots in, 158
Weaver, Robert, 208
Westmoreland, William, 171
Wilhelm, Kaiser, 64
Willkie, Wendell, and election of 1940, 113
Wilson, Woodrow, 45
  administration of, 52

Wilson, Woodrow (*cont'd*)
  attempts at mediation, 60–61
  in election of 1912, 51–52
  in election of 1916, 61
  and opposition to Treaty of Versailles, 68–69
  peace plan of, 65–66
  presidential profile of, 218–219
  reforms under, 46
  and U.S. neutrality, 56–57
Women
  employment opportunities for, 209–210
  and Equal Rights Amendment, 211
  and family, 210–211
  job-related problems, 210
  suffrage for, 40, 48
  in work force, 179–180
Women's Christian Temperance Union (WCTU),
    39, 40
Women's movement, 179–181
  reaction to, 182–183
Women's rights amendment, 180–181
Woodstock Music Festival, 178
Woodward, Bob, 188
Work relief programs, in New Deal, 100
Working conditions, and industrialization, 14
Works Progress Administration, 100, 103, 104
World War I
  American neutrality in, 56–57
  Americans in combat, 63–64
  attempts at mediation, 60–61
  casualties in, 64
  declaration of war, 61
  maritime problems, 57–58
  mobilization, 63

World War I (*cont'd*)
  opening of hostilities, 56
  peace efforts, 64–69
  postwar conservation, 71–77
  public reaction, 62–63
  state of war, 63
  Zimmermann note, 61
World War II
  African and Italian campaigns, 119–120
  allied diplomacy, 118–119
  American preparation for, 112–113
  American reaction to, 112
  and atomic bomb, 123
  beginning of, 112
  casualties, 123
  in Europe, 113–114, 119
  German and Italian aggression, 110–111
  hemispheric defense, 117–118
  Japanese expansion, 111
  mobilization and home front, 115–117
  and New Deal, 148–149
  in Pacific, 122–123
  prelude to, 109–112
  prosperity following, 141–145
  and race relations, 116–117
  rise of fascism, 109–110
  and United Nations, 123

Y

Yalta, 119

Z

Zimmermann note, 61